"AN INSPIRING HUMAN DRAMA

. . . we meet not just another fighter pilot and soldier, but a man whose character was tested for ten and a half lonely years, during which he was stripped of his soldier's rights. Behind all this is a story of a lifelong love . . . I believe this to be the most remarkable book ever written about a fighter pilot, and all the more noteworthy because it is the leading fighter pilot of all time who has lived through these experiences."

Lt. General Adolf Galland,
General of the Luftwaffe
Fighter Arm, 1941-1945

"An exciting account of personal courage and integrity in combat."
—*Richmond News Leader.*

The Blond Knight of Germany

Colonel Raymond F. Toliver
USAF (Ret.)
and
Trevor J. Constable

Introduction by
Lt. General Adolf Galland
General of the Luftwaffe
Fighter Arm 1941–1945

BALLANTINE BOOKS • NEW YORK

PHOTO CREDITS:

Except as indicated below the illustrations are from the collection of Erich Hartmann whose permission for their use is gratefully acknowledged by the authors.

8, 11, 14, 20, 22, 41; *The Toliver Collection*
9, 12, 18; *The Krupinski Collection*
15, 17; *The Chalif Collection*
16; *The Nawarra Collection*
21; *The Rall Collection*
34; *Graf von der Schulenburg*
39, 40; *U.S.A.F. Photos*
42; *NASA*

Library of Congress Catalog Card Number: 74-89076

ISBN 0-345-27847-X

This edition published by arrangement with Doubleday & Company, Inc.

Manufactured in the United States of America

First Ballantine Books Edition: March 1971
Fourth Printing: May 1978

for "Usch" who waited

INTRODUCTION

BY LT. GENERAL ADOLF GALLAND
General of the Fighter Arm 1941–1945

WHEN MY FRIENDS Colonel Raymond F. Toliver and Trevor J. Constable asked me to write an Introduction to the life story of Erich Hartmann, I was happy to do so for several reasons. First of all, I am honored to pay tribute in this way to the top-scoring fighter pilot of all time, who served under my command during the Second World War. "Bubi" Hartmann and I have been personal friends as well, ever since his release from ten years of Soviet confinement. We have remarked that if he had joined JV-44 with me when I asked him in 1945, his whole life might have been different. His desire to return to his own unit on the Eastern Front led to the personal disaster of his decade in Russian hands.

Secondly, I find it especially appropriate that Erich Hartmann's story should be presented to the world by two American authors that we of the German fighter pilot fraternity respect for their integrity and fairness. Due largely to their previous two books, the accomplishments of the German fighter pilots in the Second World War have been historically recognized on an international basis. I believe that Erich Hartmann's world combat record of 352 confirmed victories, and his other achievements, are not only endorsed but also illuminated by this book.

Thirdly, there is the quality of Erich Hartmann's story as it has been set down by his American friends after years of painstaking research. We find not only a thorough account of how Hartmann developed his unique tactics, but also an inspiring human drama. We meet not just another fighter pilot and soldier, but a man whose character was tested for ten and a half lonely years, during which he was stripped of his soldier's rights. Behind all this is the story of a lifelong love, something of which our troubled world stands in need.

I believe this to be the most remarkable book ever written about a fighter pilot, and all the more noteworthy because it is the leading fighter pilot of all time who has lived through these experiences. I recommend this book as a worthy addition to aviation history, and as a further contribution of the authors to international good will and mutual understanding.

I have to say to the authors: "Please accept our thanks; we former fighter pilots of the Luftwaffe appreciate what you have done."

CONTENTS

x

ACKNOWLEDGMENTS

THE AUTHORS wish to express their gratitude to a number of men and women whose assistance in the preparation of this book was indispensable. The late German air historian, Hans-Otto Boehm of Munich, who introduced the authors to each other and to Erich Hartmann, played an important part in bringing this story to the world public. Herr Hans Ring, Documentation Expert of the German Fighter Pilots' Association in Munich and onetime assistant to Hans-Otto Boehm, rendered signal services with his translations of Boehm's work into English.

The assistance of Erich Hartmann's family has also proved of inestimable value. His wife Ursula (Usch)* and her mother, his brother Dr. Alfred Hartmann and his mother Elisabeth Hartmann have all made substantial contributions to this book. Numerous German fighter pilots, flight surgeons and other personnel of JG-52 allowed us to impose on them with hundreds of questions, and many former German prisoners of the Soviet Union supplied painful reminiscences of the Russian jails. Heinrich "Bimmel" Mertens, Erich Hartmann's crew chief throughout his combat career, contributed from his unique perspective to this portrait of the world's most successful fighter pilot.

A special accolade goes to that surviving member of JG-52 who made available the Daily Operational History of III/JG-52, after smuggling it out of the Eastern Zone of Germany.

* Usch is pronounced *Oosh*, as in *whoosh*.

He must remain nameless, but we are deeply in his debt for documentation that materially reduced our labors.

An effort to name all those who have assisted in the past ten years would undoubtedly fill several pages, and still there would be unintentional omissions. To all who have helped therefore, we extend our heartfelt thanks.

THE AUTHORS

AUTHORS' PREFACE

HISTORY HAS treated most air heroes generously. Nearly all the leading personalities in aviation's brief span have seen their achievements recorded in detail for future generations, and fighter pilots have been accorded pride of place among air heroes. They were not only a new breed of warrior native to the twentieth century, but also the only soldiers not immersed in the inhuman mass effects of modern warfare.

Fighter aces were able to keep alive for a few brief decades, albeit in tenuous form, the now archaic concept of a fair fight. Man-to-man encounters in which individual martial skill and fighting spirit could affect the outcome disappeared from land and naval battles even as they became the central elements of aerial combat. Chivalry thus found a modern echo among air fighters.

Romance inevitably surrounded the leading fighter aces of all nations, because individual birdmen battling it out still had the potential for glorification while war itself became mechanized mass murder—not only for the combatants, but also for women, children and the elderly. Aces like von Richthofen, Mannock, Fonck, Rickenbacker, Boelcke, Bong, Johnson, Galland and Bader have found fame, but missing from the famous until now is the most successful fighter ace of all the nations and all the wars—Erich Hartmann of Germany.

Erich Hartmann is still practically unknown nearly a quarter of a century after the end of the Second World War. He is recognized, of course, within that devoted circle of air history buffs to whom the achievements of fighting airmen have almost the status of a religion, but even among the faithful there is only an inkling of the drama consummated in Erich Hartmann's life and career.

Postwar events no less than postwar attitudes conspired against the telling of his story, even as they conspired against Erich Hartmann the ex-soldier. With the hot war finished, he passed into Russian imprisonment and was illegally confined for ten and a half years. The postwar world went on without him. During this ordeal he became an unseen and unheralded hero of the same Cold War that was in time to touch and change the lives of millions. His lonely struggle against the Russian secret police, in the view of the authors, far eclipses anything he achieved as a fighter pilot.

His attainment of the staggering tally of 352 confirmed aerial victories was the ultimate achievement by an air fighter. The high scores of the German fighter pilots were not well received on the Allied side in the postwar years, because their victory tallies ran in multiples of the best Allied totals. Explanations had to be found for victory totals that were by all Allied measure completely incredible.

Half-truths and misunderstandings, as well as outright falsehoods, were widely circulated in Allied countries in this regard, so that the unwary allowed themselves to be convinced that the German scores were questionable. Typical assertions were that the German pilots counted every engine on a downed aircraft as a victory, and that squadron leaders took personal credit for all the victories scored by their squadrons. Such apocrypha enjoyed wide currency until coauthor Colonel Toliver, then C.O. of the USAF 20th Tactical Fighter Wing in England, undertook a full investigation of Luftwaffe scoring procedures in the middle 1950s.

This effort left no doubt of the authenticity of the German victory tallies. Furthermore, the meticulous procedures under which the Luftwaffe credited victories to fighter pilots were found to be far more strict than the confirmation procedures of either the USAAF in World War II or the RAF. The German victory confirmation methods have been elaborately detailed in the authors' two previous books, *Fighter Aces* and *Horrido! Fighter Aces of the Luftwaffe*. The reader may therefore regard Erich Hartmann's 352 confirmed victories as a solid and verified achievement.

The investigation of the German victory-accrediting procedures led in due course to a warm personal friendship between the authors and Erich Hartmann and his family. As his decade in Russian prisons fell farther behind him, he became able to tell more about this period of privation and diabolical cruelty. The authors became convinced, as this modest man was led to talk more and more of his experiences, that his story should be told, not only as an indictment of war, but as a clear warning of what awaits the world should it ever fall under the sway of the NKVD-type mind.

COLONEL RAYMOND F. TOLIVER USAF (*Ret.*)
TREVOR J. CONSTABLE

Los Angeles, California
1970

CHAPTER ONE

CALIBER OF A HERO

The world is in a constant conspiracy against the brave.
—*General of the Army Douglas MacArthur*

EIGHT YEARS AFTER the end of the Second World War, the emaciated German ex-soldiers in Camp Diaterka in the Urals had little hope left in life. Confined deep in Russia by a still vengeful Soviet government, stripped of all rights as soldiers and human beings, half-forgotten in their homeland and deprived of every humanizing influence, they were men who were literally lost. Few of them believed they would ever again see Germany and their loved ones. Their attitude to life rarely rose above a stoical apathy in the normal course of prison routine, but one October morning in 1953, the rumored arrival of a certain German prisoner of war charged them with new hope.

Major Erich Hartmann had the special qualities of mind and heart that could kindle again the vital fires of these haunted and bereft prisoners. His was the name whispered through the grim barracks at Diaterka, and whose arrival was a signal event. The most successful fighter ace of all time, Erich Hartmann had won the coveted Diamonds to his Knight's Cross of the Iron Cross—Germany's highest award. These external trappings of heroism meant little to the prisoners. Hartmann to them was the hero of bigger battles in their years-long struggle with the Soviet secret police. He was a symbol of resistance.

His true measure as a man and leader revealed itself in the scene that unfolded upon his arrival at Diaterka. The gaunt

1

inmates of the prison camp dashed into the compound and pressed against the wire as a prison truck pulled up in a cloud of dust. As the choking pall subsided, the new arrivals began getting down under the watchful eyes of armed guards. A wiry, middle-sized man with a thatch of flaxen hair and piercing blue eyes stood out among the shambling group of prisoners in their shapeless convicts' clothes.

"It's *him*," croaked one of the prisoners hanging on the wire. "It's *Hartmann!*"

The scrawny mob behind the barrier burst into a ragged cheer, waving and yelling like the crowd at a home-town football match. The blond man grinned and waved at their spontaneous greeting and the cheering burst out anew. Nervous guards hustled Hartmann and his fellow prisoners inside the inner wire barrier. The armed Russians had heard about Hartmann, too. Like the destitute Germans they guarded at Diaterka, they knew that a real leader had come among them —one of the Soviet Union's most prized and problematical prisoners.

Erich Hartmann's implacable pattern of resistance, which took him several times to the brink of death in personal hunger strikes, had been crowned with an act of open rebellion the previous year at Shakhty. German ex-soldiers, classified as war criminals, were used as slaves in the Russian coal mines at Shakhty, and Erich Hartmann's refusal to work had touched off a little revolt that lifted the spirits of every German confined in Russia.

The story was one to be savored by prisoners for whom escape was impossible, and whose life energies were consumed in the daily process of resisting their own dehumanization. The Russian duty officer and his crew inside the Shakhty camp had been overpowered, and Hartmann, released from solitary confinement by his comrades, spearheaded the drive for redress of the shocking conditions in the camp. He had coolheadedly dissuaded many German prisoners from escaping, and had asked instead for an international commission to be appointed to investigate the Shakhty slave camp.

The outraged Russians had not dared to kill Hartmann, but they had sent him to solitary confinement in another camp at Novocherkassk. Some of his comrades in the Shakhty Revolt had been sent to Diaterka, bringing with them the story of the rebellion. A maximum security camp, Diaterka was under rigid discipline, but the prisoners still managed a roaring welcome for Hartmann.

Located near Sverdlovsk in the Urals, Diaterka had a special inner compound, a prison within a prison, for German VIPs in Soviet clutches. Twelve German generals languished behind its wire, together with members of famous German families and "war criminals" like Erich Hartmann. In Russian eyes, the blond man who got such a rousing welcome to the maximum security pen was no longer a soldier who had done his duty under the laws of his own land and under the traditional codes of military service. His relentless antagonism toward the Soviet secret police led to his "conviction" as a war criminal in a Russian kangaroo court.

Turned over to the Russians in 1945 by the U.S. Army tank unit to which he had surrendered with his *Gruppe* from Luftwaffe Fighter Wing 52, Hartmann steadfastly refused to work for the Soviets or with their East German stooges. His resistance continued through six years of threats, lures and attempted bribes. He even resisted the supreme incentive of return to his family in Germany if he would work in his native land as a Soviet agent. After six years, the Soviets realized that Hartmann was never going to aid their cause, and they then brought him to trial as a war criminal, sentencing him to twenty-five years at hard labor. His response was to ask for a bullet.

Soviet confinement was a prolonged and debilitating test of human character. German men from every walk of life were exposed to its soul-corroding rigors, and many succumbed. America is gathering its own experience today of these nightmares of confinement, with many of its sons, similarly branded as war criminals, in the power of Asiatic Communists. Even the seemingly indomitable Erich Hartmann had his breaking point, and those who endured Soviet jails for untold years are unanimous that everyone has a breaking point under such inhuman conditions.

Senior generals in Russia proved no stronger than privates, and indeed, were all the more pitiful when they broke. Officers demonstrated no superiority over NCOs in meeting the challenge of the NKVD. Age, experience, family background or education—the traditional forces dominant in the development of character and intellect—provided little or no protection against disintegration. Those who survived the ordeal best, and for the longest time, were men who drew their strength from one of two main sources.

Religion provided men in Russian prisons with a powerful personal bastion. Whether he held his religious faith as an abiding conviction or as a fanatic, the religious man could resist his captors. The other men who could maintain their integrity were those who had known an absolutely harmonious family life, and therefore had faith that their homes and marriages would endure. These men wore a kind of armor of love. They were at once protected and powered by this arcane energy. Erich Hartmann belonged to this latter group.

His wife Ursula, whom he calls "Usch," was his spiritual and moral power source while he was under the Soviet yoke. She was the light in his soul when the glory days of war vanished and the black veil of Russian imprisonment was drawn between him and the rest of humanity. She never failed him, and she is an integral part of his achievements. Without her, he never would have survived the Russian prisons for ten years, nor would he have wrought the miracle of his rebirth.

By the common consent of his fellow prisoners, Erich Hartmann was not only one of the strongest men under the Soviet heel, but also one of an elite group of natural leaders. With Germany down in ruins and all military regulations automatically swept away, the German prisoners recognized only those leaders who rose naturally among them. The cream went to the top in this natural process.

Rank and decorations meant nothing, and neither did age or education. Tricks and gimmicks of leadership were of no value. In the Russian prisons there were worthless, traitorous generals and magnificent sergeants; indomitable privates rubbed shoulders with corrupt officers. The leaders who emerged were the best of German manhood in terms of character, will power and endurance.

Barely twenty-three years old when he passed into Russian hands, Erich Hartmann rose to the top despite his extreme youth. He was able to sustain himself and many of his countrymen for more than ten years under conditions of almost indescribable physical and moral hardship. Rarely in history, and never under modern conditions, has a war hero been subjected to such protracted efforts at his degradation. His survival of such an ordeal better verifies his heroic qualities than does his decorations.

The wellsprings of Erich Hartmann's strength were beyond the reach of the NKVD. Their source lay in his family background, free upbringing and native manhood, reinforced and overlaid by the undying love of a beautiful woman—his wife. His personality combines the strengths of both his parents. His physician father was a quiet, decent man with the old-time European doctor's deep feeling for his fellow humans, and a penetrant, practical wisdom largely missing from modern men. His mother, who is still living as this is written, was a vibrant extrovert as a young woman, gay, energetic, enterprising and venturesome.

Dr. Hartmann enjoyed quiet philosophizing over a glass of beer as a relaxation from his profession, while his exuberant blonde wife flew airplanes in Germany, before society had quite decided whether it was a fitting thing for a woman to do. The willingness to dare and the wisdom to know just how far to go—key elements in making Erich Hartmann the most successful fighter pilot ever—are character traits derived from the qualities of his parents. These and other inherited qualities met and mingled with individual talents that are distinctively his own.

He has a will almost fierce in its drive to prevail and conquer. His directness in thought and word are disquieting to the pretender, inspiring to the timid and challenging to the valiant. He is an incorrigible individualist in an age of mass effects and conformity. To the marrow of his bones he is a fighter, not only in the sense of being the greatest of all fighter aces, but also in terms of meeting all life's challenges head-on.

"Gandy-dancing" around an issue is something of which he is incapable, even if his life depended on it. He would be a total failure in the diplomatic service, with his punch-in-the-nose bluntness, but he is a sportsman and a lover of fair play. A fair man and an honest man has nothing to fear from him, for he shakes hands as easily as he locks horns. In an age with a diminishing regard for fair play he is in some ways an anachronism, and like the knights of old he would rush to pick up a foe he had just knocked from the saddle.

In aerial warfare as a flying soldier, he killed many enemy

pilots, but he is incapable in everyday-life of consciously doing injury to another. He is not religious in the formal sense, although he admired and respected the Germans who were so sustained in Russia. His religion is one of conscience and is an extension of his fighting heart. As George Bernard Shaw once expressed it: "There is a certain type of man who holds that there are certain things he must not do in life, regardless of the cost to himself. Such a man may be called a religious man. Or you may call him a gentleman." Erich Hartmann's code of conduct—his religion in a sense—is that he cannot be made to do anything he believes to be wrong, and he will not of himself do anything he knows to be wrong.

This variant of the golden rule arises from his black-and-white convictions, which admit to little gray in life. He has an old-time moral sense, probably inherited from his father, and the kind of feeling for Truth that wins him the adoration of today's young German pilots. In the Russian prisons, his spiritual forces found their focus in the image he carried with him of his beloved Usch. His conviction that all would be well at home, the mental picture he held of a peaceful hearth centered around his wife, did for him what formal religion did for others who survived. His faith in Usch never wavered, and it was fulfilled a hundredfold.

Was Erich Hartmann then, a self-centered individual, thinking only of himself and his Usch? Far from it. He actually never needed to expose himself to Russian jails. Right before the end of the war, General Seidemann ordered him to take a Messerschmitt fighter, leave Czechoslovakia and his unit, and fly back to central Germany. His orders were to surrender to the British. General Seidemann knew that the Russians would take vengeance on their aerial nemesis, and the order to fly to safety was the last order from higher HQ that Hartmann received during the war.

The young, blond-haired major deliberately disobeyed this order. Thousands of German refugee civilians—women, children and old people—most of them relatives of men serving in his *Gruppe*, had become attached to this unit. Militarily, an order was an order, and he should have obeyed. He accepted instead what he believed to be his unavoidable duty as an officer and as a human being. He stayed with the defenseless civilians, a decision that cost him more than ten years of his life.

His modesty is as much a part of the whole man as his blue eyes and blond hair. Typically, he never told the authors about General Seidemann's order in more than twelve years of friendship that preceded the preparation of this book. The information came from others. When asked about it, Hartmann merely shrugged.

Unrelentingly hard against himself, he could find it in his heart to forgive a comrade who caved in under Soviet pressure. Every man had his breaking point, and for some it came sooner than others—that was Erich Hartmann's view. When fellow prisoners cracked up emotionally under such ultimate strain as a divorce *in absentia* granted to a wife in Germany, he gave of his strength to pull them back together. He could talk soothingly to them, or slap them back to reality. His hard way was his own, and not for other men unless they chose, as a free act, to follow his lead.

When his release from Russia was secured by Chancellor Adenauer in 1955, there were still many German prisoners remaining in Russia. Many had preceded him to freedom in West Germany, and the occasion of his return to his native land was to be celebrated by ex-P.O.W.'s and their families. At the railroad station in Herleschausen, the first free soil he had touched in a decade, there was a noisy and exultant welcome. He was told that a massive celebration was planned later for Stuttgart, near his home town of Weil im Schönbuch. The P.O.W. associations had organized the gathering, and important public figures were scheduled to attend.

Thin and gaunt, Hartmann was obviously moved. Then he surprised his welcomers by insisting that there be no such reception. He could not take part in such festivities. Newspapermen asked him why he would not accept the heartfelt welcome home from his fellow citizens of Stuttgart.

"Because the Russians view life differently from us. They might well decide, on hearing or reading of such a celebration, not to release any more German prisoners. I know the Russians well enough to be fearful on this account for the continued imprisonment of my countrymen in the Soviet Union.

"When they are *all* home, then we will have the celebration. Meanwhile, we must not rest until all German soldiers held prisoners in Russia are repatriated."

His ten-year duel with the Soviet secret police intensified Erich Hartmann's native quality of directness, but he had his head-on nature long before the Russians got their hands on him. Forthright to a fault, he speaks out loud and clear in the presence of wrong. Even Reichsmarschall Goering, standing one rung below God when the Nazis were in power, failed to overawe Erich Hartmann when the young ace felt Goering had perpetrated a wrongful act.

He visited his mother near Juterborg in January 1944, when the air defense of the Reich was suffering from a severe shortage of pilots rather than planes. He landed at a fighter base near Juterborg when the weather was closing in. Only twenty-two years old himself, he was struck by the extreme youth of the pilots in the fighter squadron based at the field. He was used to seeing young men come to his units in Russia, but these flyers looked scarcely more than high-school boys.

When he returned from his visit with his mother, he found that the squadron had been sent up into the foul weather that had started to close in when he landed a few hours previously. Their mission was to intercept a force of American bombers. With limited training and even less practical experience, ten of the youngsters had crashed fatally in the bad weather, without ever finding or shooting at the bombers. The infuriated Blond Knight sat down and wrote a personal letter to Reichsmarschall Goering.

Herr Reichsmarschall:

Today from this airfield on your orders, fighter units took off in vile weather in an effort to find and shoot down American bombers. The weather was so bad that I would have been unwilling to take off myself. The fighters you sent into the air never found the bombers and ten very young pilots and planes were lost without firing a shot at the enemy.

Some of the young pilots I talked to in this squadron who are now dead had less than 80 hours' flying time. If we cannot win against the bombers in blue sky, then to send youngsters up to die in bad weather is nothing short of a criminal act.

We should wait until the skies are blue, and the bombers come, and then send everyone up to assault them at once, with some chance of success. It is disgraceful to waste young men's lives as has been done today.

Yours faithfully,

Captain E. Hartmann
Fighter Wing 52

Erich Hartmann sent the letter directly to Goering by regular mail, including his full current address. The tone and content of this missive were sufficient to ensure punishment even for a leading ace. The next communication he got from Goering was a telegram hailing him as the most successful fighter pilot in the world. Probably Goering personally never saw the Blond Knight's letter, but it was written and mailed with the intention that it should reach the *Reichsmarschall*.

Because Erich Harmann's life has had more than a fair measure of gruel as well as glory, and because he has been a fighter in war and peace, the light side of his nature has rarely been discussed in the limited material published about him to date. He enjoys life hugely, has his mother's gaiety and sense of humor, and at social gatherings of friends, old comrades and young pilots of the new German Air Force, the old tiger becomes a social lion. The boy is not far inside the man, and he is a boy who loves to play.

His boyishness when he went to the Eastern Front in 1942 earned him the immediate nickname of "Bubi," which in German means boy or lad. He was full of fun then, and his comrade-in-arms and longtime personal friend Walter Krupinski tells of the time when Bubi Hartmann clowned even in the rarefied air of Berchtesgaden, before getting a decoration personally from Hitler.

Four leading aces of Fighter Wing 52 were on their way on 3 March 1944 to Hitler's "Eagle's Nest" to be decorated. The aces were Gerhard Barkhorn, Johannes "Kubanski Lion" Wiese, Walter "Count Punski" Krupinski and Bubi Hartmann. The careers of all these men interlocked with Hartmann's and all will be dealt with later in this book, but on the occasion in question Barkhorn was to receive the Swords (*Schwertern*) to his Knight's Cross, Germany's second highest decoration. The other three were to receive the Oak Leaves to the Knight's Cross, the order standing immediately below the Swords.

The four men met each other on the train, and en route to Salzburg they befriended the conductor. He was attracted to the pilots because all four were wearing the Knight's Cross at their throats, and all four were happy, young and friendly. The conductor began conjuring an endless supply of beverages from his compartment—schnapps, beer, wine, cognac. As fast as he produced the bottles, the four flyers disposed of the contents.

When the conductor poured them off the train a few miles from the Eagle's Nest they were in no condition to meet their Führer. As they staggered into the railway station, they encountered tall, blond-haired Major von Below, Hitler's Luftwaffe aide-de-camp. A kindly old cavalier, von Below nearly capsized when he saw the four neatly-dressed pilots in such an unseemly condition. They were scheduled to meet the Führer in less than two hours. Countermeasures were necessary.

Typical early March weather in the Bavarian Alps prevailed outside. About three inches of blown snow lay on the ground, with continual light snow blowing off the nearby mountaintops or falling out of a gray overcast. The temperature was 25 degrees Fahrenheit. Von Below ordered the driver of the waiting Mercedes convertible to put the top down, and drive the four celebrants to the Eagle's Nest in the cold, brisk air.

They were driven up the road in the perishing cold, and then allowed to get out and walk a little. They were then hustled into the Eagle's Nest a few minutes before their appointment with the Führer. They were still far from sober.

As they entered the foyer of the beautiful building, Hartmann spotted a military cap hanging on a stand nearby. Seeing that it had some braid on it, he said, "Oh yes, there's my hat." He walked over and quickly plopped it on his head, turning to be admired by his fellow aces. They burst into laughter. The hat came down over his ears—size seven and a quarter on a six-and-three-quarters head.

Von Below didn't join in the laughter. The harassed aide, appointed by Hitler to steer visitors through the maze of protocol and procedure, rushed over and snatched the hat from Erich Hartmann's head.

"Give me that. *It is the Führer's hat!*"

The four pilots received their decorations without falling over, but the Blond Knight's inadvertent borrowing of the Führer's hat is always good for a laugh whenever any of the four men meet today. Because he excelled at a very grim business, and survived an even grimmer aftermath, Erich Hartmann's sense of humor has remained veiled from the public. Nevertheless it is an essential part of his personality, and he would not be the man he is without its leavening force.

In the annals of war history there have not been many heroes of Hartmann's dimension, and in the shorter span of aerial history, even fewer. His 352 aerial victories, all confirmed, are the all-time world record for a fighter pilot. His closest rival, Gerd Barkhorn, has fifty-one victories fewer than Hartmann. The Blond Knight of Germany downed more than four times as many aircraft as the Red Knight, the immortal Baron Manfred von Richthofen, top-scoring fighter ace of the First World War.

Even in the hard-driven Luftwaffe, only a handful of fighter pilots flew more often or entered aerial combat with greater frequency than Erich Hartmann. He took off to fight no less than fourteen hundred times, and actually entered aerial combat on more than eight hundred occasions. His physical and mental resilience were such that he endured without fatigue the constant grind of aerial combat from the fall of 1942 until the end of May 1945.

He was never wounded. His ability to keep his hide intact while taking toll of his foes was not mere blind luck. He was lucky, like all successful fighter pilots, but he developed a distinctive, individual style of air fighting that amounted to a tactical innovation. He rejected the dogfight, and since the war, his onetime adjutant, Will Van de Kamp,* has said that Hartmann's success was due to the way he drove home his attacks. They were point-blank, like the man.

Van de Kamp once told Usch Hartmann after the war that if all fighter pilots had used Erich's tactics, he would never have become the world's most successful fighter ace. Van de Kamp's view was that Erich Hartmann's success was due to

* The late Will Van de Kamp introduced the Volkswagen to the United States of America after the war.

his tactical break with the past, and the Blond Knight's own version of how he evolved his tactics, detailed in this book, bear out the evaluation of his onetime adjutant.

He is a man of many faults and failings, most of them arising from his positive personality. Analytical and intuitive, as well as realistic, he is likely to go to the core of any problem with which he deals and pluck out its primal seed. He decides and then digs in his toes. In business, these traits might well have made him a tycoon, but in today's military, they have been liabilities as much as assets.

As a youngster, his directness showed up in impetuousness, and often in dangerous conduct. In his maturity, it manifests as a devastating lack of tact. In a modern culture increasingly absorbed and fascinated by the vacillations of uncertain heroes, he emerges as a vibrant anachronism. His vital, mobile mind has kept him young at heart, and the heart of a tiger still beats inside the old tomcat he insists he has become. In today's Hartmann, the hell-for-leather fighter ace, often sloppy in dress, always venturesome, perennially romantic, is perilously close to the surface for a man in his late forties pursuing a military career.

He is a man of consummate coolness under stress, and has far more than his fair share of nerve. He often closed in to less than a hundred feet before firing at his foes in the air, a perilously close distance, and a paper-thin margin between a sure kill and a mid-air collision. He survived fourteen forced landings on the Eastern Front, taking off again each time as soon as a new aircraft was available. Despite his tender years —he was twenty-two years old when he won the Diamonds— his innate qualities of modesty and restraint were not disturbed.

Far older men than Erich Hartmann, in all the military forces of the world, sometimes failed to wear the hero's mantle with dignity and credit to themselves and their nation. As U.S. Marine Corps fighter ace Colonel Gregory "Pappy" Boyington once said, "Show me a hero, and I'll show you a bum." For many heroes, Boyington's derogatory assessment has been all too true. Many a wartime celebrity has become a peacetime emotional casualty. Erich Hartmann had to maintain his integrity not in the face of rewards heaped on him by a grateful nation, but against a regime that forced him to fight on for a decade in a lonely, soul-destroying Cold War.

Hartmann played the cards that Fate has dealt him in war and peace with an equanimity that all men can admire, but which few could even hope to emulate. When he returned to Germany in 1955 he had several bitter cups to drain. His son, Peter Erich, had died in 1947 and the Blond Knight never saw the boy. His beloved father had also passed away. His boyhood hope to follow his father into the medical profession had to be renounced on account of his age and long separation from the academic world. Nearly one-third of his time on earth had been in Russian jails.

Old fighter tigers from his glory days continually pressed him to join the new German Air Force. They put on an informal campaign to get him back into the military. With all other possibilities dim, he had to begin rebuilding his life on the foundation of his fighter piloting, the thing he knew best, the profession he had mastered.

He checked out on the new jets under USAF instructors, started a new family with a lively blonde daughter, and began the process of his own rebirth. He was and is the only member of the new German armed forces to win the Diamonds in the Second World War. His old glories, and his farsighted and serious new boss, General Kammhuber, made his appointment to command the first jet fighter wing of the new German Air Force—the Richthofen Wing—a historic and morale-building step. He became one of the most respected officers in Germany.

For all the good signs he was not yet done with enemies. The antagonists of the Blond Knight were not only the enemy pilots in war and the NKVD in peace, but also petty men in high places in the new German Air Force. Small men in big jobs envied Erich Hartmann and tried in various ways to injure his career and status. A few years ago, one such man in the uniform of a general tried to shoot the Blond Knight down from the ground, in a proceeding that will be detailed in due course. He survived this thrust and fights on.

The battered shield of the Blond Knight is still carried with honor, and its escutcheons are still bright. More names of glory may yet be emblazoned on it, for its fair-haired bearer is still a formidable participant in the tournament of life. The time has come to explore with him his story as a hero of the joust, the depth of his torment while in bondage, and his unforgettable romance with his beautiful lady.

CHAPTER TWO

THE MAKING OF A MAN

The fount of manhood has its source in boyhood.
—Anonymous

AN ADVENTUROUS keynote was struck for the life of Erich Hartmann when he departed Germany with his family in 1925 to live in China. Born 19 April 1922 at Weissach in Württemberg, Erich was a sturdy, blond-headed infant already showing a will of his own when his mother took him aboard a steamer bound for the Orient. Erich's father, Dr. Alfred Hartmann, had found conditions in postwar Germany difficult and unrewarding. A German Army doctor in the First World War, he had returned from that conflict only to confront new enemies—inflation, food shortages, political and economic chaos.

When Dr. Hartmann's cousin, who was German consul in Shanghai, came home and saw the shambles in the fatherland, he urged Erich's father to return with him and practice medicine in China. The consul assured him of a flourishing practice among the Chinese. Dr. Hartmann loved adventure, and the prospect of practicing his profession in a foreign land intrigued him, but he was initially skeptical of the rosy picture painted by his diplomat cousin. A conservative and careful man, in contrast to his exuberant and outgoing wife, Dr. Hartmann went ahead alone to China to reconnoiter. He was hardly prepared for what he found.

Compared to convulsed and hungry Germany, China was almost a paradise. Dr. Hartmann found the Chinese people eager for his services; they paid their bills and they rewarded him as well with their high regard. He was the only white doctor in Changsha, some six hundred miles up the Siang [Yangtze Kiang] River and another hundred up the Hsiang River, when he opened his practice and sent for his family. He had a pleasant home in Changsha, and later bought an island in the middle of the river, on which he built a new home.

Erich's earliest memories of life center on the wooded island, with its natural playgrounds, unspoiled beauty and secluded coves. The island was a place where a child's imagination could thrive and run free. This Oriental idyl was not destined to last long. A few years later, as the first modern revolutionary stirrings began in the Chinese people, their course became anti-colonialist and anti-"foreign devil." Civil disturbances broke out.

Dr. Hartmann had two sources of protection as agitation became worse. There was his status in the community as a physician. His good works were not lost on the Chinese. Secondly, he was lucky to be a German, because in the China of the 1920s the Germans had no status or influence, and were not a part of the decaying colonial structure.

These conditions nevertheless provided only a temporary immunity for the Hartmann family. By 1929, street violence was becoming commonplace. Assaults on English, French and Belgian residents were frequent. Dr. Hartmann had several English friends, one of whom had his home in the town of Changsha, not far from the medical office. Walking to his office one morning, Erich's father was appalled to find the severed heads of three English friends impaled on the picket fence around one of the British residences.

The kindly German doctor reacted quickly. Frau Hartmann, five-and-a-half-year-old Erich and his brother Alfred, a year younger, were packed off back to Germany for safety's sake. For several weeks they went jolting across Russia on the horrendous Trans-Siberian Railroad. On the way through Moscow, the train made a stop that was supposed to last an hour, and Elisabeth Hartmann went to get some food and drink for her sons.

"Erich," she said to her elder son, "you look after Alfred. Don't get out of your seats. I will be back in a few minutes."

She disappeared into the milling throng in the Moscow station. Before she returned, the train started pulling out. Alfred Hartmann, today a doctor in Weil im Schönbuch, has a clear memory of the petrifying experience that ensued.

"I was terrified, and soon blinded by tears. Erich was calmer. He kept soothing me, urging me not to cry and to be brave. I would have none of it, and kept bawling my head off. The train was rattling on toward Germany at what seemed like a frantic pace. The people in the train were trying to find out what was wrong with us, and Erich was manfully trying to explain our plight. Unfortunately, at that time we both spoke better Chinese than German, which contributed to the confusion and to my ever-mounting terror.

"After what seemed like an hour of agony, through all of which Erich had been my comforter, interpreter and nurse, the carriage door opened and there stood my mother, her blonde hair blown awry but a smile on her lips. At her appearance, even the brave Erich broke down. Tears rolled down his cheeks as he pointed to me recriminatingly. 'I told him not to cry,' he bawled, as our mother's arms went around us both."

In later years, the cause of Elisabeth Hartmann's strange absence has been one of the family jokes. She had been buying food after standing in line, when she heard her train called, long before the end of its scheduled hour stop. The departure whistle shrieked immediately afterward. Dropping everything, the blonde young German matron bolted along the platform as the train gathered speed. Grabbing at the handrail of the last car at the very end of the platform, she swung aboard Hollywood-style, exhausted and panting.

Russian railways at this time were a long way from possessing the luxurious rolling stock in vogue on most Western railroads. This particular train had no inner corridors in the cars behind the one in which Frau Hartmann had been riding with her sons. These coaches were like Australian streetcars, with a catwalk along the side. She had been forced to work her way forward car by car, finally reaching the closed coach where Erich and his brother were waiting.

Ater her return from China, Elisabeth Hartmann settled down in Weil im Schönbuch near Stuttgart and waited for word from her husband. After six months he wrote that things had quieted down. The civil strife had abated. "Come back to China," he wrote, "and bring the boys."

The independent Elisabeth Hartmann, however, had already decided that enough of their lives had been spent in the Orient. "I will not return to China," she wrote back, "and I am looking now for an office for you near Stuttgart, where you can settle down and practice medicine safely." Dr. Hartmann came home. The family moved into a quaint old farmhouse near Weil, and three years later the couple built a house and office at 9 Bismarckstrasse in Weil im Schönbuch, where Erich Hartmann was to spend the rest of his youth before going to war.

From his earliest years in Weil, Erich was aviation-mad. A capacity for daring began to emerge, exemplified by his first attempt to fly. He fashioned a glider out of bamboo shafts and stretched old blankets over the framework to form a fuselage. Carrying this rig, which was a blend of Clem Sohn and Leonardo da Vinci, he ran and jumped off the roof of the summer house. He landed in a specially-dug pit filled with soft earth, and he was unhurt, but he recognized his faulty engineering and forthwith abandoned his ground-hungry contraption.

Erich's interest in aviation was given impetus and focus when his adventurous mother took up sport flying. Life in Weil was pleasant, but a little on the boring side for an active and attractive young woman like Elisabeth Hartmann. She joined a flying club at Böblingen Airport, the civil flying field for Stuttgart in those days, just a little more than six miles from Dr. Hartmann's office in Weil.

A gifted pilot, Erich's mother got her private flying license on a light plane, a Klemm 27. Then in 1930, the happy Hartmann family became part owners of a two-seater, which they shared with the meteorological director of Böblingen Airport. Erich's exposure to airplanes and flying thus became constant and intimate.

Today, IBM has buildings on the old Böblingen Airport site, but in the early 1930s every fine Saturday and Sunday saw the Hartmann boys and their mother flying in the little Klemm, or working on it. After the economic collapse in 1932, the beloved little machine had to be sold. The loss of the aircraft was a hard blow.

The following year, Hitler came to power, and German

aviation began its resurrection. Hitler wanted German youth to become air-minded, and urged the formation of glider clubs as a focus for this interest. In 1936, Frau Hartmann formed a glider club at Weil im Schönbuch for the local boys, mostly farmers' sons, and served as instructress. The thrill of the snappy little Klemm was missing, but gliding had a rare charm all of its own, and it made for happy and entertaining weekends.

The club had two gliders. A Zögling 38, for primary training, was an open glider. For advanced pilots, there was a Grunau Baby. Every weekend Erich was taken by his mother to the gliding meets. He took his turn with the other boys. The grueling task of pulling the gliders into the air with a heavy rubber rope was a perfect outlet for youthful energy. With eight husky young Germans on each side, they would run forward, dragging the glider with all their might.

Often the sailplane would lift a few yards into the air, only to crunch back down on the grass amid groans of despair from the rope-pullers. The hard pull would have to begin again. The boys had to work hard for the thrill of flying. Then would come the magic words.

"Erich, you get in. It's your turn. We'll try to pull you up."

His brother Alfred has a vivid memory of Erich's gliding skill: "He was an excellent pilot, gifted from the start. I used to wish I could do as well, but there was a vast difference in our natural ability for gliding."

At fourteen years of age, Erich was a licensed and proficient glider pilot. At the end of 1937, he passed his "A" and "B" Glider Pilot examinations, and with his "C" License became an Instructor in the Glider Group of the Hitler Youth. Looking back on those days more than thirty years ago, Erich Hartmann says this of his introduction to flying:

"Gliding was a great sport, and something more besides. It gave me a wonderful feeling for the air. The sensation and subtle pressures of the wind all around you, holding you up, bearing on your glider, attune you to the air environment. You become, in the true sense, an *air man*. Powered flight, later in the Luftwaffe, came as nothing strange to me. I had seen my mother, my brother and all my young friends fly, and I had flown, so climbing into an aircraft was as much a part of me as getting into an automobile.

"The early familiarization with aircraft that I got through

gliding has helped me right down to this day. If I am sitting in an aircraft and something goes wrong, I get a bad feeling. I get this feeling often before there is any instrumented indication of a failure of some kind. I feel it in the seat of my pants. There can be no doubt that the earlier you get started in the flying business, the more highly developed your feeling becomes for everything connected with aircraft."

Erich's brother Alfred practices medicine today in the same family home in Weil built by his physician father. He is a sensitive and kindly man, who reflects strongly his father's temperament and outlook. After a brief fling as a Stuka gunner in North Africa, he was captured in Tunisia, and spent four years in British prison camps. More delicate of features, physique and manner than his famous brother, Alfred recalls Erich's formative early years in these frank terms:

"He was stronger than me in every way. He was sports-minded, athletic and accomplished in sports. In fact, there was nothing in the sporting line at which he did not excel or could not excel if he tried it. He was a natural athlete with wonderful coordination, and he was at home swimming, diving, skiing and at track. He excelled at gymnastics.

"In their own society, boys elect their leaders naturally, and Erich was a natural leader among them. His athletic prowess was only one element in this natural ability to lead. He was also clever, strong and practical—a resourceful boy. Boys his age really respected him for these qualities. Then, too, he had other qualities which his later fame might obscure. He was fair and he was gentle, particularly to me, because he knew he was stronger than me.

"Erich could not abide a bully, and he was a protector of younger boys. I exploited his well-earned fame as a bully-tamer by telling bigger boys who threatened me that they would hear from Erich if they hit me or bothered me. They left me severely alone on this account."

Even in sleepy little Weil im Schönbuch, with its population of three thousand people, the boys went around in gangs. Erich and Alfred belonged to the Glider Gang, a group of boys from Frau Hartmann's gliding club. The rival gang, because of its differing interest, was known as the Bicycle Gang. There was "bad blood" between the two gangs because of fancied insults, as there usually is between bunches of boys in rivalry. Erich's readiness to crash into action was revealed in one encounter between the gangs.

Returning home from a movie one evening, Alfred and another boy trailed along forty yards or so behind Erich and the main body of the Glider Gang. Members of the Bicycle Gang waiting in concealment sprang out of the shadows, seized Alfred and his pal, and spirited them off to their hideaway. Another member of the Glider Gang who was bringing up the rear, saw the kidnaping. He followed the kidnapers and then ran after the Glider Gang for help.

"The Bicycle Gang has Alfred—they've got him in the old barn and they're going to beat him up."

Hard-sprinting Erich quickly outstripped the Glider Gang as he ran to the rescue. He hit the barn doors at full tilt, smashing them open. Bursting into the barn, he confronted the shocked Bicycle Gang. There were fourteen of them. They had Alfred and his friend tied to a post. Erich snatched up a jack handle from the barn floor and started swinging.

"Get out! Get out! All of you. Before I whack you with this."

The blue eyes were like burning pinpoints as he advanced on his foes, swinging the jack handle in a wide arc. The Bicycle Gang broke and ran, bolting out of the barn for their lives as Erich, triumphant and panting, untied his grateful brother. In later years, the same fearless quality burning in the man would make him victorious over others who outnumbered him. He was a boy who tackled life head-on.

Erich and his brother were students in the mid-1930s at a national-political educational school in Rottweil. The character of this school did not sit well with the forming character of young Erich. He loved freedom. The school functioned under tight, military-style discipline, which ruled all aspects of the students' lives. Much silly polemic based on the new German nationalism was taught, and even leisure-time activities were regulated. Weekends at home in Weil seemed to Erich like a liberation from prison.

He carries to this day an unpleasant memory of Rottweil:

"Every teacher was God, and we were the slaves. Once in a physics lesson we had to make black powder from charcoal and sulfur, and when time came for the morning break, we had to put our combined production on an iron plate. We were told not to play with this material during the break.

"The teacher left the classroom, and we promptly gathered around the pile of powder, fascinated by the explosive power we knew it contained. A couple of the more enterprising boys put matches near the powder, but weren't game to actually ignite it. Everyone was daring everyone else to hit the powder directly with a match. Someone challenged me directly to do it, which was probably a mistake. I took a match and shoved it right into the powder. A flash and an explosion sent everyone diving under the desks, and a pall of smoke went billowing out of the room.

"Within seconds, our teacher came striding back in, obviously angry. Nobody would confess to playing with the powder, so I put my hand up and said that I had set it alight. My punishment was to clean up all the apparatus used during lessons. I was still doing this cleanup job three days later when I accidentally knocked a heavy iron glass-holder into the cleaning sink, destroying some glass retorts.

"Ever afterward it was outright war between myself and this teacher. He never forgot my prank, nor forgave me. He seized every chance to victimize me. This vendetta typified the unhealthy student-teacher relationship at Rottweil."

Erich chafed under the school's strictures, and made his discomfort known to his parents. In the spring of 1937, Dr. Hartmann transferred his sons to the "Internat" type of *Hochschule* at Korntal near Stuttgart. The school had a dormitory wing and the Hartmann boys boarded there during the week. Erich's old teacher at Korntal, Professor Kurt Busch, remembers the conditions under which the future ace of aces got his education.

"Korntal School operated on lines different from the military-type Rottweil school. I remember Erich telling me he thought the discipline too strict and all-encompassing at Rottweil. We allowed more freedom, and encouraged a good relationship between teachers and students. Every incentive was present for education and study.

"In particular, the freedom they were given encouraged their sense of responsibility, as well as the development of conscience. These kids were not angels, Erich included, but when they abused their freedom, they knew it and felt it inside. This really means something for teen-agers, and I believe Erich was happy in Korntal *Hochschule.*"

Thirty years later, Professor Busch had little difficulty in recalling the Erich Hartmann he taught in 1937–1939:

"He was a boy one liked immediately. Straightforward, open and honest, he carried these qualities over into a certain impulsiveness, but without hurting anyone's feelings or provoking them. He was aware of his winning traits and profited by them, which he thought was quite right, but nevertheless he was extremely tolerant and never carried grudges. His temperament was to enjoy himself and look for the sunnier side of life. Toward teachers he was courteous and respectful, and I thought highly of his modesty and tidiness."

Professor Busch, Erich's brother Alfred and his mother all agree that he was not the intellectual type. He was an average student who fulfilled the academic curriculum without either difficulty or ambition. He exerted only such effort as was needed to pass examinations. His energies were primarily directed to the sports he loved.

Part of Korntal school activities was an occasional week of skiing in the mountains. On these trips, Professor Busch had many opportunities to see at first hand Erich's drive to excel competitively—and also his penchant for fun. The professor was once almost too close to the scene. When he emerged from his chalet one morning, he was greeted by a whooshing sound and a shower of snow as Erich completed a free ski jump off the chalet roof, eighteen feet above the professor's head.

Warnings to Erich of steep slopes, danger, or jumping hazards were futile. A soft, self-assured laugh and the happy grin that later became a characteristic of Erich Hartmann the man, were his only response before tackling the next hazard. Alfred Hartmann recalls a time when they went to a skiing meet that featured a big jumping event.

"Erich had never done this kind of big jump before. But he simply said he was going to enter the event the next day. I told him he was a fool. When the time came, it was me, standing in the audience, that was trembling, while Erich was at the top of the slope as cool as the snow he stood on. The loudspeakers boomed his name. Down he came, then high in the air. My heart was in my mouth. But he made a smooth

jump of ninety-eight feet and landed perfectly. He was courageous to a fault, but there was nothing of the show-off in him.
He did nothing for the purpose of strutting or boasting. To
him, it was the most natural thing in the world to tackle a ski
jump like that—to meet its challenge. After his success, he
behaved with perfect modesty."

His head-on acceptance of any kind of athletic challenge
won him the boyhood nickname of "Wild Boar." Professor
Busch recalls it as a natural nickname. "The name is not too
flattering, but it described to perfection Erich's vitality and
forcefulness at this time—qualities that won him our whole-
hearted respect." They were also qualities that were later to
carry him to a place in history, and sustain him through
ordeals almost beyond the comprehension of the kindly people
of prewar Weil im Schönbuch.

Erich's first and only love affair was also a head-on adventure. At Korntal *Hochschule* he met the girl who was to be
first his sweetheart and later his wife—Ursula Paetsch. As a
young teenager, "Usch" Paetsch was as dark as Erich was
fair, and that immediately caught his eye. He declares to this
day that he simply fell in love with her at first sight. Having
made up his mind, he decided to take action. In October
1939, Usch and a girl friend were walking home from school
one afternoon when Erich came racing up on his bike. Jumping off and letting the bicycle fall to the sidewalk, he looked
into Usch's eyes and shyly said, "I'm Erich Hartmann." This
self-introduction, typical of Erich's innate directness, started a
love affair that was to survive the harshest adversity.

Erich's parents were concerned over his sudden concentration on one girl. He was only seventeen. Still more startled
were Mr. and Mrs. Paetsch, because Usch was only fifteen.
"Erich was the aggressor, we knew that," said Usch's mother
of this time. Usch's father, an engineer for a mining equipment manufacturer, voiced initial opposition but quickly recognized that he could not influence the youngsters. When
Erich was obviously going to persist, Herr Paetsch simply quit
the unequal struggle. "I wash my hands of the whole thing,"
he said.

Usch's mother tried to discourage the courtship, but it was
not easy. Usch once said that she was going to a movie with
her girl friend, which she did. Waiting in the movie by

prearrangement was Erich. He undertook to see Usch home, and she was late. Frau Paetsch imposed a three months' ban on all movies, despite the appeals and apologies of the blond-haired boy who came to her door to plead his case. Usch accepted the punishment with unusual resignation, and a couple of months later her mother found out why.

In order to become a typically accomplished young lady, Usch was taking dancing lessons in Stuttgart. Twice a week she would dutifully attend classes. At the dancing school and attending the same classes was her fair-haired beau, Erich Hartmann. They could not be kept apart, and it gradually became obvious to everyone that they belonged together. In time, both families were charmed by their young love in a world that was growing darker.

Before he could truly call Usch his girl friend, Erich had to eliminate some competition. Usch's charms had captivated a lanky, dark-haired youth who was older than Erich and a head taller. In later years, Usch smilingly referred to him as "Casanova"—a sort of youthful German version of Cesar Romero, complete with sideburns. When Erich told Usch that he wanted her to be his girl and go steady with him, she confessed that Casanova kept telephoning and wanting dates.

"I'll take care of that," said Erich.

He called on Casanova, who towered over him. Casanova listened impassively to Erich.

"Usch is my girl now, and I don't want you to call her or try and make dates any more. I know you will understand."

Casanova sniffed disdainfully, turned on his heel and walked away, giving no sign that he had even heard this polite ultimatum. A few days later, Casanova was again calling Usch and asking her to go to the movies. When Usch told Erich, his face darkened a little and he said he would see Casanova about the phone calls.

A few days later, he ran into Casanova.

"I told you to stay away from Usch," he said, and stood up for his rights with a couple of lefts—one to the nose and one to the solar plexus. Casanova sank to the sidewalk in blubbering disarray, forever elminated from the contest for Usch's hand.

Erich and Usch were seldom out of each other's thoughts from the fall of 1939 onward, and the warmth of young love filled their lives. They spent every possible moment together, oblivious to almost everything except each other. War had come to Europe in September 1939, but it had an unreal quality to Erich and Usch until the spring of 1940 and Erich's graduation from Korntal *Hochschule*. He had to make an important decision about his future.

His intention all along had been to become a doctor, and this wish had gladdened his father's heart, although Erich had no heartfelt, driving desire to become a physician. When he graduated from Korntal *Hochschule* a few weeks after his eighteenth birthday in April 1940, he realized that some kind of military service was inevitable. That could mean only one thing for Erich—the Luftwaffe.*

The war opened to Erich Hartmann the complex and expensive field of aviation. Powered flight in prewar Europe was possible only for a few, because aircraft were expensive to acquire and operate. Certainly sport flying was beyond the reach of most young men in their teens. Under the impetus of war, the same young men could become military pilots, and find themselves the recipients of an education in aviation in which no expense was spared.

By 1940 the German fighter force had begun to capture the imagination of the German people. Newspapers carried extensive publicity about successful fighter pilots. Werner Moelders, the top scorer of the Condor Legion in the Spanish Civil War, was in action again with much success. Johannes Steinhoff and Wolfgang Falck were the heroes of the Battle of the German Bight against RAF bombers attacking Germany. Erich's imagination was captured by the seemingly glamorous trade of fighter piloting. He decided to enlist in the Luftwaffe.

His humanitarian father was disappointed that Erich had chosen to be a flyer, but Erich had been raised a free man and was allowed to decide his own future in freedom. Erich's mother understood his desire to fly, for she had nurtured and guided his early ambitions toward the air. Usch was unhappy at the prospect of being separated from Erich, but then, as now, whatever he wished to do would meet with her assent.

* The German military was very sensitive about being referred to as the Luftwaffe after World War II. However, after about 1962 it became the normal term throughout the world. *Luftwaffe* is "Air Force" in the German language.

Dr. Hartmann believed the war would end in a German defeat, and that the conflict boded no good for the fatherland. Among themselves, nevertheless, they all rationalized Erich's decision. The common view of the times that the war would soon be over assisted their acceptance of Erich's desire to become a pilot. They reasoned that he could learn to be an accomplished flyer, and after the anticipated short war there would still be plenty of time for medicine.

Military life was psychologically wrong for Erich. He was a free young spirit who sought the freedom of the air. The Rottweil school had already demonstrated Erich's fundamental antipathy to military life, which had now become a pill to be swallowed with the sweetness of flying. His basic aversion to military ways has tended to adversely affect his later career in the air force, both in the wartime Luftwaffe and in the new *Bundesluftwaffe*, but he has nevertheless been able to survive as an independent spirit in an environment based on conformity.

On 15 October 1940, with the climax of the Battle of Britain already past, the fresh-faced Erich Hartmann joined Air Force Military Training Regiment 10 at Neukuhren, about ten miles from Königsberg in East Prussia. Flying was now uppermost in his mind. He would become a pilot come hell or high water.

The training of German fighter pilots at this time was not invested with any special urgency. The full impact of heavy pilot losses in the Battle of Britain had not penetrated the Luftwaffe General Staff. Little was done to accelerate the painstakingly thorough courses by which the Luftwaffe produced its pilots, and aircraft production had not even replaced Battle of Britain losses by March 1941, when Erich reported to the Air Academy School at Berlin-Gatow for flying training.

Since October 1940 he had been learning military discipline, close-order drill and the manual of arms activities for which he never developed any enthusiasm. There had also been theoretical studies in aviation subjects—the history of aviation; theory of flight; operation, design and construction of aircraft and aircraft engines; aeronautical engineering; strength of materials, aerodynamics and meteorology. These subjects absorbed his interest, and Erich had no difficulty with this aspect of his new life. The incentive of imminent flying training was powerful enough to drive him through his studies with ease.

The flying training that began at Berlin-Gatow was to last almost a year—indicative of the leisurely attitude taken at that time toward pilot training in the Luftwaffe. Young pilots later in the war would come to Erich's squadrons on the Russian Front with barely one hundred hours total flying time —to be thrown straight into combat. Erich took his first flight in military training on 5 March 1941 in a type BT-NB trainer, with Sergeant Kolberg as his instructor. By 24 March 1941 he was ready to solo. When he touched down at the end of his first solo flight, it was his seventy-fourth landing in a powered aircraft, although it was preceded by hundreds of glider landings.

Basic flying training was completed by 14 October 1941, and he was ready for the advanced flying course. His instructors at Berlin-Gatow had already determined that he was fighter pilot material. This advanced training period occupied from 15 October 1941 to 31 January 1942, after which he was posted to Zerbst/Anhalt and the Fighter School. At Zerbst, between Dessau and Magdeburg and now in the Eastern Zone of Germany, he was introduced to the aircraft that he would ride to glory—the Messerschmitt 109.

Erich had flown seventeen different types of powered aircraft by the time he was ready for the fabled Me-109. Every young German pilot dreamed of flying this legendary machine. The spirited Me-109* with its powerful Daimler-Benz engine was a superb-handling aircraft, and a delight to fly. One of Erich's instructors at Zerbst was Lieutenant Hohagen, a former aerobatic champion of Germany, and he taught his flaxen-haired student many of the secrets of aerobatic flying. This was knowledge that Erich was to use in the future, and misuse in the near future. With basic tactical maneuvers and

---

.* The fighters at Zerbst were the Me-109-E4 at the time. Known as the Bf-109 in Europe (for *Bayerische Flugzeugwerke*, renamed Messerschmitt in July 1938), it was powered by an 1150 hp Daimler-Benz DB-601 Aa engine. Maximum speed was 357 mph and stall speed was 75 mph. Armament was two 7.9-mm MG-17 machine guns and two 20-mm cannon mounted in the wings outside the propeller arc.

the aircraft itself mastered, he moved on in June 1942 to the business end of combat flying—gunnery.

That Erich Hartmann was a superior natural marksman cannot be doubted. Nevertheless there is a discrepancy between his own modest view of his aerial shooting and the verdict of his contemporaries. He claims that he was never a good long-distance shot in the air, while experienced aces like Krupinski, who saw him in action when he first went to the Russian Front, say he was outstanding at long range. Erich deserted long-range attacks early in his combat career in favor of point-blank attacks, and hence his long-range marksmanship was seldom subsequently exhibited. At gunnery school his shooting ability was obvious.

On 30 June 1942, in his first aerial gunnery effort, Erich fired fifty shots at a drogue with the 7.62-mm machine guns in the Me-109D, and scored twenty-four hits. Anyone with a knowledge of fighter pilot training will find this achievement remarkable. Many of the top aces of the Luftwaffe spent months, and in the case of Erich's comrade Major Willi Batz,* *years*, vainly trying to score hits in air-to-air combat. A shooting eye is the most important asset of a successful fighter ace. Erich Hartmann was one of those rare individuals gifted with this talent that came so hard and slowly to others.

The long grind through fighter pilot training had been arduous and demanding. When he was commissioned Second Lieutenant on 31 March 1942, Erich felt he had earned his wings and his commission. He also felt like letting his hair down, like a young boy getting out of school in the afternoon.

On 24 August 1942, while attending the advanced gunnery school at Gleiwitz, he flew down to Zerbst and demonstrated some of Lieutenant Hohagen's aerobatics over the airfield. He buzzed and beat up Zerbst with snap rolls and Cuban eights, and flying back to Gleiwitz climaxed his air show with a maneuver that might have been lifted out of an old James Cagney flying movie. He came howling across Gleiwitz Airfield at thirty feet altitude and upside down, while spectators stood bug-eyed with a mixture of wonder and terror.

The Gleiwitz C.O. was waiting when he landed. Erich was bawled out, sentenced to room arrest for a week, and fined

* Major Wilhelm Batz, 237 aerial victories in World War II.

two-thirds of his pay for ninety days. His air show had been expensive. This potentially dangerous stunt showed that the impulsiveness discerned in him by his schoolteacher had not yet been eliminated by military discipline. His wild aerobatics evidenced a certain immaturity that was to cause his commanding officers at the front concern about giving him too much responsibility too quickly.

Erich's punishment had its positive† side as well, and he looks back on the incident today without regret:

"The week of room arrest saved my life. I was scheduled for a gunnery mission that afternoon. When I was arrested, my roommate took this mission, in the aircraft I had been flying, as my substitute. Shortly after take-off, on the way to the gunnery range, he had engine trouble and belly-landed beside the Hindenburg-Kattowitz railroad. He was killed in the crash."

His impulsiveness had two sides, as we shall see in due course, but in the beginning it made his military progress lag far behind his warrior prowess. As his training ended, the demand for replacement fighter pilots on all fronts was urgent. He was able to wangle a three-day leave at home in Weil on his way to the Eastern Front.

A farewell party was staged in his honor. Erich's parents' friends gathered to say their farewells to the young pilot. The fathers and the rest of the men exuded pride and confidence, while the mothers had only quiet tears. Erich had never known anything quite like this celebration in his life. For those assembled, he was the hero, going to fight. His inner feeling was that he was going to kill himself, a disquieting and almost tipsy sensation he had never known before.

Between Erich and Usch there was a final, tender, lovers' agreement.

"I would like to marry you, Usch, when the war is over. Will you wait for me?"

"Yes, Erich, I will wait."

The dark-haired Usch would indeed wait, longer than any woman could reasonably be expected to wait, before Erich

† On the other hand, news of his arrest preceded him to the Soviet Front and many Luftwaffe officers heard that he was sent to the East as punishment for the escapade. In fact, this story will be revealing to some of them as to what actually happened.

would finally be hers to hold. He took a train the following day to Krakau, 145 miles south of Warsaw in Poland, where the Luftwaffe had a large supply base for the Eastern Front. From there he would fly to join the unit to which he had been assigned, Fighter Wing 52 (*Jagdgeschwader* 52, or JG-52). He was a hot rock fighter pilot, hot for action, but conditions in Russia could cool down the hottest flyer. In the coolness born of hard experience he would become the most successful fighter pilot who ever flew.

CHAPTER THREE

TO WAR

The most important thing for a young fighter pilot is to get his first victory without too much shock.
                    —*Colonel Werner Moelders*

THE C.O. OF THE Luftwaffe Eastern Front supply base at Krakau riffled through a pile of requisitions and shook his head. He looked up at the four young second lieutenants assigned to JG-52.

"I have no request for any replacement aircraft for JG-52, so you can't fly down to Maykop in Me-109's. However, I have some Stukas to be ferried to Mariupol on the north coast of the Sea of Azov, and you could easily get to Maykop from there."

Second Lieutenants Hartmann, Wolf, Stiebler and Merschat exchanged glances with each other and nodded their assent to the base commander. Erich had never flown a Stuka dive bomber, but a plane was a plane. He wasn't afraid to fly a Ju-87 or any other kind of bird. A few minutes later he was clambering into the unfamiliar cockpit of the dive bomber.

Basic controls were not much different from the Me-109. The kite was bigger and slower, with some minor differences in instrumentation. Erich ran up the engine and everything checked. Wolf, Stiebler and Merschat taxied out and took off satisfactorily. Erich eased the Stuka toward the take-off point.

A controller operated from a wooden hut near the take-off area and Erich prepared to skirt the little building. He squeezed the left brake to pull around the controller's hut. No response. He chomped on the binders. Full brakes! Still no effect. The dive bomber kept going right for the hut, as Erich fought the defective brake. He glimpsed the controller bolting out of the hut, and an instant later the Stuka went plowing into the structure.

Rapid loud bangs racketed across the base as the Stuka's propeller hacked the hut into matchwood. A blizzard of shredded paper and wood splinters filled the air, and swirling around under the propeller's blast beat like a snowstorm into the cockpit. Erich killed the engine and jumped out shamefaced to assess the damage.

Half the Stuka's propeller had disappeared. Two splintered wooden stumps about eighteen inches long stuck out from the propeller boss. The controller's hut had been chopped down to half its size, and the documents and logbooks inside had been reduced to confetti. The dazed controller picked his way slowly amid the shambles.

Officers and other personnel, headed by a livid base commander, came apprehensively out of nearby buildings to view the wreckage. Almost fainting with embarrassment, Erich stood red-eared and awkward beside the ruins. As the base commander advanced on him, he was ready to be bawled out, but one of his young comrades saved him.

A second Stuka of the four destined for Mariupol came limping in for a landing with its engine missing and trailing smoke. Before the horrified gaze of the already furious base commander, the second Stuka touched down, rolled forward briefly, and as the inexperienced pilot hit the brakes a little too hard went up on its nose and stayed there, its tail reaching for the sky. A second crestfallen young pilot crawled out and stared uncomprehendingly at his Stuka. Appalled by the attrition these "baby pilots" had caused, the base commander decided that they would fly to the front at Maykop in a Ju-52 transport—with someone else at the controls.

Conversation was impossible inside the Ju-52 due to the engine noise, so Erich settled back amid ammunition cases, crates of spare parts and gasoline drums to give his attention to a two-day-old Berlin newspaper he found among the freight. Reports of the war were optimistic. Leningrad was under siege. Battering-ram attacks were being launched against Stalingrad. The German drive into the Caucasus, where he was heading now, would soon culminate in the capture of Baku and its limitless oil—according to Dr. Goebbels. Reports of air battles showed that at all points on the Eastern Front, aerial combat was taking place at least 750 miles deep in Soviet territory.

Pilots returning from the Eastern Front had spoken in awe of JG-52 and its high-scoring aces. The Fighter Wing he was joining had won great fame. Since Erich had yet to fire his guns in anger, and with the Stuka disaster fresh in his mind, he felt his inexperience sharply. His nerves grew taut as the transport began its let-down at Maykop, 150 miles northwest of Mt. Elbrus. Maykop was the HQ of JG-52.

The wing adjutant was awaiting them as the new pilots climbed stiffly out of the transport. Captain Kuehl was a smallish man, neat and trim, with a pressed uniform and shining boots. He epitomized the staff officer as he checked their names off a list.

"All of you come with me," he said. "You're going to meet Colonel Hrabak, the wing commander, before joining your individual squadrons at other airfields."

Captain Kuehl led the way into an underground bunker. Headquarters for JG-52 was little more than a big foxhole. On one wall hung a huge map of the front. Two bomb cases served as tables, with a telephone to HQ and another telephone connecting to the three groups of JG-52 deployed along the front. One officer and two soldiers were on duty at the tables, and away in one corner were the radio operators. One operator was keeping a running log on the Wing's official traffic; the other operator was monitoring the Russian R/T conversations. Crates that once contained 20-mm cannon shells served as chairs.

This grim and businesslike setup was presided over by a short, chunky man with thinning blond hair, Colonel Dietrich Hrabak. Erich immediately noticed the difference between the wing commander and his adjutant. Hrabak's uniform was soiled and rumpled and there were oil spots on his trousers. His boots were crusted with dried mud and hadn't contacted a brush for a long time. Erich had never seen a colonel like this before. Back in the rear areas, at the training bases, a colonel was like a god and usually wore a uniform to match. Hrabak was a different kind of colonel in more ways than just his clothes.

Hrabak spoke and moved softly, easily. His penetrating, light blue eyes looked directly at each new pilot as he shook hands with each of them. Erich felt an immediate rapport with Hrabak. As the wing commander briefly explained the command setup Erich could see that while Hrabak was no old-time ramrod, he was a competent and thorough professional. If this was the kind of officer that you encountered at the front—a real old fighter tiger*—Erich felt he could find a place with such men.

"Living to rise in the Luftwaffe," said Hrabak to the new pilots, "is a question of learning as quickly as possible to fly with your head, and not with your muscles."

The wing commander at this time had over sixty confirmed victories, and the Knight's Cross of the Iron Cross hung at his throat. The things he was telling Erich and others now were not taught back in the training schools.

"Up to now, all your training has emphasized controlling your aircraft on operations, that is, making your muscles obey your will in flying your aircraft. To survive in Russia and be successful fighter pilots you must now develop your thinking. You must act aggressively always, of course, or you will not be successful, but the aggressive spirit must be tempered with cunning, judgment and intelligent thinking. Fly with your head and not with your muscles. . . ."

The R/T loudspeaker broke in on Hrabak. Erich stood rooted to the spot as a typical front-line fighter pilot drama unfolded.

"Keep the base clear. I've been hit. I can see the field and I'm going to land immediately. . . ."

A buzz of concern arose in the bunker. Then the R/T rasped again.

"Goddam! I hope I can make it. My engine's burning now. . . ."

Erich, Hrabak and the other new pilots scrambled out of the bunker just as a duty officer fired a red flare to clear the field. Near the end of the grass strip, an Me-109 was making its approach, trailing a plume of heavy black smoke. The fighter's gear was down, the pilot stroked the stick back and

---

* The term "old" among fighter pilots is relative. Hrabak was barely seven and a half years older than Erich Hartmann, but an "old man" by the youthful standards of fighter pilots.

the crippled kite hit the grass. The machine rolled a few
yards, then something in the undercarriage let go and flew
away from the aircraft. Burning and smoking, the Me-109
made a swerve to the left and ground-looped with a thunder-
ous explosion.

"It's Krupinski!" someone shouted.

Crash crews went racing out to fight the fire, but the
Messerschmitt's ammunition started exploding and tracer and
cannon shells spouted away from the pranged bird at all
angles. Erich stood with his gaze anchored by the fiery spectacle, fascinated by its drama and violence. Bursting through
the smoke, the pilot bolted clear of the inferno. His survival
seemed like a miracle. A rescue truck drove him back to
where Erich was standing.

He was a husky, big-bodied young man, and he was smiling
widely as he approached Hrabak, even if his face was pale.

"I got some flak hits over the damned Caucasus Mountains," he said to Hrabak.

"Krupinski, we will have a birthday party for you tonight,"
said the wing commander.

Hrabak turned to the new pilots, whose mouths hung open
with awe at the sight of Krupinski, and at the narrowness of
his recent escape.

"Every time something goes wrong like this, and the pilot
lives through it," said Hrabak, "we give him a birthday party
because he's born again."

"What happens, sir, if a pilot dies?" said Erich.

"Then we drink his skin (*Versaufen wir sein Fell*), so
everybody can forget quickly."

Erich was deeply impressed by his meeting with two of the
Luftwaffe's more famous fighter tigers. He liked the informality, the manly directness with which things were handled. Two
days later, on 10 October 1942, he was posted to III/JG-52,*
which had its HQ at Soldatskaya, a little village north of the
Caucasus Mountains, hard by the river Terek. He clambered
again into a Ju-52 transport on the last leg of his journey to

---

* The abbreviation III/JG-52 designates No. 3 *Gruppe* (Group)
of Jagdgeschwader 52 (Fighter Wing 52). Each wing consisted
usually of three *Gruppen*. The 7th Squadron of No. 3 *Gruppe*
would be written 7.III/JG-52. The 7th, 8th and 9th Squadrons of
JG-52 composed III/JG-52.

war, with Krupinski's crash and Hrabak's instructions burning in his mind.

As the transport flew southward to Soldatskaya, Erich marveled at the beauty of Mt. Elbrus off to the right, thatched with snow, wearing a small boa cumulus cap, and glowing whitely in the bright sunshine. Over 18,000 feet high, Elbrus made an imposing sentinel at the eastern end of the Black Sea. Erich thought to himself what a splendid landmark Elbrus would be to any fighter pilot flying in the area. Off to the left, flat plains stretched endlessly into the distance. As the heavy ship let down for a landing, Erich spotted the airfield at the northwest corner of the little village. Acres of melons and sunflowers surrounded the region. A pretty spot, thought Erich, marred only by the grim silhouettes of about sixty Me-109's on the airfield—a grass strip lined with tents for the pilots and ground personnel.

At Soldatskaya, III/JG-52 was directed from another underground bunker much like the one in which Erich had met Hrabak. As Erich walked into the bunker with the other replacement pilots, a tallish man with slicked-back dark hair and a long, small face looked up and grinned.

"Hello there, you innocent young babies!" he said. "I'm the *Gruppenkommandeur*, and my name is Major von Bonin. Hartmann and Merschat are assigned to the 7th Squadron, Stiebler and Wolf to the 9th. Now, what kind of news do you have for me from home?"

Erich responded immediately to yet another tough old fighter tiger. Men like this didn't exist in the training schools. Again the uniform was rumpled, the trousers baggy and uncreased, the boots something to give a drill sergeant apoplexy. Von Bonin also dispensed ideas that weren't taught in the training schools.

A fighter pilot veteran of the Condor Legion in the Spanish Civil War, von Bonin had downed four aircraft in that encounter, nine more flying with JG-26 in the Battle of Britain and more than forty on the Eastern Front. Thirty-two years old, he was wise in the ways of fighter leadership, and Erich liked what he heard.

"Only aerial victories count out here, not rank or other trivia. On the ground, we have military discipline, but in the air each element is always led by the pilot with the most aerial victories and the greatest combat skill and experience. This regulation applies to everyone—including me. If I fly with a sergeant who has more victories than I, then he leads the element. This eliminates all question between pilots as to who is to lead. There is never any dispute, because only victories count.

"In the air, in battle, you'll say things you'll never say on the ground—especially to a superior officer. Under the strain and tension of combat this is unavoidable. Everything that passes in the way of comments—even abuse—in the air, is forgotten the moment you land.

"You young second lieutenants will mostly be flying with sergeants.* They'll be your leaders in the air. Never let me hear that you didn't follow their orders in the air because of rank."

Von Bonin clearly meant what he said. The following month Erich heard Lieutenant Grislawski, an accomplished and successful fighter pilot, talking to Major von Bonin, his wingman, on the R/T. They were engaged in a heavy dogfight with Ratas. Grislawski got excited, and von Bonin did not respond to his instructions.

"If you won't listen to me, then you can kiss my backside," barked Grislawski into the R/T.

Still no response.

"You damned son-of-a-bitch . . ." Grislawski kept hurling abuse at his group commander.

When they landed, Major von Bonin came smilingly up to Grislawski, and told him that he had heard his instructions, but could not answer because his transmitter was dead.

"Now that we are on the ground, you will agree with me that your backside is too dirty for me to kiss."

The pilots all roared with laughter, and Grislawski apologized to his C.O., but it was not necessary. Von Bonin practiced and lived what he preached.

As he finished his informal talk to Erich and the other three new pilots, von Bonin seemed more like an older brother than any military officer in Erich's experience. He aroused a warm feeling of confidence, trust and comradeship.

* The United States Army Air Corps, during World War II, used commissioned officers as pilots. Many other nations used enlisted ranks as well as officers as pilots.

There was no empty formality, no leadership tricks, but Erich felt he could follow Major von Bonin into hell.

When he joined the 7th Squadron, Erich met a small, black-haired man to whom he was to feel a debt for the rest of his life—Master Sergeant Eduard "Paule" Rossmann. An improbable personality to become a fighter pilot, Rossmann was of artistic temperament, with a sunny disposition and a fine singing voice. Second Lieutenant Hartmann was to fly as Sergeant Rossmann's wingman.

On the ground, Rossmann was a perennial funmaker, joker and playboy. His mercurial temperament could take him in an instant from womanlike tears over the death of a comrade to laughter at a dirty joke. He burst into song when he arose in the morning and was often singing when he went to bed. In between times he reconciled antagonisms between tense pilots, dissolving animosities with his humor. He was as far from the stylized conception of a dogfighter as a pilot could be, and, as Erich soon found out, Rossmann *wasn't* a dogfighter. The mercurial Rossmann once airborne was a steady, reassuring teacher. The things Erich learned from this diminutive mentor would carry him to the top of his lethal trade.

When other officers in the squadron, dogfighters and toughies most of them, heard that Erich had been assigned as Rossmann's wingman, they thumped the baby-faced Hartmann boy on the back.

"Paule is our best man, Hartmann. He is a sharpshooter with over eighty victories, and he always brings his wingman home. You'll be safe with Paule."

For two days Erich heard from every quarter what a good man Rossmann was, a real first class honcho. He heard it also from another individual whose services were to be an integral part of his success as a fighter pilot—his crew chief, Sergeant Heinz Mertens. Erich met Mertens soon after his arrival at 7th Squadron, and there was an immediate contact between the two men.

Chunky, dark-haired Mertens was a square-cut individual, and he looked right at Erich when the two men met. Erich liked the solid impression he got from Mertens, and it was mutual. Today a happy family man in Düsseldorf, Heinz Mertens recalls his first meeting with the twenty-year-old blond boy who was to fly the planes he serviced to fame and glory:

"I couldn't picture a better young fighter pilot. The personnel, including me, liked him very much. His first words to me when we met were that we would meet every morning for breakfast. He said we would map out the day and set everything up for briefings. He seemed like such a young youngster, with that boyish face, but he had a mature, businesslike manner. From then on, I would not let anyone else touch his aircraft except under my direct supervision, and we were together from the day until the end of the war."

Mertens made a practice of using a swearword, "Gebimmel!" when anything went wrong. Erich thought it was funny that his crew chief bore down so heavily on this one word, so he simply nicknamed him "Bimmel," and the name stuck. Between Bimmel, the good reports on Rossmann, the sound impressions made by Hrabak and von Bonin, and the dashing example set by Krupinski, Erich was desperately eager to do well when he took off with Rossmann on 14 October 1942, on the first mission in which he entered combat.

The two Me-109 G-4's had just taken off for a sweep between Groznyy and Digora when the R/T came alive.

"Seven fighters and three IL-2's are strafing the roads near Prokhladnyy. Intercept and attack."

Nerves taut, Erich followed Rossmann up to 12,000 feet, and they flew down the line of the Terek River to Prkhladnyy. He tells his own story of his first air battle:

"After a fifteen-minute flight, Rossmann's voice rasped over the R/T. *'Attention, eleven o'clock low. Bandits. Close in near to me in fighting position and we'll attack.'* I searched below for sight of the enemy aircraft Rossmann had called out. I couldn't see anything. I closed in on my leader to about one hundred feet behind him as we dived down.

"Still I couldn't see any enemy aircraft. After about a five-thousand-foot dive we leveled off, and at high speed I first saw two dark green aircraft in front and a little higher than we were. They were about a thousand yards away from us.

"My heart leaped. My first thought was to get my first kill. Now! That thought took possession of me. I went to full power and overtook Rossmann to get in front of him in firing position. I closed very fast and fired from three hundred yards. I was shocked to see all my tracer hurtling over and to the left of the target. There were no hits. Nothing happened. The target grew so big so quickly that I just had time to pull up and avoid a collision.

"Instantly I was surrounded on all sides by dark green aircraft, all of them turning behind me for the kill. . . . *Me!*

"I felt desperate. I had lost my leader. I heeled over and raced for a little layer of low cloud, climbed through it and found myself all alone above it in beautiful sunshine. I felt a little better. Then came Rossmann's very quiet and reassuring voice on the R/T. *'Don't sweat it. I watched your tail. I've lost you now that you've climbed through the clouds. Come down below the layer so I can pick you up again.'* That calm voice sounded wonderful. I pushed the stick forward and went down through the cloud layer.

"When I burst out underneath the clouds, I saw an aircraft head-on to me about fifteen hundred yards away. I panicked. I split-essed down and went barreling westward along the line of the river, calling to Rossmann that an unknown aircraft was following me. Back came that reassuring, quiet voice. *'Turn to the right so I can close with you.'*

"I turned right, but the aircraft pursuing me cut across my turn and got perilously close. I panicked again. I firewalled the throttle. Down I went to treetop height, roaring westward at full bore. I could hear Rossmann on the R/T but his voice was distorted and unintelligible. I went hurtling along, all the while pulling my head down into my body, crouching behind the cockpit armor plate in mortal terror. I was waiting for the crash of enemy shells and bullets into my fighter.

"When I dared to take a look, the other aircraft was still tailing me. I kept going a few minutes more, and to my relief found I had shaken off my pursuer. I heard Rossmann again, still garbled, but I was near delirious with joy at having thrown off my tormentor. Climbing a little, I tried to establish my position. One clear landmark—Mt. Elbrus to my left. But now it was too late. The red glow of the fuel warning light told me I had less than five minutes flying time.

"After the shortest five minutes in memory, the engine coughed and blurted, then went dead. I was going in. I had a thousand feet altitude. I could see a little road with military convoys moving along. The kite started to fall like a stone. I flattened out and belly-landed in a monstrous cloud of dust. I opened the canopy and in less than two minutes I was surrounded by German infantrymen. I had bellied in about twenty miles from my base at Soldatskaya, and an army car took me back."

Erich winced his way through a noisy, vehement and cold turkey debriefing by Major von Bonin. The experienced Rossmann followed up with a lecture on elementary tactics while von Bonin listened grimly. On his first flight in combat, Second Lieutenant Erich Hartmann had violated virtually every established rule of aerial tactics. His tactical sins included:

1. Separating from his leader without orders.
2. Flying into his leader's firing position.
3. Climbing through the cloud layer.
4. Mistaking his leader for an enemy aircraft. The "enemy" from whom he had bolted after descending through the clouds was Rossmann.
5. Failing to follow Rossmann's order to rejoin.
6. Losing orientation.
7. Destroying his aircraft without inflicting any damage on the enemy.

Major von Bonin then told the crestfallen Erich that he would have to spend three days working with the maintenance crew as punishment for these breaches of flying discipline. A contrite blond boy turned to in the following days with the fitters and armorers. For the future ace of aces, it was an ignominious beginning.

He flew more missions with Rossmann. Each time, he learned something new. Rossmann had an injured arm, and couldn't dogfight like the other tough tigers in the wing. Artist that he was, Rossmann had developed a compensating technique that Erich could see was better than the grueling and dangerous turning battles. Rossmann was a fighter who flew with his head. Surprise attacks were his forte.

Erich noted how Rossmann waited before striking. He would see his enemy and wait while he made a quick study of the situation. The decision to attack was only affirmative if it could be thrust home with surprise. The other tough tigers in the squadron couldn't contain themselves if they saw an enemy aircraft. They ripped into the enemy immediately. Erich saw that Rossmann was making kills steadily, and not taking hits. When Erich talked about Rossmann's tactics to other pilots, they did not seem to know what this "see and decide" was before striking. Erich knew it was right.

He also overcame his neophyte's combat blindness, the inability to see other aircraft that had bedeviled him on his first mission with Rossmann. He describes this handicap of the new pilot in these terms:

"This combat blindness is utterly confounding. Your leader calls on the R/T to take care, that there are five strangers at one o'clock. You stare in that direction, combing the sky with your eyes. You see nothing. Unless you have actually experienced this, it is hard to believe.

"Later on, you develop an acumen for combat flying. The handling of the aircraft is no longer uppermost in your mind. The senses adjust to new demands, and then you see the enemy aircraft just like an experienced leader. But if the man you are assigned to fly with does not give you a chance to develop this acumen—to find yourself as a combat pilot—you will be shot down for sure.

"This happened more and more as the war dragged on, and there were fewer and fewer good leaders who cared to break in new pilots, most of whom, in the period from 1943 onward, came to the front with but a fraction of the training I had been given. All kinds of fighters make up a fighter unit, and we had plenty of rough dogfighters who simply said to themselves, 'I'll make the kill and to hell with what happens to my wingman.'

"To be sent out as a little, inexperienced boy on your first missions and lose your leader, or have him lose you through not caring what happens to you, must be a devastating experience. Inexperience is the handmaiden of panic, and panic is the father of mistakes.

"If I had been assigned to another leader, without Paule Rossmann's qualities and skill, I would have followed a different pathway, developed a different attitude and probably would not have lasted as long. In the education of a fighter pilot it is what he is shown *first* that helps him survive, and later equips him to bring his new comrades through.

"When I became an element leader and later a squadron commander and group commander, I did everything in my power to guide new men through these important first few flights. I made it a rule of my life to do this after my experience with Rossmann. I was a young boy, blind like a kitten. Suppose they had started me off with a tough and ruthless leader—we had plenty of them. I was rigid with fear of what might happen to me as it was, even with Rossmann's reassuring presence. He not only brought me through this critical period, but he taught me the basic technique of the surprise attack, without which I am convinced I would have become just another dogfighter, assuming that I didn't get the thing I sat on shot off first."

On 5 November 1942 Erich took off with First Lieutenant Treppe, the group commander's adjutant, in a four-ship *Schwarm* scrambled near Digora at noon. Erich's combat sight was already good, and he called out the enemy first, counting them up quickly: eighteen IL-2 Stormovik ground-attack aircraft with an escort of ten Lagg-3 fighters. The odds were long numerically, but the Germans were already accustomed to Soviet numerical superiority, which had been growing since the summer of 1942.

In a portent of things to come, it was the experienced Lieutenant Treppe who could not see the enemy this time. He ordered Erich to take the lead, and attack. The Germans split into two-ship elements, and from their perch above and behind the Russians, went into a steep dive. The main mission was to disrupt the IL-2 attack against forward German transport.

Erich and Treppe went slashing through the Red fighter screen firing briefly at selected targets as they tore down through the enemy ships at high speed. Leveling out at about 150 feet, Erich took the IL-2 on the far left of the formation. Closing in at lightning speed, he opened fire at less than a hundred yards. Hits! Hits!

He could see his cannon shells and machine-gun bullets striking the Stormovik. They were bouncing off! Damn that heavy armor plate. All the old tigers had warned about the IL-2's armor. The Stormovik was the toughest aircraft in the air. He remembered a talk that ace Alfred Grislawski had given him about the IL-2 as he watched his ricocheting bullets. There was a way to nail the Stormovik. Grislawski had told him and he thought about Grislawski's method now. "Try it, Erich. Try it." He was shouting aloud to himself over the roar of his guns.

Pulling up and banking around, he made another run on the IL-2. Coming in in a steep dive to just a few feet above the ground, he dropped below the enemy machine and came up underneath. This time he held his fire until the Stormovik was about two hundred feet away. The blast of his guns brought an immediate belch of black smoke from the IL-2's oil cooler. A long tongue of flame came stabbing out with blowtorch intensity. The empennage of the IL-2 was quickly enveloped in flames.

The stricken Stormovik lunged eastward, leaving formation. Erich followed hard behind, his throttle at full idle, both aircraft in a shallow dive. A short, sharp explosion and a flash of fire came from under the IL-2's wing, and pieces of the Stormovik were hurled directly into Erich's flight path. His Me-109 trembled from a muffled explosion under the engine cowling. Smoke came billowing back into his cockpit and streamed from under the engine doors.

Erich took a quick survey. Altitude: too low for comfort. Position: still on the German side of the lines. Good. He went rapidly through the preparations for another belly landing. Power back, fuel master switch off, ignition off. None too soon. Flames began leaping out from under the engine doors as he bellied in. The fighter set down with a deafening roar of crumpling metal. A parching cloud of dust swirled into the cockpit and left Erich choking as the aircraft slithered to a halt.

The dust pall had smothered the fire. As Erich pulled his canopy back he saw his late adversary take a death plunge. A little over a mile farther east the IL-2 went roaring to earth, trailing a plume of smoke and fire. Crashing thunderously, the Stormovik was enveloped in flames, and then disintegrated with a convulsive explosion that rocked the air.

Erich Hartmann had scored his first aerial victory. Confirming the kill would present no difficulty. Lieutenant Treppe circled the scene of Erich's crash, rocked his wings and flew away when he saw the victor was alive and mobile. Infantry swarming in the area picked up the quietly exultant Erich and took him back to his unit.

Two days later, Erich was stricken with fever and spent four weeks in the hospital at Piatigorsk-Essentuki. He had time there to mull over all he had learned to date. Again and again he analyzed his actions in the air. He dared to think that he was beginning to learn his trade now. He had not repeated the disaster of his first mission three weeks previously. He had not broken flying discipline, had held his fire better, and the second firing pass against the IL-2 had taught him a good lesson. *Get in close before firing.*

His first victory had another important aspect that Erich had time to contemplate and analyze as he lay in the hospital. He had not lost his own aircraft through panic, stupidity and inexperience as in his first engagement, but he should have broken away more rapidly. A quick breakaway would have seen him stay airborne. He could have avoided the debris from the exploding IL-2 by breaking quickly.

In the coming months he would perfect his four-step mode of attack: "See — Decide — Attack — Reserve, or 'Coffee Break.' " The basic lesson of this mode of attack was inherent in his first victory. His good fortune in flying first with Paule Rossmann had not only kept him alive, but had set the pattern for the distinctive aerial tactics that he would develop in the coming months. These tactics would carry him to an unprecedented pinnacle of success, and on the way he would pass every tough old dogfighter that ever flew.

CHAPTER FOUR

WINNING HIS SPURS

In war, if you are not able to beat your enemy at his own game, it is nearly always better to adopt some striking variant. . . .
—*Winston Churchill, 1916*

WHEN HE REJOINED his squadron after his bout with fever, Erich felt in himself a distinct tempering of his earlier impetuous aggressiveness. Plenty of time to do things to the hilt when you found out what your limits were, he reasoned. He was determined that no enemy would nail Paule Rossmann while he was protecting him. Paule would show him how it was done when you became good enough to lead an element and do the firing yourself. His admiration for Rossmann's elegant surprise attacks and long-range sharpshooting continued to increase, but the time came soon afterward when he had to fly with other aces of the 7th Squadron. His education in air fighting was expanding.

Experts with long strings of victories and all winners of the Knight's Cross of the Iron Cross, these tough aces for the most part used completely different methods from Rossmann, who was a "head" flyer without the muscles for dogfighting. Erich's natural analytical ability easily discerned the difference in techniques. By observation and intuition he knew Rossmann's way was the best, but from each of three hardened dogfighters with whom he now flew he learned something important.

There was rugged Sergeant Dammers, a square-set, thirty-year-old veteran who had won the Knight's Cross in August

49

1942. Dammers was a "muscle" flyer, a hard-turning, aggressive dogfighter who could physically wear down his foe before moving in for the kill. Keeping Dammers's tail clear taught Erich some of the cardinal drawbacks of dogfighting, including vulnerability to other aircraft in the attacked formation and loss of overview.

Alfred Grislawski was more of a head flyer than Dammers, but still used lots of muscles as well. He also had won his Knight's Cross the previous summer, and it was he who had apprised Erich of the vulnerable oil cooler underneath the IL-2. As analytical as he was aggressive, Grislawski was one of the top Stormovik-busters in JG-52 and a thoughtful tactician. Later in the war, he stepped on a mine at a Black Sea beach and was badly injured, but he survived the conflict with 133 victories and Oak Leaves to his Knight's Cross.

First Lieutenant Josef Zwernemann was a fifty-fifty muscle and head flyer. Twenty-six years old when Erich flew with him as his wingman, Zwernemann then had over sixty victories. He died in action on 8 April 1944 near Lake Garda in Italy after a wild dogfight.

One of his conquerors ignobly shot him in his parachute after he bailed out.

These three tigers all did something that was markedly different from Rossmann's tactics. They closed in to fire. Their short-range assaults were at first a surprise to Erich, because Rossmann's skill at long range had made shooting down aircraft in this fashion seem relatively easy. Nevertheless, there was no doubt of the ability of Grislawski, Dammers and Zwernemann to down their foes. Erich remembered, too, that his own first kill had come from a close-in strike against an IL-2. He found himself wondering if the best method might not be Rossmann's surprise tactics *plus* point-blank firing.

Flying with these experts as a wingman, Erich got few chances to shoot again himself. Keeping the leeches off their tails was no easy task. Furthermore, the almost constant movement of the 7th Squadron from airfield to airfield did not allow Erich to settle down. In January, 7th Squadron moved from Mineral'nyye to Amavir to protect retreating German ground troops, but within a few days the advancing Red Army made the new base untenable. Erich watched in anguish while nine good Me-109's were blown up because bad weather made their flight out impossible.

Makeshift bases subsequently at Krasnodar, Maykop and Timoshevskaya all had to be evacuated in turn. After a short operational period at Slavyanskaya, 7th Squadron finally shifted to Nikolaev, where it was reunited with III *Gruppe*. They were hard, hectic times for a new combat pilot, and there were signs that conditions were getting even harder.

When Captain Sommer, the C.O. of 7th Squadron, scored his fiftieth victory on 10 February 1943 he was refused the Knight's Cross to his Iron Cross. In the past, fifty victories on the Eastern Front had been sufficient for the Knight's Cross, but now the requirements, like the struggle against Russia, had significantly stiffened. The Knight's Cross seemed a remote and unattainable goal to Erich in January and February 1943.

He did not score his second victory until 27 February 1943. Soon afterward, a new and dynamic personality appeared on the 7th Squadron scene, an officer who was destined to give Erich solid impetus toward the top—First Lieutenant Walter Krupinski. Appointed to replace Captain Sommer, Krupinski was the same smiling tiger who had escaped so narrowly from his crash-landed Me-109, the day Erich arrived at the front at Maykop. The new C.O. of 7th Squadron took over his command in typical fashion, earning Erich's immediate respect and awe.

Krupinski arrived at Taman Kuban, introduced himself as the new squadron commander, and asked immediately for a serviceable fighter. He went up, was promptly shot down and bailed out. Brought back to the field by car, he demanded another Me-109, took off again immediately, and this time scored two kills, returning intact to the airfield. There was no doubt about this squadron commander: he was a tiger, and he obviously didn't need any tightly ordered discipline in leading his soldiers. Erich liked Krupinski immediately.

The new squadron commander's next request was for a wingman to be assigned to him. His hell-for-leather reputation had preceded him, and the NCO pilots were reluctant to assume the responsibility of protecting him. Paule Rossmann came to Erich as a representative of the sergeants.

"Would you please fly as First Lieutenant Krupinski's wingman, Erich?"

"Why? Don't the sergeants want the job?"

Rossmann appeared a little embarrassed.

"The old timers say that he is a sharp officer," said Paule, "but he can't fly. They think it is better all around if an officer is his wingman. Will you do it?"

Erich found Rossmann hard to refuse. He agreed to see Krupinski. Erich was unhappy about the whole thing when he offered himself to the new squadron commander, because many of the sergeants were decorated veterans and usually knew a good fighter pilot from a bad one. Erich felt a little like a lamb going to the slaughter. Krupinski's bullish bluntness did little to ease Erich's mind.

A strapping, five-foot nine-inch dynamo, Krupinski was already famous in the Luftwaffe by the spring of 1943 as one of its outstanding characters and playboys. Walter Krupinski was a ripe, mature personality who looked and acted—on the military side of his life at least—far beyond his years. After six months' duty in the Reich Labor Service he was drafted as a *Fahnenjunker* (Cadet) in the Luftwaffe on 1 September 1939.

He had been flying as a senior cadet, and later as a commissioned officer, since the end of 1941 and had once flown as the great "Macky" Steinhoff's wingman. He was a successful and famous JG-52 ace with over seventy victories at the time Erich Hartmann offered his services as a wingman. Krupinski was destined to end the war as the fifteenth-ranked fighter ace of the world with 197 victories, and at the surrender he was a member of Adolf Galland's elite Squadron of Experts in JV-44, flying the Me-262 jet fighter.

Krupinski's exploits through the years had earned him a reputation for toughness that preceded him to Taman. He had a penchant for getting himself into impossible situations, and for wounds, bail-outs and crash landings. He once bellylanded near the Kuban River, coming down in a meadow which the German infantry had mined. As his shattered kite slid along the grass it tripped a series of mines, and Krupinski immediately concluded that he was being bombarded by artillery.

Krupinski's first impulse was to jump out of the plane and bolt for cover. His life was saved by a German infantry sergeant who bawled out the explosive facts about the field to him as he clambered clear of the cockpit. The soldiers took two hours to extricate him, walking out to him and testing the ground with sticks as they came. His career was a skein of similar incidents, culminating in the last months of the war when he was enjoying himself on recuperation leave at the Fighter Pilots' Home in Bad Wiessee. At Steinhoff's urging, he took reluctant leave of a big barrel of cognac provided for the pilots and flew the Me-262 in Galland's JV-44. Krupinski's crash arrival at Maykop, with the burning fighter spewing live ammunition in all directions, was fresh in Erich's mind as he confronted this formidable personality.

"Sir, my name is Hartmann. I am to be your wingman."

"Been out here long?"

"No, sir. About three months."

"Any victories?"

"Two, sir."

"Who have you been flying with?"

"Rossmann mainly, but also with Dammers, Zwernemann and Grislawski."

"They're all good men. We'll get along all right. That's all for now."

Walter Krupinski is today a brigadier general in the new German Air Force, and is stationed in the U.S.A., at Fort Bliss, Texas. His only recollection of his first meeting with Erich Hartmann is an indelible impression of Erich's extreme youth.

"He appeared not much more than a mere baby. So young and full of life. As he walked away from me that first day I thought to myself, 'Such a young face.' "

This same impression of Erich was shared at this time by Captain Guenther Rall, who had become *Gruppenkommandeur* of III/JG-52 in place of von Bonin, in the same shuffle that brought Krupinski to command No. 7 Squadron. Later we will make fuller contact with Guenther Rall as one of JG-52's greatest aces, but his recollection of Erich at this time parallels that of Krupinski.

"I saw him [Erich] first in the 7th Squadron mess, and I

thought only, 'What a young boy—a baby.' He stood out first for his extreme youth, but quickly came to everyone's attention because he was a good marksman."

Erich and Krupinski took to the air the following day with disturbing initial impressions of each other. Erich was sure that he was flying with a wild tiger who could not fly, and Krupinski was sure he was flying with a baby on his wing. The first mission was sufficient to change Erich's mind about his new leader.

The new squadron commander waded into the enemy like a barroom brawler, a batteringly aggressive and fearless pilot who could not only fly like a demon, but also keep a clear tactical head. Krupinski's purported inability to fly was obviously a yarn without foundation. Nevertheless, Krupinski could not shoot straight and most of his ammunition went wide.* Krupinski's weakness was therefore supplemented by Erich's strength as a marksman, for Erich had been a natural sharpshooter from the day he riddled his first drogue in training. Together, Krupinski and Erich formed a winning combat team.

Erich began by sticking close to Krupinski, and as they entered shooting range, decreased his air speed and went to his leader's reverse as he pulled up or broke. This gave Erich a few seconds to shoot, "filling in the holes Kruppi had left." A couple of additional victories came this way. Soon they realized that they could depend on each other, and as Krupinski coached Erich they began to read each other's minds in combat, as have all the great fighter teams in history.

When Krupinski went into an attack, Erich would stay "on the perch," watching his leader's back and telling him what to do if another enemy aircraft intervened. During Erich's attacks, Krupinski stayed on the perch and called out instructions to Erich to improve his attack or take evasive action. Erich heard Krupinski's voice on the R/T rasping the same order over and over again.

"Hey, Bubi! Get in closer. You're opening fire too far out."

Erich was emulating Rossmann, with long-range attacks. He was hitting well every time he fired, which impressed the

---

* Straight shot or not, the indomitable Krupinski shot down 197 enemy aircraft in slightly over 1100 sorties.

poorer-shooting Krupinski, but it was obvious he would do even better if he closed in on his targets. As Krupinski later said: "We had so many young pilots come to us who could not hit anything in the air that Erich stood out immediately with his accurate long-range gunnery."

From Krupinski's constantly calling him "Bubi" in the air came Erich's nickname, which he has retained to this day. The whole squadron was soon calling him "Bubi," and the name stuck.

Krupinski's steady urgings, "Hey, Bubi, get in closer," encouraged Erich to close his ranges. The closer he got to his foe, the more devastating the effect when he fired. Few shots went wide. Often the other aircraft could be seen to stagger under the multigun blast at close range. Even more often, there was an explosion in the air as the other machine disintegrated. When they went down that way, they would never come back up again.

Soon Erich had fully developed the tactics of air fighting from which he would never subsequently depart. The magical four steps were: "See – Decide – Attack – Reverse, or 'Coffee Break.' " In lay terms, spot the enemy, decide if he can be attacked and surprised, attack him and break away immediately after striking; or if he spots you before you strike, take a "coffee break"—wait—pull off the enemy and don't get into a turning battle with a foe who knows you are there. The rigid observance of this tactical sequence carried Erich Hartmann to the top.

Erich's successful partnership in the air with Krupinski led naturally to a warm friendship on the ground. Krupinski's nickname, "Graf Punski," was not something conjured out of thin air, but was appropriate to a debonair ladies' man and social lion. "Count Punski" enjoyed life in the huge fashion which his physique, stamina and dashing manner united to make possible. All guts and claws in the air, he was all charm and polish on the ground, a happy, handsome fighter pilot.

Flying came first with Krupinski, but the second requirement was the construction of a bar wherever the squadron was quartered. Every eligible German girl within thirty miles belonged to the zestful Krupinski. As Erich says of him today: "From Graf Punski I eagerly learned many bad things. He was the Frank Sinatra type, charming, sharp and a lover.

A 'criminal' gentleman both in the air and on the ground, he grew serious on the outside after the war, but inside lies the old Kruppi—a tiger without teeth, like me."

Under Krupinski's guidance, Erich ran his score to five victories by 24 March 1943. His first five kills were scored as follows:

5 Nov 1942	2 Missions Flown	1 IL-2 Shot Down
27 Jan 1943	2 Missions Flown	1 MIG-1 Shot Down
9 Feb 1943	2 Missions Flown	1 Lagg-3 Shot Down
10 Feb 1943	5 Missions Flown	1 Douglas Boston Shot Down
24 Mar 1943	2 Missions Flown	1 U-2 Shot Down

Erich's fifth victory entitled him to the award of the Iron Cross, 2nd Class—his first decoration. He was not yet entitled, under the Luftwaffe system, to the honorary status of ace. The Germans adhered at this time to the First World War criterion of ten aerial victories for acedom.

Near the end of April 1943, with 110 missions as a wing-man to his credit, Erich was well qualified to become an element leader (*Rottenführer*).* With eight victories at the time he was given an element, Erich added three more by 30 April 1943. Flying with Krupinski had been an unforgettable experience, but Erich had his own ideas about tactics, based on his first missions with Rossmann and enlarged by dozens of missions flown with experienced dogfighters. As an element leader, he could at last do things his own way.

Erich already had his lethal four-step attack method set in his mind. He was resolved on one other aspect of leadership that he would never change or modify. Like his attack method, it had been born of his first experience with Paule Rossmann: *"Never lose a wingman."*

In the years the authors have known Erich Hartmann, and in all the hours they have spent discussing his life and career, there is only one aspect of his military achievements in which the man himself takes pride. That was his ability during the

* In the Luftwaffe	In the U.S.
a *Rotte* consisted of 2 aircraft	= element
a *Schwarm* was 2 *Rotten* (4 aircraft)	= flight
a *Staffel* had 12 aircraft	= squadron
a *Gruppe* had 3 *Staffeln*	= group
a *Jagdgeschwader* had 3 *Gruppen*	= division

worst of the Russian Front air war to live up to his own rule
—"Never lose a wingman." The long string of victories, the
decorations all the way up to the Diamonds, even the moral
triumph of surviving ten and a half years of Russian jails, he
can discuss with detachment, objectivity and modesty. His
ability to keep his young and inexperienced wingmen alive—
and never lose one of them—is a memory and an achievement he rightly cherishes.

Only one wingman who flew with the ace of aces was ever
shot down, and he survived the experience uninjured. He was
a former bomber pilot named Major Guenther Capito, who
was sent to Erich Hartmann's *Gruppe* near the end of the war
without any conversion training. Aged thirty-two, Capito was
making his transition to fighter piloting rather late, but it was
the only way for him to avoid being grounded. In Capito's
own words: "It was not an easy adjustment to make."

The reaction of the two men to each other was to have
many echoes in the new German Air Force in the 1950s and
1960s. Capito gives his 1945 impression of Erich Hartmann
in these terms:

"The first impression I had of Bubi Hartmann was not
earth-shattering. What stood in front of me was a dangling,
sloppy young man with untamable blond hair under a completely wrinkled cap. He had a tedious slow drawl. I thought
to myself that he deserved his nickname, and I asked myself,
'This is supposed to be a commander?'

"During the next few days these thoughts were not dis-
pelled, except for the fact that he did have some sort of
temperament. When one spoke about flying, fighter pilots or
combat, then he came to life and spoke up, loud and clear.
Then one could feel that he was a wholesome person, and
thanks to his youth, completely uninhibited. However, I still
couldn't see him as a commander, and this impression never
changed until the end of the war."

A peacetime-trained professional and an older man to boot,
as well as a bomber pilot, Capito was not at home with a
fighter unit. The freewheeling informality of the front-line
fighter pilot's life, which Erich had found so much to his
liking and so suited to his temperament, tended to jar on
Guenther Capito.

The former bomber pilot was nevertheless eager to fly as

Erich's wingman and asked him every day for this opportunity. Erich's response was to try and dissuade Capito, telling him that the war would soon be over, and that a bomber pilot in an Me-109 would inevitably have grave difficulties. Capito continued to press for his chance to fly as Erich's wingman.

The ace of aces finally agreed, and to better orient the former bomber pilot to the greater pace and heavier demands of single-seat fighter piloting, specifically briefed him on the need to stay close to his leader. Capito was warned of the tight turns that were an integral part of fighter action.

In an air battle with Airacobras, Hartmann and Capito were bounced by two higher Russian elements. Erich tells the story of the ensuing action in his own words:

"I let the Russian fighters close in to firing range, calling to Capito to stay close to me. It was just the kind of situation concerning which I had briefed him earlier. When the Russians fired, I broke into them horizontally in a very steep turn, but Capito could not stay with me. He made a standard rate *bomber* turn. After a one-hundred-and-eighty-degree turn he and the attacking Airacobras were opposite me.

"I now called to him to turn hard opposite, so that I could sandwich the Red fighters, but in his second, standard-rate bomber turn he got hit. I saw the whole thing and ordered him to dive and bail out immediately. To my immense relief I saw him leave the aircraft and his parachute blossom, but I was brassed off at his inability to follow instructions.

"I got behind the Airacobra, closed right in, and after a short burst the enemy fighter went down and crashed with a tremendous explosion about two miles from Capito's touchdown point by parachute and about a mile from our base. I was happy to get this Airacobra down, but I was mad at myself for not harkening to my intuition not to fly with Guenther Capito."

Erich flew back to base, got a car and picked up the crestfallen Capito. They drove over to the crashed Russian fighter. The pilot was a captain, and he had been hurled out of the ship on impact and killed. He had a huge amount of German money on him, something close to twenty thousand marks. This was the only occasion in fourteen hundred combat missions that one of Erich Hartmann's wingmen met with a mishap.

Guenther Capito survived uninjured, and like Erich Hartmann, serves today as a colonel in the new German Air Force. He describes his feelings after being shot down:

"I was terribly humbled and felt that I should be on my knees. Not even a visit to the crash of my enemy could lift my spirits. The dead Russian had twenty-five victories, and I was his twenty-sixth.

"My conqueror was therefore not such a rabbit as I was. Only in the evening, at the 'birthday party' traditionally given to all pilots who survive death, did I slowly begin to recover."

Colonel Capito was taken prisoner at war's end with Erich Hartmann, and later was tansferred by the American Army to Soviet custody. He was in Russian jails until 1950. Today he resides in Troisdorf, near Bonn.

Although Erich's chances to score kills were multiplied once he began leading an element in the spring of 1943, he was determined to keep his wingmen safe. He went through a period of running-in as an element leader while he developed his distinctive attacking style and maintained a constant eye for his wingman's safety. For a time, the impress of the ebullient Krupinski could be seen on his leadership. This emulation of Krupinski was only natural in a young and impressionable man who deeply admired another, and especially his quality of leadership. Events, experience and new responsibilities soon caused Erich to abandon his efforts to be like Krupinski.

He couldn't be like another man and still be himself. As his own man going his own way, he developed his own quality of leadership and men followed him naturally. Bimmel's devotion on the ground exemplified this spirit. In the air, his regard for the safety of his wingmen not only helped temper his natural impulsiveness, but also evoked confidence and devotion among those who flew with him. He always brought them back.

By 25 May 1943 he had added another six victories. He took off at dawn on that day and within minutes had driven home a bounce on a Soviet Lagg-9. Breaking off the attack he went climbing into the sun, and while half-blinded, collided in mid-air with another Lagg-9. Cautious flying and an old glider-pilot's skill allowed him to get his crippled Me-109 back into German territory. He made his fifth belly landing just inside the German lines. His nerves were jangled enough by this encounter to warrant sending him home for a brief leave. Hrabak issued orders and he was soon on his way to his personal idea of luxury—a month in Stuttgart.

Getting back to Germany after the discomfort and hardship of the Russian Front was a big boost for Erich's morale. Usch looked lovelier than he could ever remember. There were deep armchairs to sit in, soft beds with clean sheets at night, and none of the incessant pressure of the front.

Once at night he snapped upright and awake in bed to the imaginary cry of "Break! Break!"—the warning yell of a wingman. Feeling foolish, he slumped back down in the bed. The war was hundreds of miles away. Or was it still so far? Lying quietly in the gloom, he thought about events as they were unfolding.

Until the spring of 1943 the Allied bombing raids on Germany were not alarming. The German night fighter force had been fairly successful and the effectiveness of the RAF at night had not been cause for too much alarm. Nevertheless, the enemy was unquestionably getting stronger, dropping more bombs, and conducting bigger raids. When a thousand bombers tackled a target at once, the damage was massive. The RAF assault on Cologne the previous spring had started this trend.

German propaganda minimized Allied attacks, especially the recent RAF attack on the Möhne and Eder dams in the Ruhr. Whole villages had been wiped out by the rampaging water released in these attacks, and part of Kassel had been flooded. British radio propaganda was promising an increasing air assault on Germany. For a fighter pilot battling his heart out on the Russian Front, it was a disturbing thought that thousands of Allied bombers ranged over the fatherland every day and night.

The next day Erich walked into the living room of his parents' home in Weil during a radio speech by Reichsmarschall Goering. His father sat listening to Goering's ranting fantasies with a quizzical expression on his face. Turning down the volume control, he looked directly at Erich.

"Listen, my boy. Today, 'hosanna in high places. Tomorrow, put Him on the Cross.' Never, *never* will we win this war. What a mistake and what a waste."

Dr. Hartmann knew the world too well, with his rich background and knowledge of human beings, ever to be hoodwinked by propaganda. He had been saying similar things to Erich since 1939. His theme was constant—the war would end in disaster for Germany. Goering's reassurances meant nothing. Word about the massive new bombings was spreading through Germany, and Dr. Hartmann met many people in his medical practice who had seen the damage in other cities.

For the first time, Erich felt the disquiet of the German civil population. His parents were anxious about his safety. Usch could not conceal her unhappiness. For all the gaiety of the final days of his leave, the depth of concern felt by his loved ones at home could no longer be concealed. Hardened to do his best by what he saw and felt at home, he hurled himself back into the air war with all his vigor. On 5 July 1943, in four missions, he downed four Lagg-5 fighters, his best single day's score to date. Marring this triumph was another typical Krupinski disaster that left Erich saddened.

In a wild battle over 7th Squadron's airfield, Krupinski's Me-109 was heavily hit in the empennage, including strikes in the oil cooler area. With only partial control of his rudder, Krupinski came in for an immediate landing, knowing that the damage to his aircraft precluded any kind of go-around. Just as he made his emergency landing, the alert flight took off at ninety degrees to his landing direction. Fighting his stricken ship down, Krupinski could see that he would have to make a ground loop or collide with the departing alert flight.

Around he went, and as the kite swung laterally he applied too much outer brake. The fighter nosed over onto its back, the violent motion smashing Krupinski's head into the gunsight. He was hanging half-conscious in his safety belt when the crash crews reached him two minutes later. Smothered in blood and drenched in gasoline, he almost panicked because he thought the gasoline was clammy blood in his clothes. The crash crews dragged him clear and he was whisked away for medical attention. He had fractured his skull and was out of combat for six weeks. His departure hit the squadron a heavy blow, and left Erich anxious for his comrade.

Erich kept flying hard. Good comrades were being lost all the time. Five other pilots, one-third of the entire squadron, were lost the same day as Krupinski. The war could not stop on that account. Two days later, four more Lagg-5's went down under Erich's guns and three IL-2's as well—seven kills in one day. He now had twenty-two confirmed victories and the 7th Squadron total rose to 750.

The next day, four more Lagg-5's went down. There was no longer any question in Erich's mind that he had found a sound and effective mode of attack. "See – Decide – Attack – Reverse, or 'Coffee Break.' " His shooting eye continued to improve and in action after action he deliberately went in closer and closer before firing. At the point where most attackers broke away, Erich found that he was still too far out. He fought down his natural apprehension of getting too close to his enemy. The closer he got before opening fire, the more devastating the effect and the more certain the kill.

By 1 August 1943 he had forty-six confirmed victories. Two days later at 1830 hours near Kharkov, a Lagg-5 went down in flames and brought his tally to fifty kills. At one time, this would have been sufficient to win him the Knight's Cross, but now more victories were required. He had conquered much of his earlier immaturity and was now clearly a young leader of promise and ability.

Guenther Rall, as *Gruppenkommandeur* of III/JG-52, had carefully watched Erich's progress. There had been times when Rall could have given Erich a squadron, but he refrained from pushing the promising newcomer too fast. By August 1943, Rall decided that Erich could handle a squadron, and appointed him to command the 9th Squadron after the previous squadron leader, Lieutenant Korts, was killed in action.* The 9th was Hermann Graf's old squadron—the first man to win two hundred aerial victories—and it had a fighting tradition.

Erich rose to his responsibilities. Four missions a day was commonplace, and with the Russian offensive in full cry on the southern sector of the Eastern Front, the enemy was not hard to find. On 5 August 1943 Erich raised his score to sixty victories, added ten more in the next three days, and by 17 August 1943 he had eighty victories, tying Baron Manfred von Richthofen's First World War record.

---

* Lieutenant Korts had been on leave most of August, was awarded the Knight's Cross on 29 August and disappeared with his element leader in combat that same day.

By the end of September 1943, with 115 victories, Erich had surpassed the lifetime victory tally of the immortal Werner "Daddy" Moelders, who had been the first fighter ace in history to down 100 aircraft in aerial combat. In the air force of any other warring power, Erich Hartmann by this time would have been a national hero. On the Russian Front, 100 victories was a relatively common achievement, and before a young knight of the air could truly win his spurs he would have to reach 150 victories. The flaxen-haired young squadron leader kept racking up the triumphs, and days of multiple downings became more and more frequent as his confidence grew. However, Russian aircraft and pilots were getting better too. Victories came much harder, now.

On 29 October 1943, Lt. Erich Hartmann scored his 150th victory. He was all but level now with Krupinski, who had scored his 150th kill on 1 October 1943. But Krupinski had been in combat since 1939–1940. Since 27 February 1943, Erich had scored 148 kills, an outstanding achievement in eight months.

This feat won Erich Hartmann the Knight's Cross of the Iron Cross, the coveted badge of achievement among German fighter pilots. When news of the award reached squadron HQ, Bimmel Mertens was exultant. He pumped his young chief's hand.

"If you keep going like this, I know you are going to be the greatest of all the fighter pilots—none will stand above you."

Bimmel's enthusiasm knew no bounds, and Erich quietly thought to himself, as his crew chief wrung his hand, how much he owed to this devoted comrade.

"Bimmel," said Erich, "you are completely crazy, but if I reach the top it will be because my aircraft never failed me—thanks to you."

On 29 October 1943 Erich had the formal trappings of a Knight of the Air. He was one of approximately thirteen hundred Luftwaffe flyers who won the Knight's Cross. His escutcheon was a big, red, bleeding heart painted on the fuselage of his fighter. The heart was labeled "Usch" and an arrow pierced it. In the air he was Karaya One (Sweetheart One) and at his throat was the coveted Knight's Cross. The Blond Knight had won his spurs, and with them a prize he valued far more—two weeks at home with his beloved Usch.

CHAPTER FIVE

IN THE BEAR'S GRASP

Only he is lost who gives himself up for lost.
—*Anonymous*

THE THUNDER OF the Russian artillery throughout the night of 19 August 1943 was heavy enough to keep Erich awake for long periods. He had flown his three hundredth mission that day and was bone-tired, but the rolling timpani of the guns denied him sleep. A big Red push was afoot. In the uneasy predawn minutes the bad news spread through the 7th Squadron's base at Kuteynikovo in the Donets Basin. The Russians had broken through. The encirclement of large German Army units was threatened.

Erich rolled off his cot and pulled on his clothes as the squadron prepared for a panic scramble. Rumors were being babbled back and forth as the sleepy pilots came boiling out of their tents in the half-light. The base came alive with the shattering roar of fighter engines bursting into action. Since Krupinski's crash in July, Erich had been acting as commander of 7th Squadron. He strode over to the hut where Colonel Dietrich Hrabak, *Kommodore* of JG-52, was directing operations.

Cool and precise as always, Hrabak quickly apprised Erich of the situation.

"Your squadron will take the first mission, Hartmann. We will be flying overlapping missions all day to keep the air clear of Russian fighter-bombers." Hrabak's finger stabbed down on an area map. "The main breakthrough is here. Rudel's Stukas will be giving them hell. Protect the Stukas and make the Russian fighter-bombers your primary target. If no enemy air opposition appears, strafe the Red Army. Get going and *Hals und Beinbruch*."*

Erich gathered his seven pilots around him and briefed them. They would fly in open battle formation.

"If I give the order to attack, every wingman stays like glue to his element leader. If I give the order to attack, every element leader fights his own air battle with his element. Number One target is the fighter-bombers and bombers. If I attack first, the second element stays on the perch, and when I pull up, the second element attacks while I watch from the perch. If we run into huge gaggles, then every element attacks on its own initiative. I hope nobody blames me for any breaches of air discipline. *Hals und Beinbruch!*"

Minutes later, Erich strode up to Bimmel, waiting anxiously with Karaya One all ready.

"All O.K.?" said Erich.

Bimmel nodded. Erich knew his crew chief was always ready. Probably Bimmel had been up for a couple of hours fussing over the aircraft. As he scrambled into the cockpit and tucked his parachute under him, Erich thought again how fortunate he was to have the trusty Bimmel in charge of his ship. Erich hooked up his safety belt but let it lie loosely on his lap, so he could operate comfortably in the tight cockpit. He ran through the drill.

Fuel selector open . . . throttle one-third open . . . prime three, four, five times . . . water-cooling closed . . . propeller to automatic . . . master ignition on both. . . . All went smoothly while two mechanics cranked the inertia starter. The whirring grind rose in pitch.

"Free!" The mechanic's cry signified the propeller was clear.

Erich pulled the clutch and the prop began turning. The engine caught immediately, blurting into life and filling the air with its smooth thunder.

Erich checked his oil pressure, fuel pressure, ammeter and

---

* German sporting term used by flyers, skiers and others in hazardous work. Literally, "break your bones," but through usage a valediction of good luck. The superstitious flyers thought it bad luck to be directly wished good luck, so took the opposite approach.

cooling system, then each of the two magnetos in turn. The rpm held solidly. Taxiing across to the take-off point, he gave Bimmel a high sign, a pilot's silent thanks for a well-serviced aircraft. Erich made a final all-around check. His bird was ready to fly. Tightening his seat belt, he gunned the Messerschmitt into the soft wind and she went racing across the grass. Lifting easily to his touch, she soared aloft as the first fingers of sunshine stroked the high cloud.

His landing gear came up and locked in with a gentle thud. He checked his flaps and moved the trim and turned on his gun switches. The electrical gunsight and his R/T were operative. Now his bird was ready to fight. Climbing away from the field, Erich began turning east into a bloody sunrise. Black palls of smoke roiling up into the heavens to the northeast marked the battle zone. "Not more than ten minutes flight, Erich." He spoke aloud to himself. Then he craned around, looking again at the rest of his fighting flock.

Quickly he counted them. Lieutenant Puls on his own wing. Lieutenant Orje Blessin leading the second element, with Sergeant Jürgens as his wingman. The second section was in good shape, too. Lieutenant Joachim Birkner was leading, a pilot Erich had broken in as his own wingman. Birkner was a head flyer and a good shot. Sergeant Bachnik led the second element with Lieutenant Wester on his wing. Battle-ready and confident, eight Me-109's with the Blond Knight leading went racing to their rendezvous with Rudel's Stukas.

Pillars of smoke and the stabbing flashes of shellbursts over a wide area below showed the line of the barrage and the heavy, front-line fighting. As Erich and his squadron closed in on the battle scene, they could see about forty dive-bomber Stormoviks plastering German infantry with bombs. For every Stormovik there was a Russian fighter over the area, about forty Lagg-5's and YAK-9's circling warily.

Erich went diving down through the fighters, firing briefly at selected targets on the way through. Then the Messerschmitts fell on the low-level Stormoviks. Every one of the hated steel-clads they downed would take pressure off their comrades in the infantry.

Coming up into firing position behind an IL-2 at high speed, Erich carefully watched the closing distance. Two hundred yards . . . 150 yards . . . 100 yards . . . the range diminished in a twinkling. Looming in a vast black mass, the Stormovik filled Erich's windshield at 75 yards or less. A short burst from all guns. A massive explosion blasted downward from the Russian machine and its port wing sheared off. Erich broke away instantly after firing and went racing at high speed after another low-flying Stormovik.

The second Stormovik was intent on his ground targets. Oblivious to Erich's presence, he was hosing the German infantry with fire. Karaya One closed the distance to firing position astern in an instant. Erich again held out till the last possible moment. Down to 100 yards. "Not close enough, Erich. This IL-2 is the toughest bird in the air." At 50 yards Erich squeezed his triggers for a stiff burst from all guns.

The Stormovik sagged, shuddered and flared alight from nose to tail. Erich pulled up hard over the stricken IL-2, ready to swing back into the other ground-strafing Stormoviks. Explosions like backfires banged and jarred under the fuselage of Karaya One. Erich saw one of his engine doors fly off and whip away astern in the slipstream. Choking blue smoke came belching back into the cockpit.

He was talking aloud to himself again. "What in hell has happened, Erich? Flak, ground fire, stray shells from the air battle? Which? Never mind! Get out of here and head west while you can. Quick! Before this damned bird goes in." He made a steep turn to the west and pulled his throttle back. Ignition and fuel switches off. "Yes, she's going in. But where? There's a field, a large one, lots of sunflowers . . . head for it. Ease her down . . . ease her down, Erich . . . just like the gliders your mother taught you to fly"

The fighter came down easily, and bucked its way to a halt with a grinding of metal. Erich would walk away from this one. He unbuckled his parachute and made ready to leave the "bent" fighter. Reaching forward to the instrument panel, he began undoing the retaining studs on the aircraft clock. Standing orders required all pilots surviving belly landings to take these precision instruments with them, since the clocks were in short supply.

Struggling with the milled studs that anchored the clock, Erich felt a little let-down from the action. "Damn it, Erich. You didn't get any breakfast this morning—" He broke off his monologue as movement caught his eye through the dusty windshield. A German truck came rumbling into view. He felt relieved. He didn't know how far he had flown west before the belly landing, but the German truck was reassuring. Luftwaffe pilots landing behind Soviet lines were seldom heard from again. He went on battling with the clock, and glanced up as he heard the truck brakes squeal. He did an alarmed double take.

Two hulking soldiers jumped down from the truck bed wearing a strange-looking uniform. German infantrymen wore green-gray tunics. These soldiers were clad in yellow-gray uniforms. Then the two men turned in the direction of the crashed fighter and Erich felt his skin crawl with fear. The faces were Asiatic.

These Russians were using a captured German truck, and now they were about to capture a German to go with it. Erich broke out in a cold sweat as the two Russians approached. If he tried to get out and escape, they would shoot him down. Only one choice remained. He must feign injury. He would deceive them into thinking he had been injured internally in a crash landing.

He feigned unconsciousness as the soldiers jumped up on the wing and gawked into the cockpit. One of them reached down under his armpits and tried to lift Erich out. The Russian smelled sickeningly sour. Erich cried out with pain, and kept crying and sobbing. The Russian let go of him.

The two men jabbered in Russian and then called to Erich. "Comrade, comrade. The war is finished, Hitler is finished.* It doesn't matter now."

"I am wounded," sobbed the Blond Knight, pointing to his abdomen with his right hand and cradling it with his left. Through lowered lids, Erich could see they had swallowed the bait.

The Russians carefully helped him out of the cockpit, while Erich blubbered and sobbed through an Academy Award performance. He fell on the ground, unable to stand up. The Russians went back to the truck, got an old tent, and laid the "wounded" pilot on the folded canvas. They toted him over to the truck like a bundle of wet washing and laid him out carefully on the truck bed.

* The Russians do not say "Hitler," but "Gitler." Thus, in this instance, they said "Gitler kaput"—Hitler is finished.

The soldiers tried talking quietly to Erich, in friendly fashion. Their mood was happy, because the previous night's action had won them a big victory. Erich kept on groaning and clutching at his belly. Exasperated and unable to alleviate his pain, the Russians finally got back in the truck and drove him to their HQ in a nearby village.

A doctor appeared. He could speak a few German words, and he tried to make an examination. The physician stank of a sour perfume. Every time he touched Erich, the Blond Knight cried out. Even the doctor was convinced. His captors brought him some fruit, and he made as though to eat it. Then he cried out again, as though some penetrating strain had been placed on his organism by the act of biting.

For two hours the theater continued. Then the same two soldiers came again, laid him out on the tent and carted him back out to the truck. As they went jolting eastward back behind the Russian lines, Erich knew he would have to make a break—and soon—or spend the rest of the war in a Soviet prison. He weighed the situation. The truck had gone about two miles back into Russian territory. One soldier was driving, the other was in the truck bed guarding the injured German captive. As Erich's thoughts raced, from the western sky came the characteristic whining roar of Stukas.

The German dive bombers passed low overhead, and the truck slowed, ready to ditch. As the guard in the back of the truck stared apprehensively upward, Erich sprang to his feet and charged the Russian with his shoulder. The guard slammed into the back of the cab with his head and collapsed in the truck bed.

Dropping off the tail gate, Erich went bolting into a field of man-high sunflowers beside the road. As he made their cover, screeching truck brakes told him his escape had been discovered. Plunging and staggering deeper and deeper into the sea of sunflowers, Erich heard the crash of rifle fire and the whine of bullets as his captors fired at the waving indications of his passage.

Diminishing to a distant popping, the rifle fire soon ceased to be a menace, but Erich maintained his lung-bursting pace for at least five minutes. He hadn't run like this since the athletic meets at Korntal *Hochschule*. Every yard between him and his ex-hosts was a yard closer to safety. Gasping for breath, he suddenly burst out of the sunflower sea and into a little valley, a place that might have been lifted out of a fairy tale.

Trees, green grass and wildflowers grouped around a little stream seemed out of character with a life-and-death escape. He threw himself down on the grass and gulped the cool air into his lungs. As his heartbeat subsided, his thinking clarified, and he began assessing his plight and how to get back to German territory.

He stood up and started walking westward. From the sun, he judged it to be about nine o'clock. Half an hour's cross-country trudging, almost pleasant in the summer morning, brought him out by a road leading into a small village. Screened by some bushes, he began gathering intelligence that would ensure his escape.

On the other side of the road, not far away, he saw several people wearing fur clothing. He watched them for some minutes, and saw that they were Russians. There was no question now that he was still on the wrong side of the lines. Moving carefully along the line of the road for half a mile, he reached a spot where he could see a hill in the distance. Soldiers were up there digging foxholes and trenches. That meant the front line was not far away—perhaps on the other side of the hill.

The icy coolness of his combat head was ruling his thinking now. He fought down the temptation to keep going in daylight and work his way around the digging Russians. The German Army might be on the other side of the hill, but there was no gunfire. Furthermore, Russian soldiers and peasants seemed to be everywhere as the morning wore on. He talked to himself quietly, as he always did in a tight spot.

"One thing is sure, Erich. You can never go through here in the daytime without being captured. Go back to your valley and wait till dark."

He retraced his steps to the security of his fairy-tale valley, with its stream and trees. Picking out a little dry meander near the stream, he piled up sand and stones into an unobtrusive ridge. He lay down behind this low screen and went to sleep. He awakened to a dying afternoon, and made ready to move out with nightfall.

Bimmel had waited on the line after Erich took off into the dawn. He always waited. The other crew chiefs went in and drank coffee or sat around and swapped yarns until the fighters came back. Bimmel preferred to wait on the line, alone, his gaze never long removed from the sky. That morning, Bimmel's chief didn't come back with the others. Apprehensive and worried, he paced up and down, watching the eastern horizon, alert for the first sight or sound of the returning Me-109.

Appearing progressively more distraught, Bimmel maintained his vigil for hours after all Erich's fuel would have been exhausted. No one among the returning pilots knew for sure what had happened to Erich. Lieutenant Puls saw him going down trailing smoke, but he himself was jumped by Russian fighters at that moment and could watch Hartmann no longer. The rest of the pilots were too busy, in their every-man-for-himself battle with eighty Red aircraft, to see what happened to Erich.

Bimmel's pacing grew more rapid. His visits to the HQ bunker for news became more and more frequent. Still no word. His crew-chief comrades next saw Sergeant Mertens in his tent, rolling up a blanket and stuffing some food in a rucksack.

"Where are you going, Bimmel?"

"I'm going behind the Russian lines. To find my chief, that's where I'm going."

"You'll be shot if you're caught."

"I speak Russian. The people will help me find Erich."

Bimmel Mertens asked for no leave or permission to depart from the base. He simply took a rifle and disappeared on foot in the direction of the front line. If his chief was alive, he would find him and bring him back. That was the bond between the Blond Knight and his faithful crew chief, a loyalty evoked from the depths of the heart, and as the square-shouldered Bimmel disappeared from view, the other crew chiefs watched and shook their heads.

Gunfire punctuated the night air and tracer and star shells laced and bobbed their way through the sky as Erich pressed on toward the front lines. Rattles of rifle and machine-gun fire sounded nearby as he stumbled through the August half-dark toward the hill with the entrenchments he had seen that morning. He made it up the hill, picking his way carefully among the diggings. On the other side, he descended into a sprawling valley verdant with sunflowers in full bloom.

Erich waded into the sunflowers, heading west, and disturbing them as little as possible. Frequent pauses made good sense. He conserved his strength and could listen for enemy movements. Slogging through the sunflowers for an hour, he paused for a longer rest. The metallic rattle of an infantryman's web gear brought him to full alert.

Crouching down, Erich watched a Russian patrol of ten men pressing through the sunflowers. Chances were this was a recce* patrol, he reasoned. They would likely know where the German front line lay, or be going somewhere near the forward positions. He weighed the chances and decided to follow the patrol.

Keeping a respectable distance behind them, Erich watched their progress in the gloom as the towering sunflowers waved and bobbed with the movements of the patrol. In a few minutes, the Russians had led him to the edge of the sunflower belt. Crouching in its fringe, he watched the ten soldiers cross a meadow, passing two small houses on their right.

As the Russians went stumbling on up another hill and disappeared for a few moments behind a clump of trees, Erich sprinted across the meadow and flung himself under the wooden steps of one of the houses. He watched from concealment as the patrol disappeared up the hillside into the gloom.

A storm of automatic fire and some grenade bursts rent the air. The remnants of the patrol, crying and shouting, came bolting and stumbling back down the hill. Their ragged figures disappeared back into the sunflower belt. Erich felt he had a good break. The German front line must be at the top of the next hill.

He ran up the slope, and as he neared the hill's crest, he started whistling a German song. He didn't want to be cut down by another blast of automatic fire. In a few minutes he stood on the hilltop. There were no Germans, no entrench-

* *Recce* is military slang for "reconnaissance."

ments, no sign of life. His shoes clicked against a pile of cartridge cases. He was at the scene of the skirmish he had heard. Erich estimated the time as around midnight.

Erich started walking westward again. For two hours more he skidded and staggered and stumbled down into another valley enclosed by hills. He headed up the western slopes of the valley, near giddy from hunger and tension. Rumbling artillery crumped in the distance. The only other sound was his own breathing. The air was almost deathly still.

"Halten!" Blam!

The challenge merged with the muffled bark of a rifle fired at close range. Erich felt the bullet rip through his trouser leg.

"Damned fool!" he yelled. "God Almighty, man, don't shoot your own people."

"Stoppen!"

"Damn you to hell, I am a German pilot. Don't shoot, for Christ's sake."

Standing no more than twenty yards away, the sentry was lucky he missed. His bad marksmanship was due to his almost paralytic fear. As Erich gingerly drew closer, he could see the soldier literally quaking with fear in the gloom. He was more frightened even than Erich, who could feel the air washing around his leg from the bullet hole in his trousers.

Erich shouted into the area behind the sentry at the top of his voice.

"I'm a German pilot who has been shot down. I am happy to be here. I've been walking for hours from behind the Russian lines. For God's sake let me come through."

"Let him come." A sharp order from the rear sounded to Erich like a redemption.

Glaring at the sentry in the darkness, the young ace stalked past him toward the voice. The sentry was not relaxing for a minute. Moving in behind Erich he jammed the muzzle of his rifle into the Blond Knight's back. Erich could feel the sweat beading out on his brow. One slip or a stagger in the darkness and this lunatic would put a bullet in his back. The sentry pushed and poked him to the top of the hill.

The entrenched infantry shoved him roughly into a foxhole. A second lieutenant in command of the unit began interrogating the bone-weary Erich. He had no identification. The Russians had emptied his pockets. He gave the suspicious German officer his name and rank, and the approximate position where he had been shot down the morning before. It was now about 2 A.M. and he couldn't blame the infantrymen for being cautious.

"Please, *Leutnant*, telephone my wing HQ."

The officer was convinced, but he had no telephone, and couldn't leave the line during the night. He also explained the reason for their nervousness and caution.

"Two days ago, six men came, all speaking perfect German, and told us they were escaped P.O.W.'s. When they got into the positions of a neighboring unit, they whipped out submachine guns from under their coats and killed and wounded ten men."

Erich pondered the hard and dirty war of the infantry, as he settled down to spend the remainder of the night with the troops in the line. His countrymen gave him a little food, and he slumped into an exhausted sleep in a foxhole. After what seemed like a minute or two, he snapped awake with one of the infantrymen shaking his arm.

"Come with me. It's an alert."

Erich looked at the luminous dial of his wristwatch. It was 4 A.M. He followed the soldier out into the trench where a machine gun was mounted. His stomach tightened into a compact ball. The sound of yelling and singing came floating up the hillside. Erich sneaked a look over the parapet. Dimly he could see a bunch of Russian soldiers staggering and weaving up the hillside. They looked like they were drunk. Talking and joking in groups, their progress was unannounced by any artillery or tanks. They might be drunk or it could be a trap.

The young lieutenant commanding the Germans was giving last-minute orders to his men.

"Wait. Don't fire until I give the order. Let them come on and get so close you cannot miss."

Erich thought how closely this infantryman's tactics resembled his own, high in the sky.

The Russians came on up the hill, whooping and bellowing out Russian songs. The Germans in the trench crouched in a fever of taut nerves. The Russians were reeling within sixty feet of the trench. They must see their foes any second, drunk or sober.

"Fire!"

Every weapon in the German platoon opened up. A withering blast of lead and steel lifted the Russians off their feet, felled them where they stood, or bowled them dead back down the hill. Caught cold and drunk they had no chance. In a welter of blood and rags the savage ambush was over in half a minute. Not a single Russian survived.

This was Erich's first exposure to the brutal war of the infantry in Russia. This chilling experience etched itself indelibly in his memory. Twenty-five years later, recalling it would chill his spine. The infantrymen and the airmen had little in common in the way they fought.

After the ambush, in the first light of dawn a corporal escorted Erich down to company HQ. A radio and a telephone were available and the company commander soon contacted Colonel Hrabak at Kuteynikovo. Erich's identity was confirmed and he was sent back by car to his base. After telling his story to Hrabak, he went in search of Bimmel.

Erich was aghast when he learned of his crew chief's impromptu rescue expedition. Bimmel was still gone. Krupinski had returned from the hospital during Erich's absence and he recalls the Blond Knight's return to the 7th Squadron:

"The day Bubi Hartmann returned from his sojourn behind the lines in Russian territory is a day I will always remember. He was one happy boy to get back to his squadron safely, but he was really frightened by his experience. His tired eyes were very wide and big, and he was obviously exhausted.

"He had lived through an experience very few of our men survived. It seemed to me that in these few harrowing hours he had grown much older."

The cloud of concern that settled over Erich when he learned of Bimmel's absence dissipated the next day. The erect, unmistakable figure of Mertens came plodding back across the airfield the following morning. Dark circles surrounded Bimmel's eyes, and his cheeks were sunken. He was obviously near collapse as he trudged dejectedly back to the base. Then he saw Erich.

Bimmel's haggard face blossomed into a happy smile. His chief had got home. As Erich strode over to him he could see that the Blond Knight was unwounded. The two men wrung each other's hands in a silent expression of the deep bond men feel who will lay down their lives for each other. To this day, Bimmel Mertens says that the happiest moment of his life was when he saw Erich Hartmann safe and well after his crash behind the Soviet lines.

Erich's grueling experience was rich in lessons. His instinctive adoption of the wounded-man role undoubtedly saved him from either imprisonment or death. The Russians fell for the cunning ruse of internal injuries and lowered their vigilance. This was the key to his escape. The experience of other pilots in Russian hands reveals that German airmen were usually heavily guarded, with two or three armed men in attendance. Most of them were immediately handcuffed after capture.

Quick thinking is one of the successful fighter pilot's prime assets, and in this case it prevented the Blond Knight's career from ending in August 1943, when he had but ninety victories. He conveyed the essence of his experience in Russian hands to the young pilots he led later in the war, and again when he commanded the Richthofen Wing in the new German Air Force. Erich Hartmann's own summation is appropriate.

"I always told my men that if they were prisoners somewhere and able to escape, to *move only by night*. Never move during the daytime. There is the unexpected encounter with the enemy to contend with, and the ever present possibility that you will be spotted without seeing the person who has spotted you. You have too many surprises to deal with in the daytime.

"When you move by night, you cannot be surprised. The advantages are with you. You know you are a stranger, and that all around you are enemies. If you are challenged in any language you still have a moment—enough time to jump away into the darkness. At night, the majority of your enemies are asleep, so that all those pairs of eyes and hands are not around to obstruct you, spot your escape, or pull the triggers of rifles.

"I emphasized to all the men I commanded during and since the war that it takes self-discipline not to try escaping during the daytime. That burned itself into my brain that day as I lay in that dry wash in the stream bed. Don't be in a hurry. Wait till night. The darkness is your friend."

One of the strangest anomalies of the Blond Knight's often anomalous career is that when he was cast entirely on his own resources as a Soviet captive in August 1943, he made his escape through good instinct, clear analysis and self-discipline. When he was conveyed to the grasp of the Bear by his American captors in 1945, there was no possibility of escape from a situation created by agreements between governments. Another agreement between governments, ten and a half years later, was needed then to free the Blond Knight from the Bear's grasp.

CHAPTER SIX

OAK LEAVES

War is not exactly a life insurance.
—*Col. Hans-Ulrich Rudel*

ONCE ERICH REACHED 150 victories in the autumn of 1943, his climb to fame proceeded rapidly on both sides of the lines. German propaganda broadcasts began occasionally mentioning his name. His photograph appeared sometimes in newspapers, usually with other leading fighter pilots of JG-52.* To the Russians he became known first as Karaya One, his R/T designation. Later he became infamous on the Soviet side as the "Black Devil of the South."

The legend of the Black Devil began when Erich had a black nose painted on his aircraft, a distinctive pattern shaped like tulip petals. His fighter was easily distinguishable in combat, and the Soviet flyers quickly realized that the pilot of this black-marked German fighter was a foe to be avoided. He never missed. The feared but as yet otherwise unidentified German pilot was nicknamed "Black Devil of the South" by the Russians.

The Soviets had their listening posts and monitored Luftwaffe ground-to-air communications, as did the Germans in gathering intelligence about their foes. These monitored broadcasts made it obvious to the Russians that Karaya One and the Black Devil they had come to fear were the same man. He was cutting a swath through their formations, and

* Erich's *Gruppenkommandeur,* Guenther Rall, reached 200 victories on 28 August 1943, and 250 victories on 28 November 1943 —both occasions for much publicity for Rall and JG-52.

most of the Black Devil's victories were over single-engined fighters. A price of ten thousand rubles was placed on the Black Devil's head. The Russian pilot who could bring him down would win fame, glory and wealth.

These inducements proved insufficient. Red pilots encountering and identifying the Black Devil's distinctively marked aircraft quickly left the scene of battle. Erich found that his black markings, and black image in the minds of the Soviet pilots, were working against him. His scores began to diminish, as contact with the enemy declined. He was lucky to get in one strike before the enemy fighters dispersed, and the fortunes of every *Schwarm* in which Erich flew with the black aircraft declined sharply.

Erich countered first by giving the black-marked aircraft to his green wingmen. These youngsters could have had no better protection. The Red fighters left the pilot of the machine with the tulip-pattern nose severely alone, but it was still the same story. As long as the black petals were in the air, Red opponents were hard to find. Erich concluded that the black petals had to go.

Bimmel Mertens was overjoyed. Keeping up the pretty black paint job was an extra chore for him that he didn't particularly enjoy. Bimmel could also count. He knew that the trophies of the hunt had declined since the pattern was first painted on his young chief's ship. Bimmel erased the black tulips and to the unsuspecting Red pilots, Erich became just another Me-109 in a typical *Schwarm*. The difference in scoring heartened not only Erich and Bimmel, but the whole squadron. The victories began coming thick and fast again as Erich lit into the Red formations with the advantage of anonymity.

In January and February 1944 Karaya One seemed to be everywhere, and always on the victor's end of the battles. In this sixty-day period Erich ran up a staggering fifty victories —an average of nearly one kill per day. Actually, the average was about two downings for every flying day. Bad weather was almost as serious an enemy as the Red Air Force, in spite of all the Germans had learned from their Soviet enemies about contending with the weather.

The Germans were astonished in Russia when Red fighters swarmed over their airfields early on sub-zero mornings when they had been unable even to start their own aircraft. When Erich's squadron captured a Russian airman, he showed them with typical Soviet directness how the Russian Air Force maintained its operational effectiveness at 40 below zero.

The cooperative prisoner was proud of knowing something perhaps the Germans didn't know. He called for half a gallon of gasoline in a can. He went over to one of the grounded Messerschmitts, and to the horror of the watching JG-52 personnel, poured the gasoline into the aircraft's oil sump. The Germans backed away twenty yards or more. The moment that *Dummkopf* turned on the ignition and attempted a start, there would be an explosion.

Apprehensive mechanics began cranking the motor by hand, while a German pilot cringed down in the cockpit. After the gasoline was thoroughly mixed with the congealed oil, he turned on the ignition. The engine started. There was no explosion. The big Daimler-Benz burst into life and ran solidly. The Russian airman explained through interpreting Germans that the oil congealed at sub-zero temperatures and made it impossible for the starters to budge the engine. The gasoline liquefied the oil, and then evaporated as the engine warmed up. The only necessary precaution was to change engine oil more often when using gasoline for sub-zero starting.

Erich also watched another captured Russian demonstrate a sub-zero starting gimmick. He tells the story in his own words:

"This prisoner called for a spare-parts tray. Again, there was a call for gasoline. While Bimmel and others watched, the Russian stalked over to a nearby Me-109 and set the tray on the ground underneath the engine compartment. He filled the tray brimming with gasoline. Then he lit a match and sprang back.

"The gasoline vapor flared alight despite the sub-zero temperature, and a wide tongue of flame licked at the underside of the fighter's opened engine compartment. For a full ten minutes the blaze continued.

"One of the mechanics said that the electrical system would be ruined—the insulation all burnt away—as the flames died down. The Russian simply said, 'Start it.' The instant, smooth roar of that motor convinced everyone. Fighters could be started in sub-zero weather—once you knew how. We all felt indebted to the Red Air Force for this scheme, which helped us get into the air to meet their early morning sorties."

The same Russian prisoner gladly showed the awed Germans how to keep their armament functioning in sub-zero climates. Luftwaffe manuals recommended careful lubrication and greasing for gun mechanism. The grease congealed on the Russian Front and froze the breech mechanism shut. The Russian took a German machine gun and dunked it in a tank of boiling water, flushing all the grease and oil out of the weapon. Minus its recommended lubricants, the gun functioned perfectly at 40 below zero. Thanks to Russian advice, the Germans were not only able to keep flying, but also to keep firing, a problem that had dogged Luftwaffe units in the first two winters in Russia.

With Bimmel using all these tricks and more, Erich was able to rack up his impressive string of kills over the January-February period in 1944. He flew a normally camouflaged fighter, and its only distinguishing mark was the bleeding "Usch" heart on the fuselage. The Russians nevertheless matched up the plane and pilot through radio interceptions. This led to Erich's being singled out one morning by a Russian determined to down him.

Erich was flying with his wingman, Lieutenant Wester, far back in German territory on the Rumanian Front. Behind the lines there was normally little likelihood of encountering Russian aircraft, but reports had come into JG-52 HQ of ground attacks behind the lines. Erich was ordered to make a sweep.

With over five hundred combat missions under his belt, Erich had acquired something that he considered even more valuable than the 150 victories standing to his credit—an intuition for the enemy presence. The blue sky seemed empty, save for some cumulus insufficient to conceal an aircraft for long. The earth below showed no evidence of the mortal struggle seesawing across its face. Then Erich's ESP rang the little danger signal in his mind that was to save him many times. He looked back.

Sitting on the perch six hundred yards behind and above him was a single, red-nosed YAK fighter. The Russian was about to make a pass on Karaya One.

"Pull ahead of me, climb up and watch!" Erich told Wester.

As they went racing along, the Russian every few seconds would try to open fire. Watching carefully, Erich broke away each time, trying to get the Russian to overtake him on the outside. The Red pilot then did the last thing Erich expected. Pulling up, he turned and came head-on. Erich fired and the Russian fired. No hits either way. Twice they fired their way through a head-on encounter. Neither of them could get a better firing position.

After two near-misses at high speed, Erich began his out-loud talking to himself that he resorted to in tight spots.

"Erich, this Russian acts like he is mad. He is probably trying to ram you. Break away from him, come on, with negative G's."

The Blond Knight pushed his stick forward and sent Karaya One down in a negative G maneuver instead of continuing his turn. He called to Wester to escape down in a steep dive. As his fighter went plunging down, Erich watched the Russian continue his turn. From underneath, Erich could see the now confused Red pilot making a couple of quick turns, obviously rattled because he could no longer find his German antagonist. Without spotting Erich below him in the dead zone, the Russian turned east and headed for home, no doubt full of his tale of how he almost bushwhacked the infamous Karaya One . . . the Black Devil.

Firewalling his throttle, Erich followed at low level directly under his adversary. Climbing steadily, with the 109's engine wide open, in two minutes Erich had come up under the unsuspecting YAK. Throttling back less than fifty feet below the Russian machine, Erich lifted the nose, and as the enemy fighter filled his windshield with its bulk, he pressed his gun buttons.

Clunks of jagged metal flew off the Russian fighter in a deadly hail and thundered against the wings of Karaya One. Fire blow-torched out of the Russian's engine compartment and a pall of black smoke trailed back behind the stricken fighter. The YAK was done for.

The Russian pilot inverted his dying machine and bailed out. His chute billowing white against the morning sky, he hung there as his aircraft went barreling down in flames. The YAK crashed thunderously. Smoke came climbing up from the wreck as the Russian went floating down. Circling the scene, Erich watched the Russian touch down near his shattered fighter and begin gathering in his chute. German infantry from a nearby village were already on their way to the scene.

Fixing the location in his mind, Erich sped back to base, and piling out of Karaya One, clambered immediately into the squadron's flying jeep, the Fieseler Storch. The versatile little aircraft was used for reconnaissance, forward air control and rescuing downed pilots. A Storch could land in a minimum of six hundred feet, and carry three people including the pilot. A Storch was kept ready on the base at all times.

Erich took off, and a few minutes later landed in a small field close to the village from which he had seen German infantrymen move out toward the Russian pilot. Sure enough, the infantry had captured his late opponent. The Russian was a captain, with a kind face. He was obviously happy to be alive. A couple of Rumanian civilians who knew a smattering of both German and Russian interpreted for the two pilots.

Erich congratulated the Russian on his "birthday"—surviving a downing and a crash.

"For you, the war is over. You are lucky," said Erich.

The Russian nodded and smiled happily.

"Why didn't you look backward after you lost me in maneuvers, and why were you flying alone?"

The Russian captain explained that he had lost his wingman in an earlier battle. As to why he didn't look back, the Russian merely shrugged ruefully. The situation was akin to that summed up in the American expression "Don't look back over your shoulder, someone might be gaining on you."

As the young Russian talked, standing there in his dark tunic, with leather cap and boots, Erich could see he was just like any other fighter pilot—a member of his own fraternity. He was a carefree young man. He made wings out of his hands when he talked. But for his language and uniform, he could have been German.

Erich took his prisoner out of the custody of the infantry and together they walked out to the Storch and flew back to the squadron's base. With gestures and smatters of Russian Erich led the young Red captain into a mess tent. Inside were young German men just like himself. The Germans offered the Russian some schnapps and food. To Erich's surprise, the Russian became angry. One of the German pilots spoke a little Russian and discovered the cause of the enemy pilot's obvious rage.

"They told him that all Russians captured by the Germans would be shot!"

Erich handed the captain some more schnapps and food, then took him out and let him examine the Me-109 close up. The Russian was allowed to wander without an escort around the base for two days before the squadron had to send him on to wing HQ for proper processing. Enterprising enough to single out Karaya One, the Russian pilot had no ambition to escape, although he was left practically unguarded.

Air battles like his encounter with the lone Russian brought Erich into contact with every conceivable situation in air-to-air combat. He was not only confident of his own abilities—without which no fighter pilot could ever succeed—but also extended his skills through experience. He could spot aircraft now at phenomenal distances, sometimes minutes before anyone else airborne with him, and often intuit his foe's intentions. He avoided the dogfight in favor of the lethal efficiency of hit and run. The "See – Decide – Attack – Break" was a sequence never to be broken. Following it meant success, departing from it meant failure and even doom.

For joining and breaking combat Erich developed practical rules that kept him alive and unwounded while the Russian aircraft continued to fall. Under blue-sky conditions, he found the best mode of attack the high and fast approach. Where overcast prevailed, he made his strike low and fast. He waited whenever and wherever possible for this one fast blow rather than make his attack under less than ideal conditions. This was his "coffee break." Surprise was the crucial element of the successful bounce.

In winter, with Karaya One camouflaged white and the sky overcast, the low-to-high attack pass proved extremely successful. He conquered his earlier tendency to slacken speed when closing in, going right to his foe at the shortest possible distance before firing. From fifty yards the power of Karaya One's armament was devastating. Kills were scored with minimum ammunition.

The traditional tactic of turning with an enemy was something Erich had abandoned. Dogfighters could do it their way, and most of them loved the dogfight. Erich preferred his own methods. After his brief and violent attack, he would roll over wing deep and dive about two thousand feet under his foe if altitude permitted, pulling up from behind and below for a second attack. In this position, he could stay with any turn the enemy might attempt, and after firing, the Blond Knight was on his way upstairs for a third pass should his foe survive the second assault. Each pass was a repetition of the "See – Decide – Attack – Break" cycle.

In the Eastern Front air battles, the Germans were almost always heavily outnumbered. Consequently, Erich himself was often bounced by Russian fighters. In the same way as he evolved his deadly attack tactics, he developed a defensive set of rules. Just as his attack methods rolled up his score past all the old dogfighters, so did his defense tactics keep him from being wounded. The two sets of tactics went hand in hand, and led to his being consistently in action. Luck was almost always with him, but his penetrant analytical ability was ever Lady Luck's bridegroom. Physical survival and a high score were the children of the union.

When a Russian bounced him from behind, to one side and above—from "the perch"—Erich would go into a hard climbing turn, turning *into* his enemy's firing pass. Where a Red pilot came from below and behind, Erich would go hard left or right and down, again breaking into his enemy's pass, then immediately using negative G's to lose the enemy.

Erich's coolness soon became a legend among all who flew with him. He learned to observe his Russian foes as they came in to the attack and meet their thrusts with appropriate parries. Resisting the urge to turn while an attacking Russian pilot was still outside firing range required coolness. The concept of simply sitting there while an enemy aircraft rushed in with a battery of guns charged was hard to accept in theory —and even tougher to execute in actual combat. Flying straight and level, using the rudder for slight slip and waiting for the enemy to commit himself, soon convinced the Blond Knight that he could avoid being hit under these circum- stances. Vital information could often be gleaned in the split seconds before the attacking Russian opened fire.

Inexperienced or inferior pilots always gave themselves away by opening fire too early. Erich discovered that in such instances he could soon change his role from defender to attacker, but if the Red pilot held his fire and kept closing in, then it was certain that an old-timer was at the controls. A battle was then in the offing.

Erich developed only one rule for breaking away as a last-ditch maneuver, and that was to execute a movement where possible with negative G's. An attacking pilot expects his quarry to turn tighter and try to out-turn him—the classic dogfight. The attacking pilot must turn even tighter in order to pull firing lead on his quarry. As a result, his quarry disappears under the nose of the attacker. At that moment the quarry can escape by shoving forward on the stick and kick- ing bottom rudder. The forces on his aircraft change from plus five G's to minus one or minus one-and-a-half G's. This escape maneuver is almost impossible for the attacker to see or follow until it is too late. Erich made good use of this escape tactic, which threw the attacker instantly from advan- tage to complex disadvantage.

The attacker was first of all placed at the psychological disadvantage imposed by negative G's—weightlessness. Physi- cally he was disadvantaged, being lifted from his seat to hang against his belt—an impossible situation in which to track a target, due to the higher negative attack angle. Finally, the erstwhile attacker lost his overview of the area and steering the aircraft in the right direction for continued pursuit be- came guesswork.

Erich reserved these tactics for last-ditch situations. In all other attacks, his rule was to turn into his assailant's turn, using positive G's. He called these "My Personal Twist Regu- lations," and he taught them to his young wingmen to help keep them alive. His tactical skill in attack and defense took him through more than eight hundred aerial battles without a scratch—too stunning an achievement to be attributed to blind luck.

Once he clarified his tactics and got some experience, Erich's kill tally rose so quickly that he became a subject of discussion among other pilots. His consistent string of victories and seemingly charmed life made him a focus of competitive attention as 1943 wore on. There were even some pilots who thought that there must be some trickery involved in Erich's success.

Sergeant Carl Junger of the 7th Squadron, who had flown as Erich's wingman, was invited with two other pilots to visit the nearby 8th Squadron mess. This social gathering had a noteworthy sequel, arising out of squadron rivalry. During festivities, Junger heard Erich Hartmann's name mentioned in some of the noisy conversation. Second Lieutenant Friedrich "Fritz" Obleser, who had come to JG-52 about the same time as Erich, had scored well at the outset of his career, while Erich was conquering his buck fever and learning the tricks of Rossmann and the dogfighters. Once Erich settled down to lead his own elements, he rocketed past Obleser in the scoring. Fritz was expressing his skepticism about Erich's consistent skein of kills.

Junger as Erich's wingman had been witness to many of Erich's kills. He was annoyed by the implication in Obleser's remarks. The next day, Junger told the Blond Knight what Obleser had said. Erich thanked Junger and made up his mind in a flash about what should be done. He went straight to Major Guenther Rall, the *Gruppenkommandeur*, under whose command both the 7th and 8th Squadrons were operating.

"Fritz Obleser of the 8th Squadron has been saying to other pilots that he doesn't believe my kills are genuine."

Rall's eyebrows went up. "Well, I *know* they are genuine. I see the witness reports and all the details. What do you want me to do about it?"

"I would like to have Obleser fly as wingman on a few operations, sir. That is, if it can be arranged."

Rall nodded. Pilots locking horns was nothing new to him. "Of course, I'll issue the orders. He can come down tomorrow."

A somewhat embarrassed Obleser duly reported the following day for duty as Erich's wingman. Since his temporary transfer was for observational purposes, he was assigned to

the better vantage point offered by the second element in
Erich's *Schwarm*. He flew two missions and saw two of Erich's devastating close-in downings, in which the Blond Knight
blew up his opponents' aircraft.

On the ground, the convinced Obleser signed the two kill
confirmation claims as the official witness. Fritz apologized in
manly fashion for his earlier criticism and was allowed to
return to the 8th Squadron with his story. No further expressions of skepticism about Bubi Hartmann's victories came
from any neighboring unit.

Behind Erich's tactical skills, which he evolved and polished
through experience, lay yet another important talent of the
successful fighter pilot—a hunter's nose. He had an instinct
for finding his foes, even during periods of relative inactivity.
As the downing reports kept reaching Rall's desk for forward-
ing to wing HQ, he could see that Erich was getting kills
when other pilots were coming home empty-handed. So Bubi
was a hunter.

On the evening of 1 October 1943, Erich was called to the
telephone. Major Rall wanted in on tomorrow's hunt.

"What time are you going out in the morning?" said Rall.

"Seven o'clock or thereabouts."

"Good. I will come with you in the second element."

Erich Hartmann now tells the story of the only operation
the two great aces flew together.

"Rall had been flying down to Zaporozhe every morning
early to catch the worm, but with no success. I had been
flying later and having success, but I had a special route there.
I flew down from Zaporozhe to Nikopol, and near there was a
big Russian air base. I had kept my find quiet, but every day I
was able to knock an aircraft down in this area.

"Rall came with me on the morning of 2 October 1943,
and we flew south. We were circling along the front and the
line of the Dnieper River. After about thirty minutes' flight
with nothing in sight, Rall came on the R/T.

" 'What are you doing screwing around down here in the
south? There's nothing here. I'm taking my element up to
Dnepropetrovsk.'

"And so the *Gruppenkommandeur* lit out. Barely two minutes later, I spotted a P-2 recce plane at eighteen thousand

feet, with a couple of Lagg fighters as escort. I was afraid that Rall would not yet be far enough away, so I waited until I was closing in on the P-2. Then I called Rall.

" 'I have a bogey* south of Zaporozhe, and you can watch it. Turn around.'

"Back on the R/T came Rall's frantic response.

" 'Wait! Wait! Wait till I get there.'

"By then I was only fifteen hundred feet from the P-2. I closed in and shot him down, then broke into one of the Laggs and sent him down, too. Rall saw them both go down burning."

Rall's conclusion that the boy was a hunter as well as a shooter was thus proved correct, and the incident shows a certain quality of impishness that Erich Hartmann maintains to this day.

The Russian fighter pilots were the most formidable air opposition on the Eastern Front, but the toughest bird in the air, as we have said, was the redoubtable IL-2 Stormovik. The Russian fighter-bomber was not as maneuverable as the YAKs, MIGs and Laggs, nor as fast, but it could absorb quantities of bullets and shells that often left German pilots pop-eyed with incredulity. Cannon shells and tracer could actually be seen bouncing away from the heavily armored cockpit area of this incredibly tough machine.

A Stormovik had been Erich's first victory, and he learned from experience how to bring these rugged birds to earth. The IL-2's flew low, thus protecting the vulnerable oil cooler underneath the fuselage, and a rear gunner harassed attacking fighters. Erich's tactic for tackling an IL-2 with a rear gunner was to make his attack at an angle of fifteen to twenty degrees, closing fast and thus keeping the defending gun moving. He never attacked the IL-2 straight or pulled over one after firing. He avoided wounds and damage by rolling hard over one wing and diving under the Stormovik, a maneuver that no gunner could follow with his weapon and score hits.

Erich found that there were two main methods by which an IL-2 could be successfully attacked. The lightning strike from below and behind, firing at the Stormovik's underbelly, was

---

* Bogey is military slang for "target" or "stranger," and is used to indicate that an unidentified airplane has been sighted.

the best way to down the "concrete bombers." Hits in the vulnerable oil cooler would either force down the IL-2 or set it on fire. When deck-level operations of the Stormovik ruled out this attack method, Erich closed in from behind and tried to concentrate his fire on the wing root, avoiding the armored cockpit and engine area. Repeated cannon hits would cause the heavily-loaded wooden tail to shear off, and the Stormovik would crash. The two-seater version of the IL-2 proved vulnerable from ten degrees and below, as a full burst at short range would find its way through the cockpit armor.

The IL-2 was followed late in 1944 by the IL-10, an even tougher and much faster bird. These aircraft had to be almost literally "hacked down." Before the appearance of the IL-10 and during his prolific scoring period in 1943, Erich scored what were probably the most unusual victories of his combat career against IL-2's.

Erich's analytical ability served him well in the prelude to this battle. He noted that IL-2's generally came from the Russian side of the lines in balls-out, straight-for-the-target droves at low altitude. These gaggles often contained up to sixty aircraft, and rarely flew above 4500 feet.

Carrying at least two five-hundred-pound bombs under their wings, these aircraft moved relatively slowly, and could therefore be easily overhauled from behind. Erich's tactic was to climb to 15,000 feet after take-off, and from this height he could pick up the enemy gaggles at a considerable distance. Spotting an enemy formation, Erich began a shallow dive, aimed at passing high over the enemy and going in the opposite direction, with at least eight or ten thousand feet between them.

Russian pilots looking up could see the German fighters passing above and heading east at high speed. Erich's element would give no indication it had spotted the Soviet formation, whose pilots were lulled into thinking they were unobserved. Erich kept going east for several seconds, after which he would roll his fighter over on its back and smoothly stroke the stick back, executing a half-roll or split-S maneuver.

Reversing his direction and gaining speed in the dive, he would drop down to a little below the altitude of the IL-2 formation. If the sky were covered by clouds, he would approach from behind and much below the Soviet aircraft. With his superior speed, Erich could close in for the lethal hammer blows that usually meant destruction for any aircraft. Many Soviet pilots were caught napping by this maneuver.

Such tactics were studied on the Russian side of the lines, as the later account of the career of Soviet ace Alexander Pokryshkin will reveal. Each new tactic was met by increased alertness and often by counter tactics. When Erich pulled off this kind of interception near Kharkov on a formation of IL-2's, the Russians were ready for him—or so they thought.

Four Stormoviks howling along in echelon-right formation passed below Erich as he implemented his well-tried pursuit maneuver. His speed built up rapidly in a dive, and from two hundred feet astern of the fourth IL-2 he opened fire, the burst exploding in the IL-2's cockpit. The Russian leader rolled to the left in a split-S maneuver, followed in hair-trigger succession by the other two Stormoviks that had not been hit.

The altitude-consuming split-S attempt at evasion had disastrous consequences. The bombs slung under the wings of the IL-2's sharply diminished the maneuverability of the concrete bombers, and they had barely 1500 feet of altitude when they took evasive action. The split S consumed this altitude in seconds.

Four fiery blasts shook the sky as the entire Russian formation crashed with its full bomb load in the echelon-right formation in which it had been flying. Four ghastly pyres flared in four huge, debris-strewn craters, and four pillars of black smoke united in a single, swirling pall above the scene. Erich had fired one full burst. Four victories had followed in seconds.

The legend of Karaya One and the Black Devil grew out of such encounters, so devastating to the matériel and the morale of the Red Air Force. The 7th Squadron history for the period 10 January 1944 to 22 February 1944 refers to the Blond Knight in these terms: "The most successful marksman during this time was Lieutenant Erich Hartmann. Once in one day he downed five, on another day six." Despite frequent changes of operational base, Erich's tactics and consistent entry into battle continued to build up his score.

The 7th Squadron moved to Uman on 22 February, where a Royal Hungarian Fighter Squadron was assigned to III/JG-

52. On 2 March, these two units were transferred to Kalinovka, then moved on again within hours to a base at Proskurov, where they scored fifteen victories before 7 March. The history of 7th Squadron refers to this period: "Of these [fifteen kills] Lieutenant Hartmann alone downed ten enemies in air combat in one day, and thereby achieved his 193rd to 202nd victories. On 2 March 1944 the Führer awarded Lieutenant Krupinski and Lieutenant Hartmann the Oak Leaf."

The Oak Leaves were generally always bestowed personally by the Führer. Erich and Krupinski were ordered to Berchtesgaden for the investiture. Happily they formed an elite *Rotte* of their own, and squelching through the mud of the Proskurov base took off for the flight home in a high state of elation.

For a few minutes they circled the field, and away to the east Erich could see the morass of mud and snow in which the ground war was being slugged out in inhuman hardship. His thoughts turned back for an instant to the twenty thousand German bodies he had seen barely two weeks ago, littering a snow-covered valley in the Shanderovka-Korsun salient. Russian cavalry with sabers and Red tanks had hacked the trapped German unit to pieces.

Erich shuddered at the memory. More similar things must surely lie ahead, for rumors had reached 7th Squadron HQ of a pending Russian "mud offensive." Hell was not necessarily hot, thought Erich to himself, as his mind ranged over the infantryman's war. They fought in a frozen purgatory over which he and his comrades flew in their fast fighters. He was glad to be going home. With the ebullient Krupinski flying beside him, he turned westward with a profound feeling of relief.

The riotous journey to Salzburg in the train with Gerd Barkhorn, Walter Krupinski and Hannes "Kubanski Lion" Wiese, has already been recounted in Chapter One. The quartet of aces from JG-52 joined twelve other recipients of the Oak Leaves in the ceremonies at the Eagle's Nest. Winners of the decoration included Maj. (later Lt. Col.) Kurt Buehligen of the Richthofen Wing fighting on the Channel Coast, and the veteran night fighter ace August Geiger, who was later shot down and killed in action by RAF night fighter ace "Bob" Braham. There were also two colonels of Infantry. The slender, boyish and slightly tipsy Erich Hartmann was the youngest winner of the Oak Leaves and the lowest-ranked recipient of the coveted decoration at this investiture.

As Second Lieutenant Hartmann he stood near the end of the reception line looking like an overawed teen-ager. On the Russian Front he had already acquired rank and fame of a different kind than that bestowed by the Oak Leaves. He was Karaya One, the infamous Black Devil. A legend had begun around him among his enemies. In his own fraternity, he had qualified for the elite—those who had reached two hundred victories. Those few who still stood ahead of him in the deadliest scoring game of all, knew that he was the aerial jouster to watch as the war rolled on in its fifth year.

CHAPTER SEVEN

ACES OF FIGHTER WING 52

In a company of heroes, only a Titan stands tall.
                                                —*Anonymous*

A VIGOROUS competitor since boyhood, Erich Hartmann found JG-52 an environment in which he could thrive. His climb to the award of the Oak Leaves had been hard, but his progress had been stimulated by the hot pilots who were vying with each other in every squadron of JG-52. This steady competition resulted in the development of many exceptional aces who won the Knight's Cross and the higher orders of that decoration.

The most successful Fighter Wing in the Luftwaffe, JG-52 was credited with over ten thousand aerial victories in four years. A roll call of its leading personalities begins with the three top-scoring aces of Germany and the world—Erich Hartmann with 352 victories, Gerhard Barkhorn with 301, and Guenther Rall with 275. The dozens of other accomplished air fighters who served with Erich Hartmann in JG-52 at one time or another include Willi Batz with 237 victories, Hermann Graf with 212, and Helmut Lipfert with 203. The Blond Knight and these five contemporaries accounted for the staggering total of 1580 aerial victories.

Hard behind this stellar six came a covey of aces with scores ranging from 100 to 200 victories, all of whom spent a considerable portion of their combat time with JG-52. These notables included Maj. Walter Krupinski with 197 kills, Maj. Johannes Wiese with 133 victories, First Lt. Friedrich "Fritz"

Obleser with 120, and First Lt. Walter Wolfrum with 126 victories. These are the scores of the pilots as they stood at war's end. During the conflict, rivalry in squadron, group and wing was constant. Scoring leadership often changed hands, and competition brought out the best efforts of every pilot.

The urge to be top man was a driving force in all who were successful. Rivalry was keen but friendly, in the tradition of sportsmanship, and the nightly gatherings of pilots to listen to the news and see how the scoreboard stood was one of the day's chief events. Success and ever-mounting tallies kept pilot morale at a high level, and played a key role in the psychological superiority the Germans held in the air in Russia until the end, even when their Me-109's were technically outclassed and buried under the blizzards of Soviet aircraft.

JG-52 was fortunate in the high-caliber leadership that became part of its tradition. Colonel Dietrich Hrabak has already been introduced as the wing's *Kommodore* at the time of Erich Hartmann's baptism of fire, and Maj. Hubertus von Bonin has been introduced as a memorable *Gruppenkommandeur*. Other exceptional leaders who left their names on the wing's records include Condor Legion veteran Herbert Ihlefeld, Guenther Rall and Johannes "Macky" Steinhoff.

A distinguished career as a squadron leader and later as a *Gruppenkommandeur* with JG-52, proved the flying and leadership talents of Steinhoff, who heads the present-day German Air Force as Lieutenant General Steinhoff. Joining JG-52 as a squadron leader in February 1940, he was *Gruppenkommandeur* of II/JG-52 two years later. Some of Germany's most successful fighter pilots passed through Steinhoff's units in JG-52, including the immortal Captain Hans-Joachim Marseille, top-scoring Luftwaffe pilot against the Western Allies,* who flew in Steinhoff's JG-52 squadron during the Battle of Britain. Major Willi Batz was Steinhoff's adjutant in Russia, and Walter Krupinski flew as Steinhoff's wingman in his early career. Steinhoff himself scored 176 victories, most of them with JG-52.

With leadership of this character, success in fighting the enemy and continual exposure to aerial combat, conditions in

---

* One hundred and fifty-eight victories in World War II, all British-flown aircraft.

JG-52 encouraged and inspired ambitious young fighter pilots. They responded with a level of success never previously achieved in the history of aerial warfare. In the highly competitive scoring race, Bubi Hartmann rose to the top, exceeding by fifty-one victories the score of Gerd Barkhorn, his closest rival.

To accurately convey the unique human environment that brought out the best in Erich Hartmann, a few sketches of his fellow aces in JG-52 are appropriate. Since there were dozens of high-scorers, these sketches can be only a sampling of JG-52 pilot quality, although they are typical of the Luftwaffe's most successful Fighter Wing. A list of JG-52 aces appears at the end of this chapter.

Erich Hartmann rarely gets excited over old comrades, but his friend and onetime rival Gerd Barkhorn evokes from him this rare tribute: "Gerd is the one leader I know for whom every man would gladly kill himself. Father, brother, comrade, friend, he is the best I ever met." This unstinting admiration is typical of the reaction Gerd Barkhorn's name evokes among his comrades of the Second World War, for his personality and character made a deeper impression on them than did his 301 aerial victories.

There is more of the ancient knight in Gerd Barkhorn than in any other ace the authors have met. He is chivalrous, honorable and generous; strong, merciful and magnanimous —a truly heroic gentleman. Four years older than Erich Hartmann, Barkhorn in his glory days was an arrestingly handsome man with thick, dark hair, an olive complexion and penetrating blue eyes remarkably like those of Erich Hartmann. The five-foot nine-inch Barkhorn is today Brigadier Barkhorn of the new German Air Force. His dark hair is laced with gray, but he is still trim and deeply admired by all who serve with him.

Lieutenant General Steinhoff says of Barkhorn: "He is my choice of all the Second World War fighter pilots. Steady, reliable, a good leader, he never made a victory claim that wasn't confirmed." To the old aces of the Royal Air Force with whom Barkhorn has formed friendships, as well as to NATO officers with whom he has served, he is a throwback to the days of chivalry, and his are the ways of grace.

When Erich Hartmann passed him in the scoring race,

Gerd was delighted, for his character is such that he enjoys another man's success as he would his own. In combat his chivalrous spirit expressed itself frequently in a heroic quality that is often forgotten—mercy. Hartmann and others have told of Barkhorn's efforts, after disabling a Soviet aircraft, to persuade the pilot of the stricken machine to forsake his plane for a parachute, flying alongside his foe and gesturing for him to jump. Gerd Barkhorn never lost his humanity in the bitter Eastern Front struggle. He fought but did not hate. To his comrade Erich Hartmann he is the most unforgettable character of the war.

Major Johannes Wiese was one of Erich Hartmann's celebrant comrades at the Oak Leaves investiture at Berchtesgaden, and a fellow ace of JG-52. Called the "Kubanski Lion" by the Russians because of his success in the heavy air battles above the Kuban Bridgehead, Wiese was a professional officer who entered the Luftwaffe in 1936.

He came to JG-52 in the summer of 1941 as adjutant of II/JG-52, after a long spell as an instructor and reconnaissance pilot. He made a specialty of downing the IL-2 Stormovik, and about seventy of the heavily-armored ground-attack machines fell to his guns. On his big day in 1943, Wiese got twelve confirmed kills in the Orel-Kursk-Byelgorod area, and on the same day made five forced landings himself. He ended his JG-52 career in command of I/JG-52, and was promoted to *Kommodore* of JG-77 as Steinhoff's replacement at the end of 1944.

His war career ended with a wild battle over the Ruhr against Spitfires. Forced to bail out, the Kubanski Lion's damaged parachute failed to open properly and he was seriously injured in the resulting heavy fall. He became a prisoner of the U.S. after the surrender.

When Wiese was released by the U.S. in September 1945 and returned home, he was recognized by Communist-sympathizing Germans. As a highly decorated German professional officer who had fought against the Soviet Union, he became the victim of some postwar political intrigue. The police picked him up and handed him over to the Soviet government.

Wiese joined Erich Hartmann in the Russian prisons, and was released in 1950. He moved to West Germany in 1956 and joined the new German Air Force, and when he was assigned to the new Richthofen Wing in 1959, he found the first jet-fighter wing of the new Luftwaffe under the command of his former JG-52 and Russian prison comrade, Erich Hartmann.

Dynamic Guenther Rall, with 275 aerial victories, has found his career intertwined with that of Erich Hartmann since Erich arrived at the Russian Front in the autumn of 1942 as a fledgling. A prewar professional officer, Rall made a brilliant war record, not only as an ace and leader, but also as a man of surpassing will power and courage. He flew in the Battle of Britain, the Battle of France, the Balkan campaign, in the Battle of Crete, on the Eastern Front, and in the final defense of the Reich against the Anglo-American air assault.

He is best remembered by his war comrades as an aerial marksman of uncanny gifts, capable of hitting and destroying his foes from incredible angles and distances. The late Lt. Col. Heinz Baer, whose 225 victories included 120 over British-and American-flown aircraft, was a superb judge of fighter pilots as well as one of the Luftwaffe's greatest aces. Before his untimely death in a light plane crash in 1957, Baer told the authors he considered Guenther Rall the greatest angle-off shot in the Luftwaffe—superior even to the legendary Hans-Joachim Marseille.

Aggressive in the air, a fine leader and excellent administrator, Guenther Rall is today a vigorous, friendly man in his early fifties and a major general in the new German Air Force. He was perhaps the keenest competitor among all the top-scoring German pilots during the war, and he held the top spot for a considerable time. He may well have ended the war as the greatest ace of all time, had his luck not run out on two crucial occasions.

Following a Russian flamer near dusk he momentarily forgot his victim's wingman, and seconds later the fair-haired young German found himself riding an Me-109 with a dead engine. The ensuing freak belly landing broke Rall's back, and when German infantrymen dragged him out of his wrecked aircraft hours later one side was paralyzed. Condemned by the doctors never to fly again, Rall fought an epic battle back to health and strength, aided by a beautiful young lady doctor whom he later married.

Consumed by the thought of his squadron mates at the front running up large scores while he lay prostrate in the hospital, Rall broke down all his doctors' objections and forced his way back into combat flying after nearly a year on the sidelines. Flying with a cushion under his leg and another at his back, he began piling up a tremendous score, and by April 1944 he was the top fighter pilot of the Luftwaffe. At this time he had to leave the elite formation with which he had found fame.

Transferred to the Western Front, he shook hands with Erich Hartmann at the farewell party staged in honor of the departing C.O.

"Now, Bubi," said Rall, "I won't be in your way any longer. You will be the top scorer."

"Sir," said Erich, "all our doings are kismet."

Rall was proved right by events, and they never saw each other again until after Hartmann's return from Russia in 1955.

Not long after leaving JG-52, Rall lost his thumb in a battle with USAAF Thunderbolts over Berlin, and subsequently had to fight a different kind of battle. The enemy this time was infection. His thumb took nine months to heal, while he flirted again with paralysis. Erich Hartmann and Gerd Barkhorn both passed him in the scoring while he was out of action, but Rall himself has no regrets concerning this period: "The attrition of Western Front pilots at this time was fierce. If I had flown on, I probably would have been killed. I was glad to trade my thumb for my life."

For many months Erich's C.O. in Russia, Rall again filled this role in the new German Air Force in the 1960s. When the Blond Knight began his service as a Tactical Evaluation Officer at Wahn Air Base near Cologne, General Rall was his boss. Rall contrasts with Erich because he is a man attuned, suited and devoted to his chosen military career. He exemplifies the best type of officer, keen, energetic and thoroughly professional, while Erich Hartmann's basic antipathy toward conventional military life is a structural attitude formed in boyhood.

When Erich came to the Eastern Front in the fall of 1942, Guenther Rall was already a mature, experienced officer with an outstanding combat record. Erich's boyishness, inseparable from his then extreme youth, made his rise to responsibility slow and difficult. Rall had to make some hard decisions involving Erich, but the two men have been friends for years. General Rall's insights into Erich Hartmann's problems have helped the presentation of his life story, and within the German Air Force, Rall has been one of Erich's defenders in the controversies that have sometimes boiled around him since 1959.

Rall, Barkhorn and other top aces were the men to beat in the scoring race. They were the pacesetters. There was also competitive pressure from below, provided by the upcoming young pilots. Among the lesser-known but talented youngsters of JG-52 was Hans-Joachim Birkner, who was broken in as Erich Hartmann's wingman in the fall of 1943.

Modeling his fighting style somewhat after Erich Hartmann, Birkner downed his first enemy aircraft on 1 October 1943. One year later he confirmed his one hundredth victory and had won the Knight's Cross in a career of brilliant promise. Birkner was a squadron leader with 117 kills and a second lieutenant's commission by mid-December 1944, when he was killed in a test-flight crash at Krakau, Poland.

Some pilots appear to have led charmed lives in combat, which may be due to luck, but can be due to skilled piloting and tactical savvy. More often than not, the ability to stay in one piece rests on a combination of luck and skill. Erich Hartmann admits he was lucky, but his emergence unscathed from over eight hundred aerial battles was more of a tactical triumph than consistent luck, as his own earlier account of his methods reveals. He paid strict attention on a methodical basis to the business of keeping himself alive and unwounded.

Another brilliant JG-52 ace who survived multiple crashes and extensive combat without injury was Captain Helmut Lipfert. He ended the war with 203 confirmed aerial victories, and is today a schoolteacher near Cologne. Lipfert was shot down fifteen times, twice by Russian fighters and thirteen times by the deadly Russian flak.

Helmut Lipfert joined JG-52 shortly after Erich Hartmann, and they flew together frequently during the ensuing two years. Scoring his first victory in January 1943, Lipfert racked up two hundred victories in the next twenty-seven months, ending the war with the Oak Leaves to his Knight's Cross as

Captain Helmut Lipfert. In later years, Erich Hartmann likened him to Paule Rossmann in temperament, perennially happy and on top of life.

A young contemporary of Erich Hartmann in JG-52 who was later to figure in the lives of Erich and Usch Hartmann was First Lt. Walter Wolfrum, who joined the most deadly wing in the Luftwaffe about ninety days after the Blond Knight. The dark-haired and handsome Wolfrum had trouble finding his shooting eye, and did not score a victory until six months after his arrival at the front.

Between July 1943 and June 1944, Wolfrum ran up a hundred kills, but the following month was shot down and seriously wounded. Forced to leave the front for over six months while recuperating, he fell behind in the scoring race, and by the war's end had 137 kills. He is among those pilots who flew with Erich Hartmann who insist that the Blond Knight could hit targets at fantastic distances, on occasions when his point-blank attacks were not feasible.

Walter Wolfrum was leading a squadron in Erich's *Gruppe* at the surrender, and went into Russian confinement with his C.O., even though he had been wounded a short time before the end of the war. A month later, the Russians turned Wolfrum free because of his wound. He smuggled a letter out of prison camp for Erich in the lining of his coat, and this missive was the first uncensored contact between Erich and Usch after the Blond Knight's capture. Wolfrum is today a prosperous West German goldsmith and owns his own light plane. He is one of Germany's top trick flyers.

Even an outline sketch of JG-52 aces cannot be complete without reference to Major Wilhelm "Willi" Batz, whose 237 aerial victories make him the fourth-ranking living ace of the world. Erich Hartmann was for a time a squadron leader in the *Gruppe* commanded by Batz, and they have been friends for years. Batz by his own admission was for years a "lousy fighter," until a period in a hospital turned him from dove to hawk and saw him write one of the most amazing personal records of the air war.

A peacetime-trained professional Luftwaffe pilot, Batz forced his way into combat flying in December 1942 after thousands of hours of flying as an instructor. He was eleven months getting his first victory, so disquieted was he by the successful and competitive atmosphere of JG-52. He had an inferiority complex.

He added a few more victories at the painful rate of one or two per month, and was then hospitalized with a minor infection. He returned to combat with his perspective renewed, and in a year between March 1944 and March 1945 he ran up a staggering 222 victories. There is no other achievement like it in the history of fighter piloting.

He finished the war in command of II/JG-52 as Major Batz, with 237 victories and the Swords to his Knight's Cross. With admirable foresight he was able to extricate his *Gruppe* from the Eastern Front, sparing his men the pain of Russian confinement by getting them back to Germany. In today's German Air Force, Lieutenant Colonel Batz occupies an office in the same building as Erich Hartmann.

The most famous personage in JG-52 during the war was Lt. Col. Hermann Graf, whose misfortune was to be selected as a typical hero for Dr. Goebbels's propaganda build-up. A onetime blacksmith, Graf joined the hard-fighting 9th Squadron of JG-52 in July 1942. Eight months later, he had been awarded the Knight's Cross, Oak Leaves, Swords, and the coveted Diamonds.

In one savage, seventeen-day period he scored forty-seven confirmed victories, and by October 1942—the month that boyish Erich Hartmann joined JG-52—Hermann Graf had become the first pilot in history to reach two hundred kills. Transferred later to the Western Front, Graf came back to JG-52 as its *Kommodore* in October 1944. He was with Erich Hartmann when the remnants of the once-proud JG-52 surrendered to the Americans in Czechoslovakia. Graf and Hartmann went into Soviet confinement together when the Americans turned them over to the Russians one week after the surrender of JG-52.

A list of leading JG-52 aces follows. These impressive tallies testify to the long and hard fighting that won JG-52 its place in air history. They also demonstrate the challenging and competitive environment from which Erich Hartmann emerged as the most successful fighter pilot of them all.

Gerhard Barkhorn	301
Wilhelm Batz	237
Hans-Joachim Birkner	117
Hubertus von Bonin	77
Adolf Borchers	132
Hans Dammers	113
Adolf Dickfeld	136
Peter Duettmann	152
Otto Foennekold	136
Adolf Glunz	71
Hermann Graf	212
Karl Gratz	138
Alfred Grislawski	133
Gerhard Hoffmann	125
Dietrich Hrobak	125
Herbert Ihlefeld	130
Gerhard Koeppen	85
Berthold Korts	113
Walter Krupinski	196
Helmut Lipfert	203
Rudolf Miethig	101
Friedrich Obleser	120
Guenther Rall	275
Heinz Sachsenberg	104
Franz Schall	137
Heinz Schmidt	173
Leopold Steinbatz	99
Johannes Steinhoff	176
Heinrich Sturm	158
Rudolf Trenkel	138
Hans Waldmann	134
Johannes Wiese	133
Franz Woidich	110
Walter Wolfrum	137
Josef Zwernemann	126

CHAPTER EIGHT

FAME AND SWORDS

The sterner the challenge to man, the finer the response.
            —*Arnold Toynbee*

IMMEDIATELY BEFORE THE Oak Leaves investiture at Berchtesgaden, Erich and the other pilots had been instructed not to give Hitler any bad reports concerning events at the front, weapons, tactics or other matters that might properly have been discussed in response to Hitler's probings. "The Führer's health is not the best," was the excuse given to the pilots for protecting Hitler from unfavorable tidings. Erich soon saw what this process of insulating Hitler against reality had done to the German leader's mind.

After awarding the decorations, the Führer spent half an hour with the blond-headed second lieutenant from Stuttgart and the other pilots. Hitler's powerful presence soon dissipated what remained of the celebrations on the train to Salzburg, and Erich found himself a thoroughly sober young man as he listened to the dictator. Pacing the huge main room at the Eagle's Nest, with one whole wall of glass providing the snow-crested alps as a backdrop, Hitler exuded a personal dynamism that riveted Erich's attention. Strongly positive personalities like General Heinz Guderian have testified to Hitler's power over even mature officers of high rank. He ruled them by the sheer power of his will. Now the twenty-one-year-old Erich got a brief but unforgettable insight into Hitler's personality.

The Führer showed a detailed grasp of the air situation on the Eastern Front—circa 1942. He knew all about the superiority of the Me-109 over Soviet aircraft—circa summer 1941 —when most Russian machines were of older design and inferior performance. Hitler knew the caliber of the armament and numerous technical details, but it was yesterday's knowledge.

Erich felt distressed as it became evident that Hitler, obviously possessed of the power to comprehend the facts, nevertheless had no grasp of the true situation facing the Luftwaffe on the Eastern Front. All precautions were being taken to ensure that the facts were denied him on the basis of his health. Erich asked himself the unavoidable questions: Was Hitler being deliberately misinformed, and if so, why?

When Hitler turned his talk to the Western Front, he asked the assembled pilots for their views on attacking the American bomber boxes. The Führer frankly admitted to the weakness of the German air defense. Ace Kurt Buehligen and others who had fought hard on the Western Front asked for long-range weapons like rockets with which to tackle the heavily armed Fortresses. They asked also for more fighters to beat down the far-ranging and formidable USAAF fighter escorts.

Hitler listened carefully and comprehendingly. He said that fighter production was being increased rapidly. Rockets were being developed and improved. He then summarized the war situation for his assembled fighting officers:

"When the Anglo-Americans launch their Second Front, we will push them back into a Second Dunkirk. The submarine arm is getting new U-boats to cut the Atlantic supply lines. On the Eastern Front, we are building a big defense system against which the Russians will bleed themselves to death."

The Führer spoke quietly and positively. The magnetism to which so many who knew him have testified was so powerful as to be almost physical. Erich found himself enveloped in this arcane flux, being carried along by the confidence the Führer exuded. His impression as he shook hands with Hitler before departure was that he was in the presence of an idealist surrounded by ugly lackeys and opportunists. That the Führer was walled off by lies from reality was beyond doubt. The situation was hardly inspiring to a front-line soldier, but Erich was not the only one who was troubled by the war.

In Stuttgart he found his sweetheart anxious and upset,

despite her obvious happiness at their reunion. Usch's lovely face clouded as conversation returned again and again to the war—the tyrant that kept them apart and rationed their happiness to a few ephemeral days between Erich's flirtations with death.

"Erich," she said, "the war is getting worse and worse for Germany. Even the propaganda cannot hide the truth. The Americans come by day, and the British by night. Even Berlin has been bombed again and again."

Erich tried to reassure his sweetheart.

"The Führer told us about new weapons that are being built and tested. Perhaps they will turn the tide and end the war."

Erich spoke the words, but his heart wasn't behind them. Usch knew it.

"Erich, we don't know how it will all end. Shall we get married now, while we have the chance, and take what happiness we can even while this awful war goes on?"

Erich wanted desperately to say yes, but the experiences of the grinding Eastern Front were too raw in his mind. Good pilots were being shot down, killed and captured all the time. He might be next. That was no way to begin life together—with Usch perhaps a widow, or worse—possibly the wife of a crippled or maimed ex-fighter pilot. When he took her lovely face in his hands, he almost caved in, but he managed to say what he felt was right.

"Usch, darling. We *must* wait. Perhaps in a few months all will change." Erich was not quite twenty-two years of age and this may have been a factor in his decision.

Erich found no stimulus for his shaky optimism in the outlook of his wise physician-father. When he walked into the house at Weil, his mother was delighted to see the Oak Leaves at his throat.

"See, Papa," she said, "look at the beautiful decoration your son has won."

A glow of pride beamed briefly out of Dr. Hartmann as he took in the happy scene of Erich and his mother smiling together. He took a look at the Oak Leaves, mumbled something about their being handsome, and then sat down in an easy chair. His expression became grave.

"It is good that you do well as a pilot, Erich, very good. But you must know that Germany is already beaten. Irretrievably beaten."

Dr. Hartmann picked up the Stuttgart newspaper.

"Even the fantastic writings of Goebbels can no longer hide the facts."

"But Papa, the Führer said . . ."

"Erich, the Führer has said many things since 1933, most of them proved untrue. Goebbels has our armies in Russia 'advancing' back to our own borders. Surely you believe what your eyes tell you when you look down from the air over the Eastern Front. Which way are we going, Erich?"

Erich threw up his hands.

"You are right, Papa. We are retreating everywhere."

"Then be prepared for the end of all this. I am making arrangements for you to study medicine at Tübingen, because I don't believe this terrible struggle can go on much longer. Mankind has gone mad."

The two weeks in Stuttgart flew by, and when Erich said his farewells to his family and to Usch, he felt for the first time that there might not be many more leaves or much more flying. Perhaps his father was right. As he flew back to III *Gruppe* of JG-52 on the Eastern Front, the words of his father and Usch mingled in his mind with the confident predictions of the Führer. He could not decide between optimism and pessimism, and when he touched down at the 9th Squadron's base at Lemberg the mental debate ended. The stern business of duty came first.

His return to the front on 18 March 1944 opened with good news. As Erich slid back his canopy the squadron adjutant was waiting. Erich clambered out and turned the fighter over to Bimmel. He took the adjutant's outstretched hand.

"Welcome back, Bubi, and congratulations."

"Congratulations on what?"

"You are now First Lieutenant Hartmann, and official confirmation has come through for your two hundred and first and two hundred and second victories."

At the promotion party that night, Erich found the somber mood of his last leave permeating the festivities as the pilots sat drinking his health and good fortune. Shoptalk didn't help. The pilots were discussing the disquieting ability of the American fighters to fly all the way into Germany with the Allied bombers. Factory towns in northern Germany were being pounded. Pilots' relatives in these areas seemed in more danger than the men flying combat every day on the Eastern Front. The snatches of conversation contributed to Erich's gloom.

"I wish we could tackle the Mustangs. . . . I'd like to see how tough they are. . . ." "Rall says that they are faster than the Spitfire and more rugged. . . ." ". . . Did you know that Mustangs shot down Muncheberg in North Africa?" "*Ja*, and I heard they got Oesau near Aachen, too. . . ." The shoptalk dragged on interminably. When the final round of congratulations and drinks was over, the pilots went stumbling back to their tents in the rain. There would be no operations tomorrow—even if Mustangs appeared over the field.

The makeshift strip at dawn was a mass of waterlogged ruts and slippery, sodden grass. Conditions were perfect for accidents in the Me-109, with its narrow undercarriage and tricky take-off and landing characteristics. For at least six months 7th Squadron had been operating under conditions of extreme pressure, constantly moving from base, dogged by the Red Army, the weather and a straitened supply situation. They had operated from no fewer than thirteen different bases in the final four months of 1943. The JG-52 War Diary describes the conditions at Lemberg in the spring of 1944:

12 March–23 March 1944:

"Due to the bad weather, the field is very soggy. Since the tank trucks cannot get through, the planes have to taxi to the filling station. This affects operational readiness adversely and considerably, because the oil coolers must be continually sprayed with water to prevent overheating."

And later:

"On 22 March the *Gruppe* was to transfer to Kamenets Podolski. However, this was impossible because of weather conditions. The staff flight tried, but had to come back because of a heavy snowstorm. The transfer was actually carried out 23 March with a cloud ceiling of 100 meters [328 feet], and in a heavy snowstorm. In the meantime, the enemy had come so close that our own artillery had to move into position on the field."

So much for the Eastern Front fighting conditions that have so often been depicted as easy for fighter pilots.

Operations continued sporadically throughout March, and the major attainment was by III *Gruppe*. This unit scored its thirty-five hundredth aerial victory on 21 March 1944. By the end of March, the entire *Gruppe* had left Soviet territory to join the 9th Squadron at Lemberg, where Erich had added a few kills after his return on 18 March 1944.

The jam-packed Lemberg strip was playing host to far more fighters than its hard-pressed facilities and single runway could support. Long taxiing times and waiting for take-off sharply reduced operational range and made an early return from strikes essential. Erich was often compelled to return from the hunt after only a few minutes in the action zone, because he knew the situation at the field. He would have to wait ten to fifteen minutes in the pattern before he could land. Aside from the runway itself, the Lemberg field was little more than a treacherous bog.

The air situation on the Eastern Front, already precarious in February and March during the German retreat, became worse early in April. The Americans mounted four-engined bomber attacks on Rumanian targets. Colonel Dieter Hrabak, JG-52's *Kommodore*, had often cast an apprehensive eye to his southern flank, knowing that American bombing missions from Italian bases were inevitable. Mustangs would come with the bombers. The American offensive led to orders for the transfer of JG-52 squadrons to Rumania.

Accustomed to crash transfers to makeshift airstrips, Erich and his 9th Squadron initially viewed the shift to Rumania as routine. The 9th was assigned to the town of Roman. Flying the aircraft down proved no problem, but the movement of ground personnel and essential maintenance equipment proved hazardous and time-consuming. When a Ju-52 loaded with equipment tried to fly across the Carpathians, the machine iced up, then crashed and burned on the heights. The other Ju-52's were accordingly routed via Vienna, Belgrade and Bucharest when the bad weather persisted.

The pell-mell situation that had begun to rule in the Luftwaffe is exemplified by the High Command's next decision. Having sent III *Gruppe* of JG-52 to Roman, including Erich's 9th Squadron, the High Command was forced to immediately retransfer these units to the Crimea. A last-ditch effort had to be made to stop the rout in the South and provide protection for the retreating German Army against the hordes of strafing Russian aircraft.

Operating from Zarnesti near Zilistea by mid-April 1944, Erich's squadron began taking a heavy toll of the Red Air Force, despite supply difficulties. Erich's burdens were increased when the High Command ordered that a number of pilots with five or more victories be transferred to the Reich Defense. Raw young pilots came in their place, some with less than a hundred hours' total flying time. They were hurled into the air at odds of up to thirty to one, but Erich kept intact his record of never having lost a wingman.

These young pilots came to the front not only inexperienced in flying, but also steeped in the old tradition of dogfighting. In the brief time available for such instruction, Erich would pass on to them the quintessence of his own experience.

"If you see enemy aircraft, it is not necessary for you to go straight to them and attack. Wait and look and use your reason. See what kind of formation and tactics they are using. See if there is a straggler or an uncertain pilot among the enemy. Such a pilot will always stand out in the air. Shoot *him* down. It is more important to send one down in flames— so that all the enemy pilots see the loss and experience its psychological effect—than to wade into a twenty-minute dogfight in which nothing happens.

"There are some things that are more important in the overall picture than just scoring a kill. The Russian Air Force is numerically large and getting larger all the time. If you score a kill and lose your wingman, you have *lost the battle*. Anyone who does this will not lead an element after it happens. From the day you make your first flight here at the front you must think, think, think, as never before. Fly with the head and not the muscles. That's the best advice I can give you."

That advice, when followed, kept a lot of young Germans alive.

On 18 April 1944, orders were received from Galland's HQ transferring Guenther Rall and Walter Krupinski to the Reich Defense. They were two of JG-52's best leaders and most formidable fighters. Rall still held a scoring lead of about fifty victories over Erich Hartmann, but his best scoring days were now behind him. As *Kommodore* of JG-11 in the West, he would secure a few more victories to bring his tally to 275 kills, but another wound and ensuing infection virtually put him out of the war.

In his farewell to Erich, it seemed as though Rall knew intuitively that the dynamic youngster would reach the top of the tree. Rall was right; Lt. Willi Batz took over as *Gruppen-kommandeur* from Rall, and Erich was temporarily assigned to direct *Gruppe* operations in the Crimea. More scoring was in the offing.

In April 1944 Erich ran up another nine victories. Three, four and even five sorties a day were commonplace. He continued his streak into May. Between 10 April and 10 May 1944, Erich and his former wingman, Technical Sergeant Joachim Birkner, each scored twenty-one victories. Erich's success did not blind him to the writing on the wall. The Crimean retreat was becoming a rout. JG-52 was ordered out. Eight aircraft were left behind under Erich's orders as a rear guard, but by 9 May 1944, incessant Soviet attacks left only one Me-109 operational. Evacuation was essential.

The Me-109 proved itself a veritable work horse under conditions of emergency. Several battered fighters were made operational, and then the R/T's and armor plate were removed from behind the pilot's seat. Ground personnel who had made these emergency modifications then crawled into the pencil-thin fuselage—two to an aircraft—and were flown out in relays by Erich and his 7th Squadron pilots.*

Erich Hartmann personally provides a reminiscence concerning this emergency evacuation, a useful addition to the history of the Me-109:

"After pulling out the cockpit armor plate and radio, you have a baggage compartment perhaps four to four and a half feet long. A small man can crouch in there, with his head alongside the pilot's head.

* Hartmann, Rall and Krupinski have all recounted to the authors details of crowding two mechanics into the after-fuselage of the Me-109. The emergency measure saved ground personnel from capture by the Russians.

"During the emergency evacuation from the Crimea I put two men in the fuselage after removing the radio and armor, saving them from capture by the Russians. The inspection plate for the R/T, when removed, provides a hole big enough for men to crawl inside.

"If they lay on top of each other, you could actually put *four* men in the Me-109 fuselage. There is no problem with power, because the engine was big enough to lift them with plenty of spare capacity. I carried a couple of 30-mm cannon slung under the wings, and two men in my aircraft, and if the cubic space were available, I firmly believe the Me-109 could have carried five or six men."

Erich got his squadron out of Zilistea, and I *Gruppe* staged a rally of sorts out of Zarnesti to keep the ever-present Stormoviks off the backs of the German infantry. By 18 May 1944 the Crimean venture was over, and Erich's squadron was again ordered to Roman in Rumania, where an advance commando unit had prepared the base. From Roman, operations began against the American B-17's and B-24's that were pounding Rumanian targets to knock that country out of the war.

By the end of May, Erich had confirmed an additional thirty-two victories beyond the nine scored in April. On one May mission, his intuition again saved him from destruction at the hands of an aggressive Russian pilot. North of Jassy, the Luftwaffe monitors had determined that approximately 375 Russian fighters and 370 ground-attack aircraft faced JG-52's atrophied formations.

On 29 May Erich had flown a successful mission against these Russian concentrations, and was returning to his base at Roman with Lt. Orje Blessin on his wing. Erich was a little weary, and he let his thoughts roam to the party that was planned that night for Willi Batz, the new *Gruppenkommandeur*. Willi had shot down fourteen planes in three missions. Good comrade Willi had been several years finding himself as a fighter pilot, and now he was turning into one of the best.

Droning along over friendly territory, Erich happily mulled over the forthcoming party and the relaxation it would provide. There would be schnapps, singing and some Rumanian girls. The party would be a relief from the incessant grind of operations. These days, thought Erich to himself, we are having less and less to celebrate.

Erich's lifesaving intuition overrode these pleasant thoughts like a small, insistent, electrical shock. Snapping back to attention, Erich swung his head around to be sure his wingman was still with him. Blessin was in position, just fine, but lancing in on him was an uninvited No. 3—a Red fighter about to hold his triggers down on Erich's wingman.

"Break right! Break right and go into a steep dive," barked Erich into the R/T.

Lieutenant Blessin was a sharp young pilot, and he took immediate evasive action as a stream of Russian tracer sliced through the air where his fighter had been instants before. The Russian plunged after the diving German fighter. Erich immediately broke right and went racing after the Russian. All three aircraft went hurtling toward the deck at full throttle. As Erich began closing in on the Russian, the Red pilot never looked back or took evasive action. He had target fixation. The Russian was so utterly determined to shoot down Blessin he forgot about his own tail.

Erich knew he could shoot down the Russian if the right maneuver were executed. Blessin could be relied on to follow orders.

"Karaya Two. Pull up. Make a shallow turn to the right so I can close the enemy."

Blessin obeyed. Erich went slicing across the Russian's pursuit turn and was soon approaching point-blank range on the Red fighter's right quarter.

"Look back now, Karaya Two. See what happens when you don't watch your tail."

Erich pressed his gun buttons and the cannon and machine guns roared in a full burst. Shells and bullets hammered into the Red fighter. A blast shook the air as the Russian machine blew up and went tumbling down, shedding burning pieces and trailing black smoke. Watching the fiery, final impact, Erich shook his head. How easy it would have been for him and Karaya One to have gone down the same way. The Russian had both him and Blessin cold. But for that sharp intuitional warning—the dread feeling in the backside—the smoke might well have been climbing up from Erich Hart-

mann's funeral pyre. He flew back to Roman more in gratitude than triumph.

By the end of June 1944, Erich had 247 victories, gained in
twenty months of combat. He was still better known to the
Russians than to most of his Luftwaffe contemporaries, for to
join Germany's air immortals in the final year of the war, a
fighter pilot needed 250 victories. On 1 July 1944, Erich
Hartmann reached that score, and with it, permanent historical fame. Once more, the rugged Stormoviks figured in the
life of the Blond Knight.

Flying above a layer of ragged cloud, Erich spotted three
IL-2's doing their devil's work on German artillery positions.
The Stormoviks were intent on their victims, as they circled at
low altitude and made strafing passes. The Russians neglected
their tails.

Pushing the stick forward, Erich went into a shallow dive,
coming up from behind and below the Stormoviks at full tilt
and holding his fire until the last fifty yards. The first Russian
exploded from a full burst, and Erich breaking away was in
perfect position for a strike on the second Stormovik. Down
to point-blank range he went again, and again the Russian
staggered and went down burning. Another pass on the third
Stormovik, a full burst, and another explosion. Speeding away
from the scene of battle, Erich looked back and saw three
smoke palls marking the crashes of the Stormoviks.

When he landed, the Blond Knight was the first fighter pilot
of JG-52 since Guenther Rall to reach 250 victories. Only a
handful of aces had reached this level of success. Major
Walter Nowotny, soon to die in the Me-262 jet against the
American heavies, had been first. Rall had been next, then
Gerd Barkhorn and Otto "Bruno" Kittel of JG-54—only five
fighter pilots all told, of whom Erich was the last. No others
would share their company.

Bimmel Mertens and his crew thumped their young C.O.
on the back and took care of the aircraft. Other squadron
mates chaired the shyly happy Blond Knight from the airfield
to the mess. The celebration had just got under way when
Bimmel burst in, his obvious agitation momentarily cooling
the exuberance of the gathering.

"What is it, Bimmel?" said Erich.

"It's the armorer, sir."

"Anything wrong?"

"No sir, no. Nothing wrong. But you fired only one hundred and twenty rounds, sir. For three kills. I thought you should know."

A roar of admiration erupted from the throng of pilots and the schnapps began flowing. Willi Batz, the *Gruppenkommandeur*, celebrated with them. Just as proceedings began to slow down, advice came from Hitler's HQ that First Lt. Erich Hartmann had been awarded the Swords to his Knight's Cross, the exalted degree of the Iron Cross standing above the Oak Leaves.

Only one other first lieutenant had qualified for the Swords in the history of the decoration. As a squadron leader with JG-52, First Lt. Hermann Graf had won the Swords on 18 May 1942—more than two years previously. The fighter pilots who had won the Swords were the Luftwaffe's men of legend, classical heroes like Galland, Moelders and Luetzow; daredevils like Heinz Baer and "Gulle" Oesau; dedicated leaders like Rall, Ihlefeld and Gerd Barkhorn; and the world-famed Marseille and Nowotny.

The award of the Swords placed Erich Hartmann among Germany's famous soldiers. The dazzling news gave the celebration party fresh stimulus. The pilots boosted the Blond Knight on their shoulders once more and chaired him around the dugout bar.

"Karaya* One! Karaya One! *Schwertern* (Swords) for Karaya One! . . ."

The chanting, cheering and singing dinned into Erich's brain. Somehow, he felt out of place amid the uproar staged in his honor. The whole thing seemed almost unreal. His thoughts turned to the devoted Bimmel, probably out there on the field this minute, sweating over Karaya One to ensure the ship would never fail him. Then his thoughts raced to Stuttgart, where alone his heart could find what it really sought from life.

The Swords were wonderful, yes, because their award meant another brief leave with Usch. How crazy this war was.

---

* Karaya was the radio call sign or identification of Erich's combat flight. He was Karaya One and his wingman was Karaya Two. The leader of the second flight was Karaya Three and his wingman was Karaya Four.

He was supposed to be playing this deadly scoring game day after day. Success meant medals, adulation and parties. He chased and killed Russian boys and they tried to kill him in turn. That was crazy. All he really wanted from life was to be with his Usch.

To those who were there that night in the dugout bar, Erich Hartmann seemed detached and withdrawn. The smile that flickered occasionally on his handsome face was happy enough, but the cast of his features was sad. As the young flyers celebrated the award of the second highest decoration of the Third Reich, Erich was with them but not one of them. Generals and field marshals had won the Swords, together with a handful of valiant, front-line soldiers. The honor was great, but Erich was not an excited young man, as he had been when he won the Knight's Cross and the Oak Leaves. His ensuing visit to Hitler's HQ at Insterburg in East Prussia, to receive the Swords from the Führer, did little to lift his spirits.

On 3 August 1944 Erich entered the wooden barracks building in which Hitler had survived the 20 July bomb plot against his life. The structure still showed the effects of the blast. Splintered walls, beams out of plumb and the scorch marks of an explosion were the backdrop against which a changed Hitler moved to greet a group of ten Luftwaffe heroes.* Erich was shocked at the appearance of the Führer.

Hitler moved slowly, the compelling quality of personality that had struck Erich a few months before immersed now in his physical awkwardness. When he shook hands with Erich, Hitler extended his left hand, while the right hung slackly at his side. His right ear deafened by the explosion, the Führer had to turn his left ear toward whoever spoke. He was a shadow of the man Erich had met at Berchtesgaden, but he nevertheless had a message for his front-line fighting men. To the best of his recollection, Hartmann remembers it like this:

"Never would I have believed it possible that a German officer would be so cowardly, so untrue to all he was taught as a soldier, that he would put a bomb in this building to kill me and then try to escape himself. Any officer who was in this

---

* Decorated in the same ceremony was Major Heinz-Wolfgang Schnaufer, the top Luftwaffe night-fighter ace, who ended the war with 121 night victories.

building that day could have drawn his pistol and shot me, face to face. I have never looked in the pockets of German officers.

"I am sorry that through this cowardly act I am left alive while other good men were killed and badly wounded. God has delivered me, and my first step is to hunt down these counterreactionary cowards. I find furthermore that my General Staff officers do not tell me the truth. Most of my generals, except Schoerner, Model and Rommel, do not understand their jobs. I have them running to my HQ crying about heavy fighting and losses, but never are these generals killed or wounded with their men.

"For the future I am optimistic. I expect that the Anglo-American invasion will be turned into another Dunkirk. There are new weapons of incredible power coming to hand, that I think will change the whole course of the war. This is why I believe God spared my life on July 20, so that I may lead Germany in this hopeful period ahead."

Erich left the Wolf's redoubt overborne by a dark intuition. The Führer on one side was deeply enraged, and on the other full of hope in what seemed like a hopeless situation. His speech had been slow and quiet, but not reassuring—not something that the Führer could have you believe in spite of what could be seen at the front. The forces of disintegration were clearly gaining momentum in Hitler, Germany, and even in the Luftwaffe itself.

Erich knew that the Swords had brought him fame. Every triumph henceforth would be studied and celebrated. He was unelated by his new eminence, but deeply disturbed by the ruin he could see engulfing Germany. He felt older and wiser for the experiences of the past year, and he knew he would need all the steadiness he could summon for what lay ahead.

CHAPTER NINE

STALIN HAWKS

Seek out your enemy! Do not ask how strong the enemy
is, but where he is to be found.
            —*Motto of the Soviet fighter pilots*

RELATIVELY EARLY IN HIS combat career, Erich Hartmann
exceeded the 1939–1945 totals of the top-scoring British and
American fighter aces. Sketches already presented of Hartmann's fellow aces in JG-52 reveal that many German aces
on the Eastern Front exceeded one hundred victories. Since
the German methods of recording and verifying victories were
accurate and reliable, the conclusion seems inescapable that
Hartmann and other high-scoring Eastern Front aces faced
inferior opposition—both in planes and pilots. This conclusion
can be justified only in a limited way, because many aspects
of the Eastern Front air war bearing on fighter operations are
but little known in the West outside Germany. If Russian
inferiority in planes and pilots is accepted as a universal
explanation for the success of the German aces in Russia,
then the notable achievements of Soviet industry and Russian
fighter aces will be obscured. Dislike for an ideology or a
regime must be set aside in assessing the historical facts of
Soviet air power.

Germans, Americans and British alike have long shared a
fatuous conceit concerning Russian achievements, and the
disasters that have befallen the German people since 1941
may be deemed to have originated in their leaders' underesti-
mation of the Soviet colossus. For the Americans, the space
race should have deflated by now the sense of universal

119

superiority held by America in its attitudes toward things Russian. The Soviet Union's combination of a low standard of living with brilliant technical achievements confounds the conventional Western mind and leads to massive errors of judgment.

In evaluating the Eastern Front air war and Erich Hartmann's achievements, an error is committed if we uncritically convince ourselves that he was shooting down ducks over the Steppes. The enemy could and did shoot back, with first-line aircraft often superior in performance to the Me-109. Some of these machines were flown by the top-scoring Allied aces of the war—Russian pilots who handily outscored the British and the Americans. A fair and unbiased view of Erich Hartmann's victory tally must therefore focus primarily on the *quality* of the Russian opposition, both technical and human.

Published engineering data* precludes the theory of inferior Russian aircraft as a blanket explanation of high German scores. From the beginning of the Russo-German conflict, the Russians had at least one fighter that was superior to the Me-109 in most respects. As the war progressed, the Soviet aircraft industry not only produced other types of fighters superior to the many variants of the Me-109, but also accomplished prodigies of aircraft production, far outstripping the Germans in this sphere.

The authors in their previous book, *"Horrido!" Fighter Aces of the Luftwaffe,*† dealt extensively with the character of the Eastern Front air war and the differences between this vast conflict and the air struggle in the West. There is a natural tendency in Western countries to regard the Anglo-American air assault on Germany as the major arena of aerial conflict. In truth, the aircraft losses sustained by the Soviet Union were approximately twice those suffered by the Anglo-American air forces. The biggest air war was fought on the Eastern Front.

Reorganized in 1939 to gradually become a separate service

* See Asher Lee, *Soviet Air and Rocket Forces* (Garden City, N.Y.: Doubleday, 1961); William Green, *War Planes of the Second World War*, Vol. III (London: Macdonald & Co., 1961); and *Famous Fighters of the Second World War* (London: Macdonald & Co., 1961).

† New York: Macmillan, 1968.

from the Red Army, the Soviet Air Force had previously been hampered in its development through tight army control. The Air Division under the reorganization became the largest unit, each Air Division consisting of from three to six air regiments made up of four or five squadrons per regiment. German estimates of Soviet air strength, at the time of the invasion of Russia in June 1941, concluded that the Red Air Force had between forty and fifty Air Divisions containing approximately 162 regiments. Overall numerical strength was estimated at about 10,500 airplanes.

Red fighter forces were equipped primarily with the I-16 Rata, or its later variants, the I-151 and I-153. The Rata was a single-seat, gull-wing biplane introduced to air combat in the Spanish Civil War. Obsolescent in 1941, the Rata was being replaced by the MIG-3 and Lagg-3 fighters when the Germans struck. Less than a quarter of the Russian conversion to modern monoplanes had been achieved when the Luftwaffe arrived to make bonfires out of the Soviet air fleets parked on bases along the front. The virtual eradication of Soviet air power as a factor in the defense of Russia in the first ninety days, was one of the Luftwaffe's most complete triumphs.

Tactical ground support remained the primary mission of the Soviet Air Force even after the 1939 reorganization. As a consequence, nearly every available aircraft, including fighters, was fitted to carry bombs. In early encounters, the German air superiority fighters that accompanied Luftwaffe bomber and fighter-bomber strikes took terrible toll of bomb-carrying Soviet fighters intercepting the invaders. Subsequent Soviet Air Force orders forbade Russian pilots of fighters carrying bombs to engage German air superiority fighters, so that combat was often refused by the Russians. The Germans attributed this to a lack of aggressiveness, until interrogation of downed Russian pilots revealed the truth.

The Soviet Union was in many respects better prepared for the challenges of the air war than were Britain in 1939 and America in 1941. Special attention and planning was devoted in Russia to building up a reserve of trained pilots. Similarly, preparations for large-scale aircraft production on a twenty-four-hour-a-day basis were so far advanced by 1941 that the Russians were able to recover rapidly from the air blitzkrieg of June and July 1941. The Russians maintained a steady flow of pilots from their training schools to man the flood of fighters that poured from Soviet factories.

Russian losses were severe throughout the war, but their fighter pilots improved steadily as the war progressed, in contrast to the degeneration of pilot training that plagued the Luftwaffe fighter force. Germany's lack of a four-engined strategic bomber allowed the U.S.S.R. to operate vast armament factories and flying schools beyond the reach of the Luftwaffe. As a consequence, all this matériel and personnel had to be dealt with after it reached the front.

From late 1942 onward, Russian air power became an irresistible aerial tide that grew in strength with the passage of every month. By mid-1944 the Russians dominated the air over the Eastern Front and were far superior tactically to their 1941 status. Despite these facts, the legend that all Russian Front air combat was some kind of easy picnic for the Germans has enjoyed such long currency that it has become almost a historical doctrine. The facts rule out any blanket conclusion that flying against the Red Air Force was easy.

Erich Hartmann likens Eastern Front combat to the fighter assaults on the Allied bomber streams in the West. The hails of lead and steel that filled the air made it inevitable that a pilot constantly in action would fly into some stray projectiles sometime. "Often there were ten of us against three hundred Russians. Those are long odds. A mid-air collision was almost as likely as being shot down, too. We had to plan our attacks against these hordes with great care or we never would have survived."

As to Russian pilot quality, the experience of German aces on the Eastern Front varies widely. In day-to-day operations over long periods, the Germans felt superior, both technically and psychologically. This was especially true of the top German pilots. Nevertheless there is virtual unanimity concerning the quality of the Guards Fighter Regiments, the elite of the Soviet fighter arm. These Russians earned the Germans' respect.

Crack Soviet pilots were concentrated in the Guards Regiments. They were the real fighter types, aggressive, tactically formidable, fearless and flying some of the finest fighter aircraft in existence. Their operations were vitalized by the same kind of unquenchable morale that characterized the immortal "Few" of the Battle of Britain.

The aggressive spirit of these Soviet pilots is illustrated in a remarkable incident near Orel, involving a young Stalin Hawk named Lt. Vladimir D. Lavrinekov. An ace with thirty kills, Lavrinekov downed an Me-109 in battle, and watched the German pilot land in a flat field. The Luftwaffe pilot scrambled from the cockpit and dashed for cover in a nearby gully filled with trees and underbrush.

Circling low over the scene, Lavrinekov saw that Red Army units would probably not locate the German, and that he might therefore escape. The young Russian lieutenant landed his fighter next to the crashed Me-109, and led the searching infantry to the thickets in the gully. Lavrinekov found the downed German, and pouncing on him, strangled him to death with his hands. The Russian ace returned immediately to his fighter and took off in a cloud of dust, leaving his dead foe at the feet of the open-mouthed Russian infantrymen.

The Guards Regiments produced the top-scoring Allied fighter pilots of the Second World War. The desire to denigrate everything Russian on account of ideological enmities ill serves the recording of history. There is a widespread and irrational prejudice against considering the Eastern Front air war as comparable to the Western Front air struggle, but the facts are that no fighter pilots in history ever faced the odds that were the daily way of life of the Germans on the Eastern Front. Similarly, the Soviet Union's outstanding fighter aces have not been accorded a fair hearing by chroniclers of the conflict. The top Russian pilots, whose scores were half as large again as the best American and British scores, have remained in obscurity for a quarter of a century.

All the leading German aces on the Eastern Front were either shot down or forced down many times. The exposure rate of these pilots was the highest in history. Using Erich Hartmann as an example, his fourteen hundred sorties and eight hundred aerial battles, most of them fought against high numerical odds, made it inevitable that he would be at a tactical disadvantage in a proportion of his encounters. He estimates that approximately two hundred times he found himself under the guns of Soviet fighters. While Hartmann, Rall, Barkhorn and the other top German aces were probably the most skilled air fighters of all time, the numerical odds against them, the law of averages and sheer chance resulted in their being downed one way or another.

Wherever the Guards Regiments were operating, the Luftwaffe could be sure of solid opposition. The masses of Russian pilots stood below the Guards in skill, but still took their toll of the Germans in the long battle of attrition. The top Soviet ace of the war, Major General Ivan Kozhedub, scored sixty-two aerial victories against the Luftwaffe, and seven other Soviet pilots are credited with more victories than the top-scoring Anglo-American ace, Major Richard I. Bong, with his forty victories scored in the Pacific Theater of Operations.

Ivan Kozhedub was born in 1920 in the Ukraine, the son of a factory worker. He got into flying through one of the many aviation clubs that flourished in the U.S.S.R. during the 1930s. His career with the Guards Regiments of the Red Air Force led him to three awards of Hero of the Soviet Union, a decoration approximately corresponding to the U.S. Congressional Medal of Honor.

Kozhedub is reported to have commanded the North Korean Air Division of fighters in 1951–1952 during the Korean War. His units were equipped with MIG-15 jets, which were lighter aircraft than the USAF F-86E and F-86F "Sabres" with which they did battle. Whether Kozhedub flew any combat sorties in Korea is an unanswered question nearly twenty years later, but it is possible that he did so since he was at that time a young man of thirty-one. United States military authorities feel certain that skilled Russian pilots did fly combat in Korea, and believe it is possible that Kozhedub added to his sixty-two kills of the Second World War.

Kozhedub's autobiography, *I Attack*, was published in the Eastern Zone of Germany in 1956. What should and could have been a historical work of interest is instead a turgid, highly polemical account of his life, the supreme experience of which is his admission to the Communist party. Every aspect of his career, from early school days through to his winning his country's highest decoration, is seen through a red prism, which distorts even as it colors a brilliant flying career.

The most famous Soviet fighter ace, and one whose units frequently opposed JG-52, is Colonel Alexander Pokryshkin of the Guards Regiment. "Sacha" Pokryshkin is credited with fifty-nine confirmed aerial victories, and during the war he also won his Gold Star as Hero of the Soviet Union three times. Pokryshkin's career has many common elements with those of numerous German and Allied aces. The international fraternity of old aces could recount many similar stories. Regardless of the uniform worn or the flag served under, most fighter aces have been through the same fires in much the same way.

Pokryshkin was inspired during his Siberian boyhood by the achievements of Russian pioneer aviator Valery Chkalov. He left his home at Novosibirsk to seek his fortune via aviation school, but his enthusiasm turned to dismay when he found that the aviation school was strictly for mechanics and not for flying training.

He began filing semiannual requests for transfer to pilot training, but his mechanical aptitudes were so outstanding that his superiors consistently denied his requests to become a flyer. Pokryshkin, however, would not be put off or put down. He joined the Krasnodar Aviation Club, which operated under the Soviet Ossoaviakim scheme, and like Erich Hartmann in Germany, he learned glider flying. Pokryshkin also learned parachute jumping, and then graduated to powered flight. At the age of twenty-four he took his first hop in October 1937 in a lumbering U-2.

Still serving as an aircraft mechanic, Pokryshkin soon soloed successfully, and passed his pilot's examination. He persisted in filing requests for transfer to piloting, and eventually he wore down his superiors by sheer persistence. His transfer was finally approved.

Pokryshkin joined a fighter training unit at Kacha, and was shortly afterward assigned to a regular fighter unit of the Red Air Force. Whatever sense of egalitarianism the Russian Revolution might have induced in Pokryshkin was given a rude jolt when he joined the fighter squadron. He was still wearing mechanic's insignia on his uniform, and his fellow pilots would barely talk to him. He was stigmatized in their eyes because he was an ex-mechanic, while they considered themselves legitimate pilots.

The undaunted Pokryshkin soon proved himself to be more than just an upstart mechanic. His fine piloting skill was undeniable, and his detailed knowledge of aircraft construction and engines far exceeded that of his fellow pilots. They soon accepted him completely, but the range of his knowledge would normally have diverted him into service as an instructor.

Pokryshkin was able to avoid this sidetrack largely through his dynamic and avid interest in aerial tactics. He did historians a favor during this period by keeping a diary and setting down his tactical concepts as they developed. His Bible was *My Air Combats*, a classic book on First World War fighter tactics, written by Captain René Paul Fonck of France. Fonck was the top Allied fighter ace of the war, with seventy-five confirmed aerial victories.

Serious, determined and studious, Pokryshkin practiced Fonck's theories and maneuvers in mock aerial combat, modifying and extending them to fit the new generations of fighter planes. He introduced innovations. His mechanic's training in mathematics had endowed him with a drive for precision, and he sketched in his diary all his tactical maneuvers and those of his opponents. He maintained this routine throughout his combat career.

The trends of post-revolutionary culture in Russia had been toward the production of a mass psychology in which individualism was looked on as something inherently bad and bourgeois. This outlook became structural in the generation of young men who were to fight the Second World War for Russia. The result was that the qualities essential to success in air fighting—high individuality, quick decision, hair-trigger initiative—were blunted in millions of young Russians. Dogmatic steel nerve was the usual substitute. The experience of the Germans who fought them verifies that the Russians for the most part had to overcome a psychological barrier as pilots, far more challenging than the techniques of modern aircraft design. They conquered the latter, and battled with the former.

Born in 1913, Pokryshkin was through his formative childhood years before the compulsive elements of Soviet education had time to work on him in depth. He became a great ace because he comprehended from the outset the importance of the individual in aerial combat. Through his endless sketches and persistent studies of maneuver, he could see how an exceptional pilot in an inferior aircraft might well defeat a less competent opponent in a superior machine. This conviction was reinforced by all the experience he acquired in mock combat.

Like Erich Hartmann on the German side, Pokryshkin became a devotee of the sudden, swift and violent attack. His early guide in developing this mode of attack was a veteran fighter pilot named Sokolov, who flew with him in the first squadron he joined. Sokolov insisted that the sudden, savage strike won the psychological battle immediately, leaving the enemy pilot rattled and ready to be shot out of the sky. Pokryshkin wrote in his diary: "The factors of victory are maneuver and *fire!*"

Pokryshkin had devoted himself primarily to aerobatics and maneuvering. When he turned his attention to the actual business of bringing the other man down by gunfire, he found he had much still to learn. Sacha couldn't shoot to save himself. When he practiced with a drogue target he made one firing pass after another until his ammunition was exhausted. Hundreds of rounds flew off into the blue while the drogue suffered three or four hits.

A puzzled Pokryshkin could not understand his inability to hit the target in the air. His approaches were perfect, and he followed the gunnery instructions in the Air Force manuals to the letter. He resorted to his mathematical background for the answer.

He sat down and figured out trajectories, bullet velocities and the problems of air-to-air shooting from a mathematical standpoint. He covered pages with involved calculations, and drew many graphs. These labors brought him to the same conclusion reached by Erich Hartmann in actual combat many years later. Wrote the elated Pokryshkin: *"Success depends on firing from close range."*

Convinced that the problem was to compute the proper initial position for point-blank attack, Pokryshkin drew more maneuvering diagrams for this purpose and took off the next day in a fever of anticipation. He wrote of his experiment:

"The secret was as follows. I approached the cone from a definite angle and attacked, pressing on the firing buttons at a time when, according to all the rules, I should already be swerving aside. For a young pilot, that was taking a big risk. The slightest inaccuracy and I should be pumping lead into the towing plane instead of the cone.

"When we landed, the pilot who towed the drogue was furious. 'What in hell made you crowd in on me like that? You could kill a fellow that way!' But neither my hand nor eye deceived me. I continued firing from short range, and with deadly accuracy. That is what in-fighting in air combat means."

Pokryshkin through mathematical analysis had found the same basic tactical formula that Erich Hartmann's native analytical ability would find for him many years later. The similarity of their concepts and findings seems remarkable. Both found the validity of their conclusions verified in actual combat.

In over six hundred sorties and in fifty-nine victories, Pokryshkin found no reason to question the accuracy of his prewar findings. At the time of the German invasion of Russia in 1941, Pokryshkin was a fully-fledged fighter pilot serving in the Ukraine. Two days after the first German assault, he flew a recce mission to Jassy, an area in which the fighters of JG-52 later encountered Pokryshkin's fighters many times during the period of Hartmann's service. With Lieutenant Semyonov as his wingman, Pokryshkin in a MIG-3 sighted five Me-109's, three at lower altitude and two above his Russian element. Pokryshkin hauled back on the stick and began a swift climb toward the higher German element.

The pilot of the leading German fighter zoomed and Pokryshkin countered with a stall turn that brought him around on the German's tail. Closing in to point-blank range, Sacha sent a burst into the Me-109 from all guns. The German fighter burst afire and went roaring earthward, trailing smoke.

Exulting over his first kill, the young Russian made the same error that cost many tyro fighter pilots their lives. He watched his victim plunging downward, fascinated by the fiery spectacle. The stricken German's wingman bounced Pokryshkin while he watched the show. Sacha snapped back to business as his port wing was riven by a series of cannon shells and tracer went lancing past his canopy.

Pokryshkin put his MIG-3 into a dive to deck level, and half-crouching in his cockpit behind his armor plate—like

Erich Hartmann on his first combat mission—he went hedge-hopping home. His first triumph had been tempered by the narrowness of his escape. Fighter aces of the eminence of Adolf Galland and Guenther Rall confess to being similarly clobbered when they could not resist watching a spectacular crash. Galland almost lost his life and was wounded. Rall ended up in a crash that broke his back and put him at death's door. Pokryshkin thus learned this fundamental lesson in the same way as two of Germany's finest pilots.

The bold Pokryshkin, with his mode of attack now clearly proved in hot war, nevertheless got little opportunity for more fighter-to-fighter combat until the autumn of 1941. He flew innumerable reconnaissance missions, but seldom tangled with German fighters. He never ceased studying the art of aerial maneuver, and in later battles he found that his response to enemy attacks was prompt and appropriate. He had made moves and countermoves so much a part of his existence that he was instinctively doing the right thing in combat—and staying alive as a result.

Pokryshkin's innovations were largely responsible for breaking the Soviet Air Force out of the strait jacket of horizontal maneuver in which all prewar Soviet fighter doctrine had been confined. Taught to fly and fight in horizontal planes before the war, the Russians were rapidly re-educated to the new realities by 1941–1942 aerial combat. Improved aircraft performance and the new low-wing monoplane era opened vertical maneuver to fighter tactics, and Pokryshkin was among the most significant contributors to Russian tactical development.

He used the climbing spiral often for evasion. Against the advice of his more conservative comrades he practiced the snap-roll as a speed-killing maneuver to make pursuing Germans overshoot and thus become his victims. His leadership, knowledge of aircraft design and engineering, and his abilities as a tutor brought him to the front rank of Russian fighter pilot personalities.

What Pokryshkin taught others he had himself wrought in the fires of war. His photographic memory permitted him to recall details of every maneuver in combat. He set all these details down in sketch form, and hung his dugout walls with diagrams, graphs and performance charts. Like the top German pilots he faced, Pokryshkin was shot down many times. He made numerous forced landings and his comrades were often aghast at the shattered condition of his fighter when he staggered back from battles with the Luftwaffe.

Pokryshkin's passion for knowing his enemy was insatiable. He not only kept detailed records of maneuvers, but also flew captured German fighters, carefully noting what he believed to be their weaknesses. He put himself in the place of a German pilot in these maneuvers and wrote at length on the qualities and deficiencies of the Me-109. He considered the best Soviet fighter planes superior to the rugged German bird.

Over the Kuban Peninsula, where his regiment again mixed for a protracted period with JG-52, Pokryshkin developed his basic formula for aerial combat, distilling his knowledge and experience into four words: "Altitude, Speed, Maneuver, Fire."

With good aircraft and leaders like Pokryshkin, the Guards Fighter Regiments were afraid of no one in the air. Many times JG-52 radio monitors were startled to hear Russian R/T transmitters switch on to German frequencies. The Russians would throw down the gauntlet with a challenge in German.

"Beware, all German pilots. The ace Pokryshkin is in the air!"

This kind of fighter pilot morale was probably exceptional on the Russian side, but it was the common possession of the Guards Regiments. They painted their aircraft in wild colors, favoring brilliant red patterns, and in every way were the counterparts of the best fighter units in other air forces.

Pokryshkin resembled Erich Hartmann in yet another way. He believed in the careful guidance of new pilots, to keep them alive as a fundamental accomplishment of leadership, and as a prelude to making them aces by experience and tutoring. He took pains to explain the art of maneuver, using his profound knowledge backed up by his beloved diagrams. He taught them to bring in their shooting eye, and a number of the top-scoring Russian aces owed their success to his tutoring. Alexander Klubov, who is credited with fifty victories over the Luftwaffe, was broken in and trained for leadership by Pokryshkin. Klubov was twice awarded the Gold Star as Hero of the Soviet Union.

As Russia's best-known ace, Pokryshkin thus fought like,

and to a great degree tactically thought like, Erich Hartmann. Pokryshkin nevertheless can be equated more with Colonel Werner Moelders than with any other Luftwaffe pilot and fighter leader. The Russian was about the same age as Moelders, and his tactical insight and perseverance in developing new methods are strongly reminiscent of Moelders, who was largely responsible for freeing the Luftwaffe of old-fashioned tactics inherited from the First World War.

"Daddy" Moelders had the same kind of precise mentality as Pokryshkin, and the German leader's careful direction of young pilots has, by their own present-day admission, allowed them to enjoy a prosperous middle age in contemporary Germany. Propagandist distortions of the Russians should not be permitted to obscure Pokryshkin's achievements as a fighter ace, leader and tactician. His fame is well-earned, and it is appropriate to recognize him in this book since he fought so frequently against Erich Hartmann's units in JG-52.

There is no firm evidence that Pokryshkin and Erich Hartmann ever fought each other aloft, but nor can it be said with certainty that they were never direct aerial antagonists. In more than eight hundred aerial battles, many of them against formations commanded by Pokryshkin, it is possible that the Blond Knight did encounter the famous Russian, but no one can say for sure. Both aces were shot down or forced down many times.

For historical purposes the authors include a list of Soviet fighter aces with thirty or more aerial victories. This list originated with the Soviet air historian M. Mosskov, and reached the authors via Miss Jean Alexander of London, British air historian, and the Cassidy Group of researchers with whom she is associated. As of November 1967 it is believed to be the most accurate list of Soviet aces available.

Soviet Aces of World War II:

Kozhedub, Ivan Nikitch	62
Pokryshkin, Alexander Ivanovich	59
Rechkalov, Grigorli Andreevich	58
Gulaev, Niklaev Dmitrievich	57
Yevstigneev, Kirill Alekseevich	52
Glinka, Dimitri Borisovich	50
Klubov, Aleksandr Fedorovich	50

Pilipenko, Ivan Markovich	48
Vorozheikin, Arsenii Vasil'evich	46
Kubarev, Vasilii Nikoleevich	46
Skomorokhov, Nikolai Mikhailovich	46
Kostilev, Georgi Dmitrievich	43
Morgunov, Sergei	42
Popkov, Vitallii Ivanovich	41
Alelyukhin, Aleksei Vasil'evich	40
Golubev, Viktor Fedorovich	39
Golubev, Vasilii Fedorovich	38
Luganskii, Sergei Danilovich	37
Pivovarov, Mikhail Yevdekimovich	37
Gul'tyaev, Grigorii Kapitanovich	36
Dolgikh, Anatoli Gavrilovich	36
Kuznetsov, Nikolai Fedorovich	36
Koldunov, Aleksandr Ivanovich	36
Babak, Ivan Il'ich	35
Kamozin, Pavel Mikhailovich	35
Lavrinekov, Vladimir Dmitrievich	35
Pavlushkin, Nikolai Sazonovich	35
Gnido, Petr Andreevich	34
Kotchekov, Aleksandr Vasil'ovich	34
Lukyanov, Sergei Ivanovich	34
Sytov, Ivan Nikitich	34
Chislov, Aleksandr Mikhailovich	34
Chubkob, Fedor Mikhailovich	34
Borovykh, Andreii Yegorovich	32
Zelenkin, Mikhail Mikhailovich	32
Komelkov, Mikhail Sergeovich	32
Krasnov, Nikolai Fedorovich	32
Ryazanov, Aleksei Konstantinovich	32
Stepanenko, Ivan Nikifirovich	32
Golovachev, Pavel Yekovlevich	31
Kirilyuk, Viktor Vasil'evich	31
Akmet-Khan, Sultan	30
Arkhipenko, Fedor Fedorovich	30
Bobrov, Vladimir Ivanovich	30
Glinka, Boris Borisovich	30
Likhobabiyi, Ivan Dmitrievich	30
Likholetov, Petr Yakovlevich	30
Makharov, Valentin Nikoleevich	30
Pokryshev, Petr Afanas'evich	30
Khlobystov, Aleksei Stepanovich	30

CHAPTER TEN

300 DOWN AND DIAMONDS

If Aye be Jousting's rightful King, then Sov'reigns be my Peers.

—Anonymous

WHEN ERICH RETURNED to the Russian Front during the third week in July 1944, he found the numerical superiority of the Red Air Force more evident than ever. American and British lend-lease aircraft were present in about the same numbers as always, but the hordes of YAKs, Laggs, Stormoviks and MIGs were multiplying at an alarming rate. The Russian fighter pilots were tactically sharper now than ever before, and their red-painted Guards Regiment aircraft were manned by top-grade talent. The Guards had ace-leaders like Kozhedub, Pokryshkin, Rechlakov and others, most of whom had fifty or more victories against the Luftwaffe. These men were dangerous.

An aggressive German pilot on the Eastern Front could find targets on his doorstep in the summer of 1944. Red aircraft abounded within fifteen minutes of take-off, and this meant numerous rhubarbs and continuing success for Erich. Between 20 July 1944 and 22 August 1944, he shot down another thirty-two aircraft. With 282 victories to his credit, he had obliterated more than fifteen squadrons of Soviet aircraft. His only rival now for top-scoring honors was Gerd Barkhorn. Uncertain communications and delays in official confirmations of victories had Erich and Gerd—the man he admired most in the entire Luftwaffe—running neck and neck for several weeks.

A great dogfighter, Barkhorn stood out in what the Germans called the "circus" type of air fighting. Consistent and steady in his scoring once he found his shooting eye, he owed his eminence more to this quality than to wildly spectacular days of multiple downings. Like Rall before him, Barkhorn suffered wounds that kept him out of the air for long periods. Badly wounded in the defense of Ploesti against the USAAF in June of 1944, Gerd was kept studying the ceiling of his hospital room while Erich kept hammering away at the Red Air Force.

On 23 August 1944, Erich had a big day. Eight victories in three missions brought his score to 290 victories. He had passed Gerd Barkhorn and was now the top-scoring ace not only of the Luftwaffe, but of all the air forces in all the wars. When Barkhorn was transferred soon afterward to the Reich Defense, all challenge to Erich's leadership was over, but a challenge of a different kind still lay ahead.

A fever of anticipation gripped Erich's squadron mates as the incredible total of three hundred aerial victories drew near. The historic attainment lay within his grasp, but a lucky Ivan or an accident might rob him of the prize. The tension in the squadron became more marked as the days rolled on.

Barely four years ago, when the gifted Colonel Werner "Daddy" Moelders had first exceeded von Richthofen's First World War record of 80 victories, and then went on to pass 100 victories, Germany had been proud and almost incredulous. By comparison, 100 victories now seemed a remote historical oddity, with 300 victories an imminent possibility for Erich Hartmann.

When the brilliant but underestimated Gordon Gollob lifted Moelders's record to 150 victories on 29 August 1942 it was another historic new mark, but aces like Luetzow, Oesau and others were hot on Gollob's heels. In a blaze of glory on the Eastern Front, Hermann Graf had broken the 200 victory mark, but within a short time there were others to share his distinction. Walter Nowotny of JG-54 and later of the Me-262 jet *Nowotny Kommando,* had raised the record to 250 victories, only to be outstripped by Guenther Rall, Otto Kittel, Gerd Barkhorn and Erich Hartmann. The magic 300 mark glittered tantalizingly now, a scant eight victories away for Hartmann.

The high excitement of this time has fortunately been preserved in a contemporary account. Master Sergeant Carl Junger, onetime wingman and long-time squadron mate of the Blond Knight, had the presence of mind to write down his version of events the day after Erich's greatest triumph.

A JG-52 fighter ace in his own right, Carl Junger was an aggressive, black-haired dynamo who fought hard and lived hard. Hartmann recalls one occasion in Krakau, Poland, when a furious binge until three in the morning preceded the squadron's early departure for Warsaw. Junger lay poleaxed on his cot, stark naked save for a pair of sunglases, and incapable of rising to the challenge of the morning. The squadron left without him.

Two hours later in Warsaw, Junger appeared in a lone Me-109, bringing up the rear. While Erich and his pilots watched, Junger came in for a landing. Just as he was letting down, a Polish farmer uncomprehendingly crossed the grass strip after making a sudden change of direction with horses and two huge hay wagons.

Junger hit the bucolic convoy with a tremendous crash, and the scene disappeared behind a huge pall of dust and straw, out of which an innocent horse came flying end over end. Loud crumpling noises subsided as the pilots went sprinting over to the dust cloud. When they got to the crash site, all that remained of the fighter was a pile of twisted metal, unrecognizable as an aircraft. Erich was about to say how sorry he was that Junger had to die by accident, when stirrings sounded from under the pile of twisted structure. Junger suddenly crawled out of the shambles, stood up, and with sunglasses still in place, said, "Thank God the Earth has me again." Next day, he was back flying combat.

Carl Junger later sent the story he wrote on 24 August 1944 to Usch Hartmann. He wanted her to have it as a keepsake, when it was uncertain that Erich would ever return alive from Soviet imprisonment.

"AT THE EDGE OF AN ADVANCED AIRFIELD

24 August 1944

by

Master Sergeant Carl Junger

"Yesterday was a great day for us. A day unprecedented in the history of combat flying. My Chief, First Lt. Erich Hartmann, holder of the Oak Leaves with Swords, in two missions shot down eleven enemy planes, and with this raised the number of his victories to three hundred and one. He is the first to have passed the three hundred mark, and therefore is the best fighter pilot in the world.

"Even yesterday, good spirits were in evidence all over the field. The question that buzzed from lip to lip was: 'Will the three-hundred mark topple today? Can Bubi do it?' All of us were tense with excitement and anticipation. The day before, our Chief had sent eight Ivans into eternity and had raised his figure to two hundred and ninety. Yesterday morning the weather did not look promising. Not until noon did it clear up, thus reducing operational time to half a day. After lunch came the first mission, and our squadron leader did not waste the chance. Right after he lifted off with his wingman we started counting the minutes.

"Exactly one hour later, two aircraft appeared on the horizon and came toward our field. The familiarly-marked Me-109 of our twenty-two-year-old 'Old Man' wagged its wings, pulled up, made another pass and wagged again. And then another and another . . . five and then six times. Everyone cheered and shouted, wild with joy. The Chief had two hundred and ninety-six kills now. Only four more to go. *Hals und Beinbruch!*

"We could hardly wait for the two ships to become operational again. Refueling and rearming seemed to take forever. Meanwhile there were arguments and bets amongst the rest of us. Can he do it today or must we wait another day? Suddenly another mission is ordered. Everyone scrambles to the machines, the blond-haired Chief in the lead.

"He clambers easily into the cockpit. He buckles himself in, as steady and unexcited as ever. His features do not betray his emotions. Only a slightly harsh line plays about the corners of his mouth. A cool one, this. Quietly and with deliberation he begins the cockpit check for this decisive and historic mission —one that will bring him to the head of all fighter pilots. For those who were there, it was a unique experience.

"At his sign, the crew begins to start the machines. First slowly, and then ever faster until the starter is running at the highest RPM. Then a slight jerk, a turning of the propeller, and finally the engines are running. They smooth down and the Chief starts, easing his fighter to the runway with his wingman behind him.

"They pause faced into the wind. The roar of a final run-up reaches our ears. Then comes take-off. Billows of dust swirl up from the sun-dried earth as the slender fighters race forward and lift gracefully into the air. Two ships, course east. What will the next hour bring? With a reporter we drive to the advanced area, where already everyone is in a fever of anticipation. We walk to a man with earphones who is listening to the R/T conversations between the ships. He hands us earphones and we plug in and listen. . . ."

The reporter with Sergeant Junger on that historic day was war correspondent Heinz Eckert, who plugged in headphones during the epic mission and gave this contemporary account of the ensuing action.

"The air-to-air communication, by which the pilots inform each other, is very terse. Only the most essential is said, and even this by words of certain meaning, where one word may stand for a whole sentence. Sometimes, there are long breaks between the individual dialogues, sometimes address and reply follow each other in staccato counterpoint, and often in dramatic crescendo when within a few minutes one enemy aircraft after another is being shot down. Then, two words, sometimes only one, characterize this happening, but the listeners on the ground are wholly absorbed by the breath-taking excitement.

"Now, everybody is gathering around the operator and those two poor receivers of his headset. It might happen any moment. The operator is fingering the buttons of his set . . . he is a little nervous, as though afraid of missing the call of victory.

"15:44: Hartmann to ground: *'Have you any enemy observations?'* *'None.'* *'Why the hell do they chase us up, then?'* 15:50: Ground to Hartmann: *'Enemy echelon over Sandowiez approaching.'*

"15:51: *'Eighth Squadron watch out! . . . Airacobras . . . damn! . . .'* 16:00 *'Bull's eye!'** 16:03: *'Bull's-eye!'* 16:06:

* Bull's-eye means "direct hit" in the fighter language employed by Erich Hartmann at this time.—Authors

'*Watch out backward and upwards! Airas to the right! Bull's-eye!*' 16:07: '*Watch out upwards!*' 16:09: '*We'll get this one!*' 16:10: '*Attention! Bull's-eye!*' Call of wingman: 'Congratulations on the three hundredth!' Ground to Hartmann "Congratulations!'

"During the next five minutes, the operator cannot take any more messages. Everything goes crazy. He cannot understand a word because of the ensuing hubbub. Then it goes on.

"16:15: '*Six kilometers west of Sandowiez. Six light bombers, height 2000 meters, circling. . . . Ah . . . there's another echelon, they're P-2's.*' 16:17: '*Eight kilometers east of Ostrowiez, height 3000 meters, fighter echelon. . . . We can't get at them, dammit!*' 16:19: '*Get at them! . . .*' 16:20: '*Bull's-eye! Impact burst!*' 16:23: Wingman to Hartmann: 'Look out, there are two aircraft behind us to the left. One fighter is with them.' 16:27: '*Single aircraft to the left! That's one of our own. . . .*' 16:29: '*Look out back!*' 'Roger!' 16:35: Wing to Hartmann: 'Congratulations!' 16:37: '*Go down for a landing. I'll rock the wings five times.*'

"Only an hour before he sat with us in front of a tent, shirt front open to a cooling wind, looking thoughtful and day-dreaming at the same time, for we had been talking about his bride-to-be. Her photo stood on the table. He had looked down at his chest and laughed the merry laugh of a youth.

"He said: 'There is a hair on my chest, now I'm going to be a man!' At that moment, he was called for take-off on this historic mission; the curtain closed over a little piece of insight into his ego, uttered lightly and laughingly, with self-irony—a joke and knowledge of himself all rolled into one."

Master Sergeant Junger again takes up the narrative at the frenetic scene on the squadron's airfield.

"The news of the 300th and 301st victories came upon us like a redemption. Everything becomes wildly busy. Wreaths are being rapidly braided in the final few minutes before the Chief's return. Shields are painted, inscriptions are painted, rough banners fashioned. The ground crew is milling around like a swarm of bees, with Bimmel proud and square among them.

"Soon the ships must come back. Everyone who can leave his post streams toward the parking spot of the Chief's plane.

There are majors and captains and lieutenants mixed cheek-by-jowl with the mob of ground personnel, united by their common desire to pay homage. I have a bottle of champagne and two glasses under my arm.

"To avoid being late in the uproar, I open the wire around the top of the champagne bottle now. There is a bang, and the cork flies through the air in a great curve. Quickly I clap my palm over the opening. Not a drop is lost. Suddenly, I am the sorrowful one in the crowd. Everyone is happy. I can only think, 'I hope my Chief comes soon. I hope he comes soon.'

"My wish was seemingly his command. Karaya One comes drumming in over the field. This time, Lt. Hartmann waggles his wings on five successive passes. The resources of energy and concentration that lie behind this feat can be understood only by a few.

"After the fifth pass, Lt. Hartmann pulls his machine up, and amidst the exultant cheering of his crowd of comrades, makes a perfect landing. He taxies his machine easily to its waiting berth, and we wait eagerly for the moment when he will stop his engine. But he will not favor us so quickly. He runs the big motor up again, and with his canopy open, lets the slip stream play about his nostrils. The only one who can squeeze his hand and congratulate him at this time is Bimmel Mertens, his crew chief. Without envy, everyone else stands and waits.

"As the engine roar dies away into a hiss and the propeller turns for the last time, there is no more restraint. The acting *Gruppenkommandeur*, Willi Batz, jumps up on the ship. JG-52's *Kommodore*, Colonel Dieter Hrabak, springs up beside him. They pump the Chief's hand. We lift him off the aircraft the moment he gets out of the cockpit, and he sits on the shoulders of two comrades, one of them the proud Bimmel Mertens.

"A lei that was fashioned at the last minute is hung around his neck. For a moment, the reporters intervene and momentarily take charge as they get their photographs. As they shoot the Chief from various angles, we become impatient, even though we know it is a one-time occasion.

"The Chief asks to be put down from his shoulder-high perch, and as his feet touch the ground, everyone is crowding in on him to shake his hand, pat him on the back, or at least to capture his glance. No one who was present will ever forget those minutes. As the peak of excitement passed, the crowd began to thin a little and we all walked toward our quarters.

"In the meantime, chairs and tables had been brought, and without restraint we all sit down around our Chief. This is his day. Colonel Hrabak is sitting beside him and is joyfully toasting him. At the Colonel's prompting, the Chief must recount the last suspenseful moments of his aerial battle. Everyone listens intently, suppressing their excitement as he tells the story.

"After an enormous feast, preparations for a little special celebration are made. The Chief wants to hold a special party with Bimmel and his technicians. Every bit of alcoholic beverage in sight is put on ice. A semicircle with straw as cushions is placed around the Chief's tent. A fire is built in the middle. At a predetermined hour, everyone is present. A deep, black night is spreading. Only the moon and stars are our spectators. The fire is lit. The leaping flames give the faces a unique expression.

"The bottles are passed, and we all drink with the Chief until shortly after midnight. When the last piece of wood falls into ashes, deeply impressed and moved by the occasion, we all stand up, bid the Chief good night and go to bed. So this adventureful day, which none among us will ever forget, came to its close."

Next day Erich was called to Colonel Hrabak's tent. There had been comradeship between them from the day Erich arrived at the front. When the time came for Hrabak to get some additional victories in order to win the Oak Leaves that now hung at his throat, Erich had been proud to fly as his *Kommodore's* wingman. Keeping such a fine comrade safe was a fighter's finest tribute to his leader. Now things had come full circle. Wreathed in smiles, Hrabak reached out and pumped Erich's hand.

"Bubi, congratulations. *Congratulations!* The Füher has awarded you the Diamonds. You are to report the day after tomorrow to the Wolf's redoubt at Insterburg, to receive the award from the Führer."

Erich had known all along that if he reached three hundred victories he would be awarded the Diamonds. He was prepared in his mind for the exalted decoration, but the official advice from the Führer's HQ still hit him with terrific impact. Hrabak was still talking.

"Only seven day-fighter pilots* have been awarded the Diamonds in this whole war. . . ."

Hrabak's words mingled with the whirl of Erich's own thoughts. One thought came uppermost. He would see Usch again, because there would be home leave after the visit to the Wolf's redoubt.

". . . before you go, Erich, we must of course have a big celebration party for the Diamonds. It is a rare honor, and JG-52 is proud of you."

Hrabak wrung Erich's hand again and he stumbled back out of the *Kommodore*'s tent. Two years ago Erich would never have believed that he would excel all Germany's air heroes within such a short time. He thought of poor Paule Rossmann, now in Russian hands. Paule was a part of this success. And Bimmel, what would he have done without him? But only one man got the award for the work of many; that was the military way.

The celebration party went boomingly, as the pilots replenished the squadron's supply of alcoholic beverages by cajoling, borrowing and bargaining. Another joyous night passed around the fire. Erich's head was still pounding when he climbed into his Me-109 the following day and checked the maps that he would use to navigate to Insterburg. As his fighter leaped into the air, an escort of his elated comrades flew around him, keeping watch over the lone Me-109 until it was well behind the lines. Then with a final wing-waggling salute they flew back to war, while Erich droned westward to the Wolf's redoubt.

Since the unsuccessful July 20 bomb plot, the Führer had moved to quickly eliminate the plotters and everyone remotely connected with those directly involved. The terror Hitler had unleashed was reflected in the changed atmosphere of the Wolf's redoubt as Erich reported to receive his Diamonds.

* Moelders, Galland, Gollob, Graf, Nowotny, Marsielle (posthumously), and Hartmann.

Fear and suspicion were evident on all sides. Security precautions were ultra-tight. The Führer's aides had divided the HQ into three zones of security, with an absolute prohibition against sidearms in the third, or inner zone. To get his Diamonds, Erich would have to enter the third zone.

Most soldiers summoned to receive high decorations from Hitler would have been glad enough to comply with the security regulation and take off their pistols. Erich felt himself balk. He felt humiliated by the suspicion inherent in the regulation. Controlling the rage that surged inside him, Erich spoke coolly to the SS security officer.

"Please tell the Führer that I do not want to receive the Diamonds if he has no *Vertrauen** in his front-line officers."

The security officer went pale.

"You want me to tell the Führer that you will not receive the Diamonds? Because of the pistol regulation?"

"Yes, please. Tell him what I said."

"Wait, please, Hartmann. I will see Colonel von Below."

"Please do."

As Hitler's Luftwaffe aide, Colonel von Below had already encountered Erich Hartmann before. He had been forced to sober up the Blond Knight when he arrived at Salzburg the previous year in a tipsy condition. He had met him again prior to the Swords award. The long-suffering von Below had a lot of experience with young fighter pilots. Now, for this brave blond boy the old cavalier would have to be a modifier of security regulations. If Hartmann refused the Diamonds, Hitler would probably go on a rampage.

The tall, blond Colonel von Below stalked out to the security officer's desk, a weary expression of resignation on his face.

"Hartmann, you can wear your pistol if you insist. Now please come in and get your Diamonds."

Erich felt himself cooling down as he walked into the Führer's reception room. In the normal way, he took off his cap and pistol belt and hung them on the stand provided. Hitler came in and took no notice of the presence of the

---

* Literally in German, "true-believe"—roughly equivalent in English to personal faith in the integrity of another.

weapon. Erich noticed that the Führer was markedly more stooped, and that the right arm still hung limply at his side.

Hitler's eyes were sunken and dull. His face was haggard and he looked completely exhausted. As the tired old man who had once held the world in thrall handed Erich the Diamonds, the Blond Knight saw that the Führer's one good arm was trembling.

"I wish we had more like you and Rudel,"* said Hitler.

After some coffee and brief inquiry after Erich's family, the Führer indicated that they would go to an adjoining building for lunch. Erich walked across the room and got his pistol belt and put it on. The Führer said nothing. Together they walked to another building containing the dining room. They sat down, and Hitler began discussing the war. This time, he spoke in different terms from those he had used on the previous two occasions when Erich was in his presence.

"Militarily, the war is lost, Hartmann. You must know this. But politically, there are such vast differences between the Allies—the British and Americans on the one hand, and the Russians on the other—that we have only to hold on and wait. Soon the Russians will be fighting the British and Americans as well as ourselves. The only alternative is for us to be overrun by the Bolshevist hordes, and you know what that will mean for the fatherland."

The Führer had heard many stories about guerrilla activity on the Eastern Front.

"Partisans, Hartmann, partisans. My generals tell me they are everywhere and do tremendous damage. What is your experience?"

"When I served in the Central Sector of the Eastern Front, sir, I came down twice in a heavily wooded area marked on our maps as occupied by partisans. Both times I walked out and never saw an enemy."

"I see. Then perhaps my generals misinform me?"

"Perhaps, *mein Führer*, I don't know. But partisans have not bothered us at any time.† I know that once in Rumania

---

* Colonel Hans-Ulrich Rudel, leading Stuka pilot of the Luftwaffe, and *Kommodore* of *Schachtgeschwader-2* (SG-2).

† Hartmann had not heard that two fighter pilots returning by train from leave in Germany had been killed by the partisans.

an air matériel depot where many aircraft were stored was bombed by the Americans, and it was reported as due to partisan activity."

"How do you know this, Hartmann?"

"It was common knowledge in our *Gruppe*, sir."

"Common knowledge? Hmmmm. Then I am more sure than ever before that a lot of my generals do *not* give me accurate information."

Hitler then abruptly changed the conversation to the air war over Germany.

"You have flown only on the Eastern Front, Hartmann. But what do you think about these bombing attacks on Germany by the Anglo-Americans?"

"From what I have seen and heard, we do not approach this problem correctly, in my opinion.

"Why not?"

"Reichsmarschall Goering has ordered that we fly any time the bombers come—day, night, good visibility or not, good weather or bad."

"And this is wrong, Hartmann?"

"In my opinion, yes, *mein Führer*. We lose too many pilots unnecessarily by forcing them to take off and land in weather so bad that a crash is a certainty. To convert all pilots to competent instrument flyers would take too long—at least a year. So I believe that we should save all our efforts for hard flying against the Americans in blue-sky weather—daylight operations. Then I think the bombing could be deterred."*

The Führer fidgeted with his lunch as they spoke.

"Tell me, Hartmann, you think training is insufficient now for fighter pilots?"

"I know it is insufficient, sir. I get young men coming to my squadron in Russia with less than sixty hours' total flying time, and only twenty hours of that in the Me-109. They have to fly combat with such slender training. This accounts for most of our Eastern Front fighter losses."

* Unbeknown to Erich Hartmann, this was the course of action being urged almost daily on Goering by the embattled General of the Fighters, Adolf Galland. His concept was to mount massive fighter strikes when conditions were favorable, a devastatingly effective tactic when he was permitted to use it.

Hitler assumed an absent expression. Erich went on with his story.

"These young boys come to us and are shot down practically immediately. They come and go in waves like this. It is criminal, *mein Führer*, and I think our home-front propaganda is to blame."

At this, Hitler sat up and showed some life.

"How?" he said.

"They know they are not ready to fly combat. They can barely get the Me-109 up and back safely as it is, without fighting. But they come to the front pleading fanatically, suicidally, to be allowed to go on operations."

Hitler looked incredibly tired, slumped in his chair.

"Hartmann, all you say may well be true. But now it is too late. As I said, the war is lost militarily. From all sides people come to me every day with ideas for rockets, tanks, guns, submarines, new operations, offensives, withdrawals, and with crazy inventions. I am the one who must decide. Now there is no longer any time. . . ."

The Führer stood up abruptly, and Erich knew the interview was at an end. Hitler's handshake was slack and perfunctory. When Erich left the Wolf's redoubt that twenty-fifth of August he knew he would never see Hitler alive again.

He flew back to Russia and his comrades crowded around to inspect the beautiful decoration and congratulate him yet again. The brave gaiety of his fighting pilots could not drive from his mind the conviction that the fatherland was disintegrating, and that final defeat could not now be averted.

Orders for ten days' leave came through the following day. He was to fly back to Berlin-Gatow for an interview with General Adolf Galland and go on leave to Stuttgart from there. In the cavernous interior of the Ju-52 transport he lost himself in his thoughts while the big motors thundered, carrying him home. Usch was only hours away now. He had 301 victories. Usch would be his 302nd victory. They would marry now, and damn the war.

CHAPTER ELEVEN

302ND VICTORY

Looking ahead is part of the challenge of living.
—*Captain Eddie Rickenbacker*

ERICH'S INTERVIEW with General of the Fighter Arm Adolf
Galland at his Berlin-Gatow HQ was brief and to the point.
Galland wanted to transfer Erich to the Me-262 Test Commando. This unit was combining flight testing of the revolutionary twin-jet fighter with limited combat operations. Erich's
piloting skill and fighting record undoubtedly suited him to
the task Galland had in mind, but the Blond Knight did not
wish to transfer.

Explaining to Galland his deep attachment to JG-52 and
his comrades, and his conviction that he was best serving his
country on the Russian Front, Erich followed with a direct
request that his transfer to the Test Commando be canceled.
Galland as a commander had an uncanny instinct for detecting hidden motives in his subordinates, and Erich's request
rang true. Galland valued comradeship as vital to the Fighter
Arm's morale, and he saw the merit of Erich's request. He
canceled Erich's assignment to the jets, and rescinded an
order that had taken the Blond Knight off combat operations
after he had received the Diamonds. Galland then cut orders
assigning Erich to the Fighter Pilots' Home (*Jagdfliegerheim*)
in Bad Wiessee, for rest and recuperation prior to return to
the Russian Front. Erich left Galland's HQ greatly relieved

that he would remain with JG-52, and more eager than ever to see Usch.

On the train journey from Berlin to Stuttgart, Erich made up his mind that previous marriage plans would be set aside. A year ago, when they had become officially engaged, he and Usch had decided to wait until he was promoted to captain before getting married. Just last month they set that arrangement aside in favor of a wedding at Christmas, 1944. Now everything had been changed by the war situation, and by Erich's receipt of the Diamonds.

Usch was waiting when Erich piled out of the train in Stuttgart. He embraced her and kissed her, his face all smiles.

"Usch darling, we're going to get married now, on this leave. We're not going to wait any more."

The future Mrs. Hartmann looked at him in surprise.

"But Erich, we just decided last month that we would wait until Christmas. . . ."

"I know. But things have changed. We have many married men in my Group at the front—men with families. They will get priority for Christmas leave. I probably won't even get home then."

"But Erich, I don't even have a dress to get married in."

Usch looked a little unhappy.

"You can buy one, Usch. Today if you like. But we must get married while I have the leave and the opportunity. Getting the Diamonds has changed things, too."

As they walked out to the car, Erich explained they could get married down in Bad Wiessee, at the rest and recuperation center for fighter pilots. He had been ordered there, and that meant they would not be able to get married in Weil or Stuttgart. Erich saw that Usch's face got a little longer as he delivered this news. Traveling about inside Germany was becoming increasingly difficult and hazardous. Sensing her disquiet, he leaned over and kissed her again as they sat down in the car.

"You will be my three hundred and second victory," he whispered.

Usch's face lightened.

"Is *that* what you're saying to everyone now, Erich Hartmann? That Usch is just another victory?"

"No, not just another victory. The only one that matters. . . ."

Erich kissed Usch again, and he knew she would come to Bad Wiessee for the wedding.

Two whirlwind days followed, which included a citizens' reception for Erich at the Sports Palace in Weil, then Erich was off to the Fighter Pilots' Home in Bad Wiessee. He left Usch preparing frenziedly for the most important day of her life. The wedding would take place on the following Saturday. Usch would come down by train via Munich on Friday, arriving at noon. This would give them time to conclude final details together. The plans were one thing, the actual events were something else.

Things went smoothly enough for Erich. The Fighter Pilots' Home was a comfortable and rambling building, with a large central banquet hall—a perfect place for the reception. Plenty of fighter pilots were on hand to assure a gay atmosphere. Tea dances were held every weekend, to which young women flocked from the surrounding areas for the attentions of the dashing young airmen. Manicured grounds and a nearby lake with sailboats for the tired fighter pilots, completed an idyllic backwater in which the war could be forgotten. Bad Wiessee was a perfect place for a honeymoon.

Installing himself in the Fighter Pilots' Home, Erich started organizing. He went to the local courthouse and arranged for the marriage license and other necessary documentation. Reception arrangements were lined up—food, champagne, general catering and an orchestra for dancing at the reception. Erich was soon irrevocably committed to a wedding, with much expense involved. He telephoned his father in Weil in a fever of apprehension.

"Everything here is set, Father. All the arrangements are finalized. Usch has *got* to come."

Dr. Hartmann's voice was reassuring.

"Of course she'll come," he said.

"Father, I want you to be sure that she gets the train out of Stuttgart on Friday. Could you telephone the Luftwaffe provost there and explain to him? Perhaps he will help her get to the railway station."

"Certainly I will, my boy. Now don't worry about it. Just be there to meet her."

As Erich hung up the phone, he reflected on the solid and quiet support he had always received from his father.

Usch was just as determined to get to Bad Wiessee as Erich

was for her to make the trip. An irresolute woman would probably have abandoned a journey fraught with the difficulties that confronted Usch. The Stuttgart railway station had been bombed out. Checking into the makeshift railway time-tables, Usch found she would have to get an early morning train from Kornwestheim in north Stuttgart in order to reach Bad Wiessee by noon. The Luftwaffe kindly sent a motorcycle and sidecar to collect her at 9 A.M., but by that time the dark-haired bride was well on her way to Munich, change-point for Gmünd, the closest railway station to Bad Wiessee.

As the train pulled into Munich, the air-raid sirens were wailing. Usch had to run to the nearest air-raid shelter as soon as she got out of the train. Three hours in an oppressive hotel cellar completely disrupted her schedule for meeting her bridegroom. For a bride on her wedding eve it was an unexpected and nerve-clanking ordeal. At the Fighter Pilots' Home meanwhile, the bridegroom with the Diamonds at his throat was undergoing a different kind of ordeal.

"Elf's Night" is a German tradition corresponding to similar prenuptial celebrations in other Western nations. The bridegroom's bachelor friends concentrate on getting him drunk for the last time as a bachelor. The celebrants then hurl old pottery and china into a fireplace, and the bride and groom clean up the mess the following day as their first domestic task as man and wife. Elf's Night began rather early for Erich.

Shortly before noon, Erich drove to Gmünd station with Dr. Alfred Rossbach, resident physician for the Fighter Pilots' Home. The doctor enjoyed the wartime luxury of a small car. Wreathed in smiles and bursting with anticipation, Erich strode quickly down the length of the train, looking for Usch. Disembarking passengers were soon all off the train, but Usch was not among them. As the train whistle blew for departure, Erich quickly checked the train again, compartment by compartment. Usch was not aboard.

"Usch must have missed her train connection," he said.

Dr. Rossbach's professional manner was soothing.

"She will get the next train, Erich. Let's find out when we can meet it."

The next train was due in two hours. Erich was upset. He was even more upset when he tried to call Stuttgart. The bombing had knocked out the telephone exchange and he was unable to complete the call. Dr. Rossbach rose to the professional challenge inherent in the crisis, and prescribed the proper palliative.

"Let's go back to the Fighter Pilots' Home and have a drink," said the doctor.

Erich nodded his agreement and off they went, chugging back over the country roads to Bad Wiessee. When they got back to the home, Elf's Night began for Erich. Today a successful physician in West Germany, Dr. Rossbach describes the ensuing events:

"Elf's Night started very early in the afternoon in my room, and in a short time we were all in a very happy alcoholic mood. We broke off proceedings briefly to drive again to the Gmünd station to meet Usch at the next train. Still no Usch. The dilemma was fought with large quantities of champagne and cognac, and after a while things did not seem anything like as serious as they had previously.

"Two more trains arrived, which we dutifully met, but still no bride. The mood of the Elf's Night party became even more critical. Walter Krupinski spoke up. 'She has thought the better of it, Bubi, she is backing out.' And for one awful moment Erich looked as though he believed him."

At the last train, after midnight, Erich had almost given up hope, but this time the bride arrived. Usch was exhausted but happy, and they drove back to Bad Wiessee. A few fighter pilots goggled approvingly through their alcoholic haze at the shy Usch, who was quickly taken to a nearby guesthouse. She was glad to fall into bed and leave her beaming bridegroom to the mercy of the elves.

Erich did not feel very strong the next morning, but he rallied to the challenge of the day, and put on his best uniform for the wedding ceremony. Witnesses and friends were rounded up and the party made its way to the courthouse. Erich's comrades from JG-52, Gerd Barkhorn, Willi Batz and Walter Krupinski, were all present, and Batz recalls the wedding:

"Gerd Barkhorn and myself were Bubi's wedding witnesses. Here we were, bride and groom at the head, Barkhorn to the left and me on the right as we entered the church. As we left the church in the same formation, we were all surprised at the portal to find a formation of Luftwaffe officers in full uniform, with swords drawn and held aloft in a saber arch. Bride and groom and then Barkhorn and myself all had to go through it. I can say today that it was a memorable and successful wedding."

The simple civil ceremony climaxed a great love. Under normal German custom, Erich and Usch would have immediately gone and repeated the ceremony in a church, but there was no Protestant church in Bad Wiessee. A church ceremony would have to wait until later—much later as it turned out. Erich's imprisonment in Russia imposed an eleven-year delay on the church wedding.

A couple of hours later, the wedding party got under way at the Fighter Pilots' Home. Champagne flowed freely at Dr. Hartmann's expense, and the fighter pilots made the most of it. A small band played for dancing, but as the evening wore on, Elf's Night and the day's events began to have their effect on Erich. The Blond Knight and his lady bade their guests good night, and adjourned to a luxurious suite prepared for them in the nearby guesthouse. While they slept, the party of reeling fighter pilots celebrated the 302nd victory far into the morning.

Honeymoon days in the tranquil countryside around Bad Wiessee made the war seem incredibly remote—until the Ardennes offensive flooded Germany with new hope. Newspapers were splashed with victory headlines as the Allied forces reeled under the German Army's assault. Berlin Radio blared out the probabilities of a second Dunkirk, with the British and the Americans pushed into the sea together.

Even the spell of the honeymoon was broken by the good news. Sugar-coated bad news had long been a steady diet in Germany. As a fighting airman, Erich knew the odds against the fatherland were long, but he heard the Ardennes news with soaring enthusiasm. He wanted to hear news like this. Such success could change a man's life.

These thoughts were racing in Erich's mind as he stepped into Dr. Rossbach's room to listen to radio reports of fresh triumphs.

"This is wonderful," said Erich. "We're going to have a big victory, and that means it's possible for me to have a family."

Dr. Rossbach was aghast.

"Erich, in times like these you would be wiser to wait to have a family. . . ."

"No, I don't have to wait, Doctor. Not now. I can have a family."

Erich was still the impulsive boy, not yet master of himself. Eight days after the wedding, when they left Bad Wiessee to return to Weil, Usch was pregnant and the Ardennes was being written down in the catalog of German failures. The happy reunion with the families at home was overshadowed by Erich's imminent return to the Russian Front. As the days passed he grew restive.

"Erich, something is wrong. What's bothering you?"

Usch already knew Erich better than he knew himself.

"It's my *Gruppe*, Usch, back at the front. I keep thinking about them all the time. I don't feel I have any right to be here in such happiness while they are out there fighting. I'm going to go back."

Usch's face fell.

"But Erich, your leave still has two weeks to run."

"I know. But I've got to go back. You understand why, don't you?"

Tears were welling up in her eyes as Usch nodded and smiled wanly.

"Do what you have to do, Erich. I'll help you get ready."

A few hours later, Erich was clambering into a Storch at Böblingen Airport. He taxied the little ship to the end of the same field from which he had taken off so many times in his gliders and in his mother's Klemm two-seater. Gunning the Storch into the wind, he felt her lift beautifully to his touch. As Usch's lovely face went flashing by below, there was a moment to wave and then she was gone. He set course for Krakau, where an Me-109 would be waiting to speed him back to the front. Under his breath he cursed the war blackly.

The newlyweds did not see each other at Christmas 1944. As Erich had feared, he was unable to get away from the front, but as the married men with families returned to their units after Christmas, others were released for a brief New Year's leave. Erich struck it lucky, but when he arrived in Stuttgart on New Year's Eve, the air-raid sirens were wailing and he and Usch had to run for it. There was time only for a brief embrace before they plunged into the shelter of the Wegenburg Tunnel.

The pressure of war on two fronts reached home sharply to Erich as bombs thundered into the city of Stuttgart overhead. Usch looked well enough, but there was no doubt that she was under a strain. She was three months pregnant, and living in the Hartmann home at Weil under Dr. Hartmann's good care, but that could not eliminate the larger tensions of the times. Sleep was fitful for the whole family, she told Erich. Every night they went to the cellar. The roar of the planes, the crash of bombs and the barking of the flak kept them all sleepless. Weil had not been bombed, but Böblingen and Stuttgart had both been pounded. Weil im Schönbuch was twenty miles from Stuttgart and only four miles from Böblingen but the bombers never touched the little town.

These somber tidings clouded the joy of their reunion, as they left the shelter of the tunnel and headed home to Weil. Erich felt deeply disturbed and was silent. Usch broke in on his disquieting thoughts.

"How long is your leave, Erich?"

His face brightened.

"Ten days. Ten whole days. It's going to be wonderful."

Less than wonderful was the telegram that came four days later. Erich was ordered to a special instrument course at Königsberg Neumark. The good-bye was hard this time, after only four days. Erich consoled himself with the prospect of another leave after the instrument course. The Russians crushed that dream with their offensive into Hungary.

The day after he arrived at Königsberg Neumark, emergency orders came through reassigning Erich to JG-52. His *Gruppe* was in the thick of the action down in Hungary, and instrument courses were not necessary to find and shoot down the hordes of Russian aircraft involved in the offensive. In the ensuing wild days of battle, the Blond Knight ran up his score to 336 victories, far ahead of Gerd Barkhorn, his closest rival. JG-52 was still fighting hard in March when Erich received another urgent telegram.

CEASE OPERATIONAL FLYING IMMEDIATELY REPORT LECH-FELD FOR CONVERSION TRAINING ON ME-262 TURBO

Erich was convinced as he flew back to Lechfeld that the war was irretrievably lost. He had seen the vast flood of men and matériel with which the Red Army was going to inundate Germany. Real fear welled up in him as he thought of the Russian hordes swarming into the fatherland. Getting Usch to safety, or at least to somewhere safer than Stuttgart, was uppermost in his mind. The baby was coming soon.

He had confided his fears to his adjutant, Captain Will Van de Kamp, whose family had a home in the country at Schongau, south of Lechfeld. Van de Kamp had immediately suggested that Usch move there until after the baby was born. Erich gratefully accepted his adjutant's offer.

After reporting at Lechfeld, Erich borrowed a Storch and flew over to Böblingen. With his father's help he managed to borrow an old truck, which he drove over to Usch's place in Rottenbuch. The shirtsleeved ace of aces piled their furniture and belongings on the truck, and drove Usch and all their worldly goods to the Van de Kamp home in Schongau, a charming old castle far out in the country. Invading troops would be unlikely to go near it, since it was remote from the main arteries.

The rural surroundings and sense of security conveyed by the old castle would help keep Usch happy until the baby arrived. Erich felt the anxiety that had been burning inside him subside as the Van de Kamp family made Usch welcome in her new home. Concern for her welfare had given him more bad moments than the Red Air Force as the war burned inexorably westward.

When they said good-bye in the German countryside, Erich's heart was happier than when he had left the front. Things in Schongau made it seem like the happy prewar years had returned. Verdant peace surrounded them. For a few precious moments they felt like carefree kids in love again, except that now their hearts sang with the thought of their child. Erich kissed Usch tenderly.

"Be brave, Usch. And don't worry for me," he said.

His lips would not touch hers again for ten and a half years. As his dark-haired and radiant loved one disappeared from view, Erich turned his thoughts to the challenge waiting him at Lechfeld—the revolutionary "Turbo" fighter—the jet-propelled Me-262 that he would learn to fly in the coming weeks.

The airfield at Lechfeld was hardly a place to inspire confidence, despite the presence there of the fastest fighter in the world. The base was bombed early every morning, and flying could not start until after the runway was patched, which usually took until about 10:30 A.M. Flying was only possible for about an hour and a half, because at 12:30 every afternoon formations of USAAF P-38's swept in at treetop height and hosed the base down with gunfire.

Mosquito fighterbombers sometimes followed up with ten or fifteen tons of high explosive. By night, more Mosquitos filled the air with the smooth but terrifying thunder of their Merlin engines. The RAF birds came swooping down to strafe any lights that showed near the Lechfeld base.

In charge of jet transition training amid this shambles was one of Germany's greatest air heroes, Lt. Col. Heinz "Pritzl" Baer. "Pritzl" was not as well known to the German public as Erich Hartmann, Hermann Graf or Adolf Galland, but in the estimation of his fellow pilots, none stood above him. A dark-haired, medium-sized man with a hawkishly handsome face, Heinz Baer was a hero's hero. He wore the Swords at his throat, and by rights should have worn the Diamonds. Two hundred and four victories stood to his credit at this time, and he had fought on every front where German fighters met the enemy. In the Me-262 he would bring down sixteen more British and American machines* to end the war with 220 confirmed victories, 120 of them aircraft of the Western Allies. Only the immortal Marseille would down more Anglo-American machines. Baer's job now was to prepare the finest pilots in the Luftwaffe to take the Me-262 into battle as a fighter.

A stellar collection of fighter pilot talent was being assembled for Adolf Galland's JV-44—an all-jet fighter unit that would later be called the Squadron of Experts. Nearly every pilot selected for JV-44 held some degree of the Knight's Cross, which was said to be the JV-44 squadron badge. Galland had fought a bitter and exhausting battle to get the

---

* Lieutenant Colonel Heinz Baer was the top-scoring jet ace of World War II with sixteen kills in the Me-262. He was the last C.O. of the Squadron of Experts, JV-44, formed by Adolf Galland.

Me-262 into action as a fighter plane, over the irrational edict of Hitler that the machine was to be used as a bomber. The young fighter general had made many enemies in his struggle, including Goering and Himmler, and the bureaucracy behind the Luftwaffe General Staff had been a frustrating drag on progress.

For years, Galland's strategic and tactical recommendations, to which history already assigns the stamp of genius, had been blocked, frustrated and nullified. After a series of increasingly acrimonious confrontations, he had been relieved of his command. Hitler and Goering then gave him permission to form a jet fighter unit and prove his contentions about the machine. Their expectation was that Galland would be killed.

This political intrigue and Galland's struggles lay outside the ken of the young Blond Knight. He was too busy battling on the Eastern Front while the drama of the Me-262 was being acted out behind the scenes. Checking out in the aircraft was therefore almost fun for Erich, with the witty and irrepressible "Pritzl" Baer making laughter out of even the hard conditions at Lechfeld. Galland came to the base at the end of March, and Erich was ordered to report to his office.

In his fourth wartime meeting with Adolf Galland, Erich found him little changed on the surface. The black-maned former General of the Fighter Arm, with his penetrating eyes, pencil-thin mustache and overpowering aura of personality was still an arresting figure. He greeted Erich with characteristic humor.

"Hello, Erich. I am now a squadron commander," he said.

"So I have heard, *mein General*," said Erich.

"I'm getting some top pilots together to take the Me-262 into action as a fighter. Colonel Luetzow, Colonel Steinhoff, Major Krupinski, Major Hohagen. . . ."

Galland was glowing with enthusiasm.

"I want you to join my squadron, Erich."

Baer had told Erich during his Me-262 check-out that Galland would probably want him to fly with JV-44. The prospect disturbed Erich deeply.

"What will I do in such a squadron, with all those big aces with long service and senior rank, *mein General?*"

"Why, you'll fly with us, of course. You are the top-scoring fighter pilot of the world."

"But *mein General*, I do not wish to fly again as someone else's wingman, and that will certainly happen if I join your squadron."

Galland hardly seemed to notice Erich's lack of enthusiasm, and a moment later a telephone was thrust into the young general's hand. He waved Erich away. The interview was over.

Walking back to his quarters, Erich pondered the Squadron of Experts idea. Steinhoff, Luetzow, Baer . . . they were all senior men, much older and more experienced than he. They were colonels, lieutenant colonels and majors and many of them had commanded Fighter Wings. He was a young captain and he had been a long time getting to be captain. He had the most victories, that was true, but beside Galland's experts in JV-44 he was a little boy of twenty-two—and he knew it.

Erich kicked a piece of shattered brick out of his way as he walked along, and cursed his luck. He'd rather be back with I/JG-52 on the Eastern Front, where he felt he belonged. There he was a *Gruppenkommandeur*, and had some control over his fate. He wondered how he was going to get out of the Squadron of Experts.

The following day an urgent telegram came to Lechfeld from Hermann Graf, *Kommodore* of JG-52, which was now operating in Czechoslovakia. Graf requested Erich's urgent return to command of I/JG-52. The unit was under heavy combat pressure. Graf's request proved a timely intervention in Erich's dilemma.

Two days later, Colonel Gordon Gollob made a fortuitous visit to Lechfeld. He was Adolf Galland's successor as General of the Fighter Arm, and an accomplished fighter ace in his own right with 150 victories. Like Erich, he wore the Diamonds, and was one of the nine Luftwaffe fighter aces to win the coveted decoration. Gollob had intense interest in new aerial armament, and wanted to see how the Me-262 training program was progressing at Lechfeld. Erich knew Gollob was the officer with the authority to send him back to JG-52. He managed an interview with the new General of the Fighters.

"I would like to request transfer back to my *Gruppe* in JG-52 on the Eastern Front, sir."

"Why? Don't you like the Me-262?"

"The Me-262 is fine, sir, but I have been with the men in

my *Gruppe* ever since I went to the front. I am proud of my unit and I believe I can do more there than flying the Me-262 here."

"Any other reasons?"

"Because we fly so seldom in the Me-262, due to the constant bombing and strafing, I feel as if I am doing nothing to help my country. With JG-52 I will be doing something positive. And my *Kommodore*, Colonel Graf, has requested my return, sir."

Gollob nodded. An Austrian with a good leader's intuition, he seemed to know what was going on in Erich's mind.

"All right, Hartmann. You may return to your *Gruppe*. I'll see that the orders are issued."

Within hours, Erich had an Me-109 in his hands again and was headed back to the Eastern Front. In later years, he would curse his precipitate desire to return to JG-52, and through the grim prison years he often wished that he had stayed with Galland in JV-44. But these ideas were far from his mind in the spring of 1945 as he elatedly sped away from Lechfeld. Awaiting him was a final series of battles that would include a new struggle with the Mustangs and the Americans of the USAAF.

1. Erich Hartmann, Luft-
waffe cadet in 1941.

2. Erich's parents, Dr. and
Mrs. Alfred Hartmann.

3. Erich's mother, in white blouse third from left, ran gliding
club at Weil and taught her sons to fly gliders. Here club members tow glider up slopes for run.

4. Hartmann and Ursula "Usch" Paetsch on June 14, 1943, the day of their engagement.

5. Hartmann sits in cockpit of his Me-109 fighter while crew chief "Bimmel" Mertens stands on wing.

6. Lt. Edmund "Paule" Rossmann took neophyte Hartmann on his first combat mission, which nearly ended in disaster.

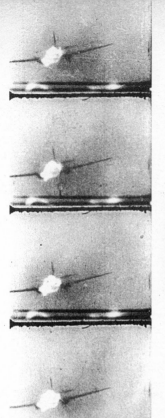

8. Major Hubertus von Bonin was *Gruppenkommandeur* of III/JG-52 when Hartmann reported to his first combat unit.

7. Gun camera on Luftwaffe Me-109 records the finish of Russian SB-2 bomber over Kerch, near Sevastopol.

9. Major Walter Krupinski was experienced fighter ace when Hartmann was assigned to be his wingman in the winter of 1942-43. The pair formed a strong fighting combination.

10. Crew chief Heinz "Bimmel" Mertens and Hartmann discuss bullet hole made by Russian bullet in windshield of Erich's Me-109.

11. Soviet IL-2 "Stormovik" dive-bomber takes hits from German fighter on Eastern Front.

12. Melting snows and spring rains turned ground into gigantic bog on Russian Front. Here JG-52 fighter is dragged through mud after landing from mission.

13. Hartmann takes oxygen test on Eastern Front during 1944, while JG-52 personnel watch.

14. Hartmann's wingman, Hans-Joachim Birkner, broken into aerial combat by Hartmann, had 117 victories in 14 months and won the Knight's Cross to the Iron Cross.

15. Most famous Soviet ace, Col. Alexander I. "Sacha" Pokryshkin was credited with 50 aerial victories.

17. Top-scoring allied ace, WW II, Soviet Major-General Ivan N. Koshedub of the Red Air Force was credited with 62 aerial victories over Luftwaffe.

16. This two-seater Ilyushin-2 ground attack aircraft was shot down north of Jassy, Rumania, on Aug. 12, 1944 by German fighters.

18. JG-52 airmen bicycle into Soviet village in Crimea.

19. Guenther Rall, for months Hartmann's C.O. on the Eastern Front, was one of the most formidable aerial fighters of all time, with 275 victories.

20. "Muscles and Head Flyer" is how Hartmann describes fighting technique of First Lt. Josef "Jupp" Zwernemann, 126-victory ace of JG-52 and early tutor of Hartmann.

21. German fighter with rapid closure rate nearly rams wounded Liberator near Bucharest.

22. German fighter bores into close range on Boeing B-17 over Bucharest.

23. Note black tulip-petal nose of Hartmann's Me-109 (Black Devil of the Ukraine). Also note spiral on propellor hub, feature believed by Luftwaffe pilots to confuse enemy ground gunners, and Hartmann's 1000 mission flight cap.

24. In 2 sorties on Aug. 24, 1944, Hartmann raised his victory tally to 301 and made 11 victory passes over bleeding-heart flight ramp. Here crewmen and compatriots wave congratulations as he signals 11th kill of day.

25. Hartmann received following telegram message: "Confirming your continued heralded accomplishments in the fight for the freedom of our people, I transmit herewith to you on your 300th victory as the 18th soldier of the German Wehrmacht the Oak Leaf with Swords and Diamonds of the Knights Cross—Adolph Hitler."

26. Hitler congratulates Hartmann after presenting him with the Diamonds award on Aug. 26, 1944. Germany's highest award was bestowed on only 27 servicemen between 1939 and 1945.

27. The wedding ceremony uniting Erich and Usch Hartmann. Ace Willi Batz is seated on Erich's left.

28. At Bad Wiessee, the Luftwaffe pilots from the *Jagdfliegerheim* made an arch of ceremonial daggers for the Hartmanns as they left courthouse. Erich jokingly called this his "302nd victory."

29. Erich and Usch Hartmann with Erich's parents.

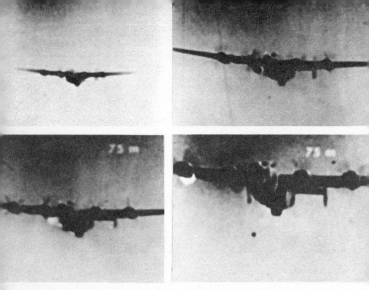

30. Here JG-52 fighter makes head-on attack on American B-24 "Liberator" over Ploesti oil fields. Last two photos show hits on No. 3 and No. 4 engines.

31. Twenty-two-year-old <u>Gruppenkommandeur</u>, with 3 squadrons of fighters under his command, Hartmann planned operations as well as flew. Here he plans sortie with aide in Czechoslovakia in 1945.

32. Lt. General Adolf Galland asked Hartmann to join his "Squadron of Experts," JV-44, formed near end of war after Galland was relieved as Luftwaffe General of the Fighter Arm. This would have kept Hartmann in the West, but he preferred to return to his old unit on the Eastern Front.

33. Hartmann pores over family snapshots while in Soviet P.O.W. camp.

34. Graf Siegfried von der Shulenburg and Hartmann became fast friends when they shared prison cell in Russia after war.

35. Harsh conditions existed in Soviet prison camps. A fitness test was administered monthly by a visiting Soviet nurse, here pinching buttocks of German prisoner for evidence of dystrophy which would disqualify prisoner from work detail.

36. Gaunt and emaciated Hartmann returns to free world on Oct. 15, 1955, after 10½ years in Soviet prisons.

37. Erich and Usch reunited after a decade. Erich chose to rejoin new Luftwaffe.

formation to oil-field protection on the Rumanian Front. Erich's squadron was ordered to operate from a grass strip at Zilistea, a few minutes' flying time from Ploesti.

He flew down to Rumania with his squadron, found the Zilistea strip and led his pilots in for a landing. Ground crews ~~t on ahead~~ to the makeshift base were waiting. Refueling ~~squadron~~ had barely finished when the order came

38. First major assignment was to raise and train first all-jet fighter wing, JG-71 Richthofen. At left is Bolko von Richthofen of famous family that produced Germany's leading ace of WW I.

39. Here The Blond Knight confers at HQ Air Defense Command, Colorado Springs, Col., with Lt. Gen. Robert M. Lee USAF, ADC COMMANDER.

40. Blond Knight beams his reaction to flight in an F-106 fighter at Tyndall Air Force Base, Fla., June, 1961.

CHAPTER TWELVE

41. Dec. 4, 1967, 12 years after release from prison, Hartmann and Ursula pose with daughter Ursula.

42. Hartmann examines space suit of astronaut John Glenn during visit to USA in 1961. Not yet 40, Hartmann was struck by mankind's progress in aerospace in the brief period of his own life.

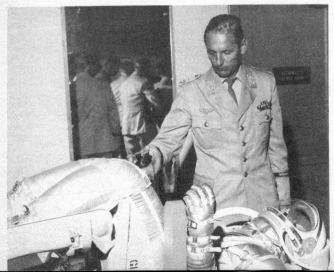

The Mustang created records from the day of its inspired
conception. . . .
    —William Green in
    Famous Fighters of the Second World War

FLYING BACK TO HIS *Gruppe* at Deutsch Brod in Czechoslovakia, Erich found his thoughts turning constantly to the earlier
battles with American fighters in Rumania. The P-51 was a
fast, maneuverable and rugged bird, as good or better than
the Soviet YAK-9. The old model Me-109's used on the
Eastern Front, which JG-52 had been forced to send up
against the Mustangs in Rumania the previous year, suffered
by comparison with the P-51. These older Me-109's, without
methanol injection for emergency high-altitude power, or for
escape, were at a serious disadvantage in combat with the
Mustangs.

Some good men and many aircraft had been lost by JG-52
in the struggle to defend Ploesti and Bucharest. Now that the
Americans were ranging into Czechoslovakia with their inex-
haustible Mustangs, Erich felt certain he would have to fight
them again soon. As he flew closer to the front he reviewed in
his mind his first, fierce encounters with USAAF fighters.

Orders leading to the first clash with the Americans came
after the disastrous Sevastopol battle and subsequent pell-mell
German evacuation of the Crimea. The USAAF chose this
time of heavy pressure on the Luftwaffe to begin its attacks
on the Ploesti oil fields near Bucharest. Crash orders pulled
I/JG-52 out of the Eastern Front battle and assigned the

161

of Erich's squadron to scramble.

He clambered back into his bird and the warm engine caught immediately. Bimmel was missing from the Zilistea advance party, so it was a strange technician who signaled all clear. Erich's *Schwarm* taxied to the end of the strip. Master Sergeant Carl Junger was flying as Erich's wingman, with Lieutenant Puls and Sergeant Wester composing the second *Rotte*. They all took off in good order, closely followed by the second *Schwarm*. The squadron's mission: protect other JG-52 fighters while they tried to get through to the "Fat Dogs" —the bombers.

The Americans had been running their bombing operations over Rumania as if their intention was to make interception of their formations by German fighters as easy as possible. Every day the Americans came over at the same time. Between 1100 and 1300 hours, the USAAF heavies hove into view with the precision of a well-run American railroad. Colonel Dieter Hrabak, JG-52's *Kommodore*, was delighted by the American penchant for accurate timing, even if a little incredulous at first. "We need no standing patrols," he told Erich. "We can bring maximum force to bear on them with minimum effort, and cause them maximum damage, because of the way they plan their operations."

Erich could hear Hrabak's words ringing in his mind as he went racing with his squadron toward Ploesti. The German flak was banging and puffing its black bursts all over the sky. The barrage was massive. Boring through the flak came gaggles of B-17 Fortresses, staggered horizontally and vertically in formations of ten to fifteen ships. Smoke trails reaching earthward showed that the flak had scored a couple of kills. Four miles farther back, droning in on Ploesti from the west, came a second huge gaggle of B-17's.

Erich was on about a level with the Fortresses. He checked his altimeter. Twenty-one thousand feet. No enemy fighter escort was in sight. That meant he would get a shot at the bombers. He drew the stick back and Karaya One went soaring upward, climbing south into the sun in a wide curve. Erich felt the sun was his friend, especially when it was at his back.

The altimeter needle spun up to 25,500 feet as he finished his climbing turn in an ideal position to attack the formation of bombers. A quick glance around him showed him that both his *Schwarms* were intact. He eased the stick forward to dive down on the bombers.

A tight formation of four Mustangs suddenly sliced across his line of vision three thousand feet below, a target too tempting to ignore.

"Attack the fighters," he said into his R/T.

The Me-109's went screaming down on the Mustangs. Erich judged his bounce perfectly, closing in rapidly behind the rear ship in the unsuspecting American formation. The distance between the two fighters shrank rapidly. Three hundred meters . . . 250 meters . . . 200 meters—"closer, Erich"—150 meters . . . 100 meters . . . the white and blue star insignia was close enough to touch. The P-51 filled his windshield. His guns roared for two seconds.

Pieces flew off the American fighter and thundered against Erich's wings. Smoke and fire billowed from the Mustang as Erich pulled left and up, the Messerschmitt easing around to his touch. More debris from the disintegrating Mustang showered against the empennage of Erich's kite. A quick glance back. A big, black and red fireball engulfed what was left of the fighter, while smoking chunks of wing and tail went tumbling earthward.

Erich snapped back to business. "No time to watch fires," he said aloud to himself. The next Mustang was already filling his windshield. Down came the distance again, even more rapidly this time. At 100 meters he pressed his gun buttons. Again he saw a Mustang sag and wobble. No explosion. No matter, Erich. The engine door peeled off the P-51 and inside Erich could see the red glare of an inferno. Emitting a plume of black smoke, the American fighter snap-rolled and fell into an uncontrollable spin. The P-51 was a goner.

Pulling up, Erich watched his second element flame two other Mustangs in quick succession. Looking down he saw the bombers still droning along below them, and nearby but closer, two other P-51's in a turn away from his position. Another perfect bounce beckoned.

"Attack the fighters again," he said on the R/T.

The Blond Knight's *Schwarm* went sweeping after the Mustangs. A perfect attack on the American wingman . . . down came the distance . . . 200 . . . 150 . . . 100 meters. A touch on the gun buttons and half the Mustang's wing sheared off with a bright flash. As the stricken machine went spinning down, Erich could see the pilot clambering out of the cockpit.

"Don't watch crashes, Erich. Get the leader."

The American leader had spotted Erich, but it was too late. He pulled his P-51 around to the left in a standard rate turn. Erich thought it was an incredibly clumsy maneuver until he saw that the American pilot still carried his external fuel tanks. Erich pulled Karaya One inside the Mustang's left turn, then pulled his fighter right as hard as he could and clamped down on the triggers. The P-51 rolled over to the other side, as Erich had expected, and flew right into the burst of fire. "Fool!" said Erich aloud. "He should have broken hard left."

Hits sparkled brilliantly on the Mustang's propeller and spangled their way back through the engine compartment and the full length of the fuselage to the tail. A long burst, it finished Erich's ammo, but it looked as though every round found its target. Red and black smoke came billowing from the Mustang, and seconds later a thick, white stream of glycol added contrast to the color pattern.

Diving under his foe and looking up at the riddled P-51, Erich saw the ten-foot tongue of flame licking backward along the empennage. The American pulled up and stalled, then went tumbling earthward. Erich watched the burning wreck for a sign that the pilot might still be alive.

"Jump! Jump! For God's sake, jump!" Erich was calling out as though the American pilot could hear him. The Mustang's canopy flashed clear of the cartwheeling fighter and the pilot struggled clear of his coffin. A sense of relief arose in Erich as the American's chute blossomed.

Erich glanced back and saw wingman Carl Junger was with him watching the crash. There was no point in stooging around here without any ammunition. High contrails were showing. More Mustangs were coming. Time to get out.

"Back to home base at Roman," he said on the R/T.

As they went barreling back in triumph to refuel and rearm, he was quietly talking to himself. "You were lucky today, Erich. Next time, maybe you won't be so lucky." At Roman, Bimmel was waiting to guide him into the parking area after touchdown, all smiles as usual. Switching off, Erich pulled back the canopy and held up four fingers of his left hand for Bimmel to see.

Bimmel beamed as he saw the sign for four victories.

"Mustangs?" Bimmel bellowed the question, knowing Erich would be partially deaf for a few minutes. Erich nodded and Bimmel whistled a little as he set to work once more preparing Karaya One for battle. He filled the ship with fuel, checked the oil, made sure there were full belts for all guns. He wiped the windshield and canopy and made a thorough visual inspection of the fighter.

Three more missions in the next few days were long on fighting but short on success. The Americans came winging in each day on their railroad timetable, so finding the bombers was easy. Attacking the heavies was a rugged task. The beating the Mustangs had taken in the first battle had put the American pilots on their toes. They were sharply alert, aborting Erich's attacks on the bombers. Hard dogfighting and whirlwind battles with the rugged Mustangs produced no results either way. Erich's *Schwarm* had some damaged aircraft, and there were hits on the enemy, but no confirmed kills. The Mustangs were doing a solid job of protecting the bombers, and a single *Schwarm* of Luftwaffe fighters heading for the bomber stream would draw whole squadrons of Mustangs in vigorous defense of the heavies.

Erich's fifth mission against the Americans began like the others, with a good interception at 20,000 feet in clear skies. He held his *Schwarm* at 23,000 feet as top cover for the attacking *Schwarm* assigned to assault the bombers. Watching the four 109's going in to attack, Erich spotted a gaggle of Mustangs plunging down on them from above, probably from 28,000 feet or higher. He hadn't seen the Mustangs, nor had anyone else in his *Schwarm*. They were lucky the American fighters hadn't seen them either, or the German top cover could have been bounced and shot down.

The Mustangs were intent now on bouncing the Me-109's a

thousand feet below Erich. Far beneath the bombers, Erich could see two more 109-s from another squadron, climbing at full boost and heading for the bombers. Behind this German element were four Mustangs in loose trail, climbing hard and closing fast on the unsuspecting Messerschmitts. Erich snapped on his R/T.

"Look back! Mustangs! Look back! Mustangs!"

The climbing pair of friendly fighters never wavered. They couldn't hear. Damn them. He couldn't do anything more for them now. His job was to protect the other *Schwarm*, with the Mustangs about to attack. Pushing his stick forward, Erich went lancing down after the P-51's, taking them from above and behind.

"Dive down and watch from below," Erich told wingman Junger.

The Mustang leader already had a lone Me-109 bore-sighted and was pouring fire into the German fighter. Three more Mustangs were lined up ready for a firing pass. "Four against one!" Erich saw red. He swept in on the American four from behind at maximum dive speed. Smoke was pouring from the stricken Me-109 as the American leader kept firing. Small pieces of the Messerschmitt were being blasted clear and whipped backward by the slipstream. The American .50-caliber guns were deadly, but not as devastating as the 20-mm cannon on the Me-109.

Four hundred . . . 300 . . . 200 . . . 100 meters . . . the distance came flashing down in split seconds. The Mustang with its checkered tail looked as big as a barn. Erich's windshield was all P-51 as he came rushing in on the rearmost American from below and behind, at a perfect thirty-degree attack angle. He pressed his gun buttons. A blast of fire and an explosion shook Karaya One as the P-51 blew up.

Erich switched instantly to the third Mustang, whose pilot seemed momentarily paralyzed. The Mustang took an all-guns volley of hits from Karaya One and began burning. The American kept flying, and now it was Erich's turn to feel the lash.

"Bubi, Bubi, behind you! Break! Break!" Sergeant Junger's alarm rasped in his headphones.

Erich stroked the stick forward, diving down hard. He felt his eyes bulging in their sockets, and his helmeted head bounced against the canopy as negative G's boosted him hard against his safety belt. In heavy left spirals at full power, the Blond Knight went plummeting down, the Mustangs hot on his tail.

"Back to base on your own. I'll make it alone," he radioed his wingman. That would give Junger a chance. There were too damned many American fighters for him to deal with anyway. The horde of them strung out behind Erich now were determined that this lone Messerschmitt would not escape their vengeance.

Erich looked in his mirror and quickly to each side. Damn! *Eight* of the deadly Mustangs were tearing after him. His negative-G break had momentarily foiled them, and he'd gained some distance as a result, but he was in a tight spot. He began talking aloud to himself, as though acting as his own guardian angel.

"All right Erich, keep your head now, and *fly*. Fly like you never flew before."

The P-51's split into two four-ship elements and sandwiched Erich neatly. They were as fast as he was. That made it rough.

"Hard turns, Erich. Real hard turns, or you'll have bullets in your whiskey stomach."

He reefed Karaya One around hard left and the aerial baseball game began, with the Blond Knight as the ball. Hard right—a blast of gunfire from two of the Mustangs . . . hard left—a storm of tracer from the other side . . . hard right—more gunfire.

"You're lucky, Erich. They're not top shooters. They open fire too soon, too far out. You're lucky again, Erich. If they knew what you know you'd be dead. . . ."

Hard right . . . hard left . . . and in the blood-draining turns where the Mustangs sometimes swung close to him, he fired his own guns.

"You know you won't hit them like that, Erich, but they'll see the tracer. May rattle them a bit. Besides, the sound of your own guns makes you feel better when they've nearly got you."

The eight relentless Americans and the lone German went rat-racing across the Rumanian sky, the roar of the American fifties ringing out at intervals and Erich dodging the tracer. In seconds he could feel the perspiration running down his body under his uniform. His adrenalin-charged body was pouring out sweat. His face was streaming as though he were sitting in a stream bath, and his vest and shirt were saturated. Even his uniform was becoming damp. Hauling the Messerschmitt round in these murderous turns was an ordeal of hard labor.

Amid the periodic hammering of the American guns and the groaning of his overstressed Karaya One, thoughts of the past poured through Erich's head. The sports of his boyhood swam before his mind's eye. "Good thing you liked gymnastics, Erich. Gave you the strength to keep your hide whole. Your coordination is saving you now."

He made another try with his guns when there was a slight chance of hitting a P-51 in one of the tight turns, but this time his guns were dead. All through the numbing turns Erich had kept slowly working his way back toward his base. He was actually gaining slightly on the Mustangs, beating them by a hair in each turn and drawing away a few yards each time.

The Americans might have been losing a few yards, but they were staying glued to the Blond Knight's tail, firing often but wildly. They couldn't quite pull enough lead on their quarry to score a hit, but they were keeping up the pressure. The kill was going to be theirs even if they had to split it eight different ways.

"Keep going, Erich. Keep going. The flak near the base will take these leeches off your tail."

Erich swung into another grinding turn.

"Damn!"

The fuel warning light on the dash glared red. Karaya One was almost out of fuel and he was too far from the base to land the fighter even if he dared.

"Make a fast bailout, Erich. Flip her over on her back, quick but easy."

He released his safety belt. As he came out of the next turn, he tripped the emergency release for the canopy. The plexiglas cover went whipping away in the slipstream and the wind howled and tore around the cockpit. Coming out of the next turn, Erich sucked back on the stick with all his strength, hauling it back into the pit of his belly. As the 109 went soaring upward and over, he released the stick and shot clear of the doomed aircraft.

Sky, earth and trees; wheeling Mustangs and his own booted feet flashed before him in a wild kaleidoscope as he went tumbling earthward. He pulled the D-ring. There was a rustling of silk and cord followed by the plumping sound of the opening umbrella. A bone-bruising jerk shook every joint in his body as he was jarred upright in the parachute harness. He was swinging helpless in his chute surrounded by eight angry Mustangs.

For German fighter pilots it was unthinkable to strafe an enemy pilot hanging in his parachute. They regarded that not as war and fighting between soldiers, but as murder. This chivalrous tradition may have seemed out of place in total war, but the Luftwaffe lived by this code to the end. Swinging under his silk umbrella, the defenseless Blond Knight wondered if his American foes would act the same way. He thought how horrible it would be if they didn't. Was he going to die by mid-air strafing, and fall to earth as a bundle of bloody rags?

A Mustang lined up on him as though for a firing pass. Erich's entrails contracted into a tight ball. For one blinding instant he thought of Usch. Then the American fighter went roaring past a few yards away. An ugly face under a white and yellow helmet glared at Erich through huge goggles that made the pilot look indescribably malevolent. The American's hand went up, there was a manly wave, and the Mustang banked around.*

Erich felt happy to be alive. He felt even happier as the eight Americans formed up on their leader and went streaking off to the north. As he came floating down to the good green earth he told himself again and again, "You are lucky, Erich. You are a lucky boy. By God, you'll have a birthday party tonight."

He came down a little less than four miles from the base, and an army truck took him back to his squadron. The air at HQ was full of bad news. Nearly half the *Gruppe's* aircraft had been shot down. Two pilots were killed and a number of others wounded. Without methanol injection, the old type Me-109 would not cut it against the Mustangs, even with experienced pilots. Higher HQ ordered an immediate halt to

---

* In general, victorious pilots of all nations avoided shooting at parachuting airmen.

fighter attacks on the Americans because of these heavy losses, and the certainty that they would become worse.

Erich Hartmann's *Gruppenkommandeur* during this period was Captain (now Lt. Col.) Willi Batz, a long-time comrade and admirer of the Blond Knight. Batz recalls the struggle to defend Ploesti in these terms:

"In the latter part of May we were forced into combat on two fronts. Fighters were direly needed everywhere, both against the Russians and in the south in Rumania guarding the Ploesti oil fields against American four-engined bombers. I remember well those hard times, because they not only called upon all our resources as fighting pilots, but also placed heavy demands on our ground support forces.

"In defending the Ploesti oil fields, I always made Bubi, at his own request, the head fighter pilot. We always went up together, the whole *Gruppe*, and Bubi would take his squadron and protect the rear against the Mustangs. He accomplished his tasks brilliantly. This type of four-motored aircraft was not familiar to us Eastern Front pilots, but because of Bubi we suffered relatively minor losses. He always managed to protect us, hold the Mustangs in abeyance and keep them off our necks. Only because of Bubi's experience were we able to find success against the bombers. Today [1967] I do not recall how many Bubi shot down in Rumania but I know he was successful against the Mustangs and saved us from greater losses."

Erich reviewed these five battles with the P-51 Mustangs, which had taken place in the spring of 1944, as he droned through his air journey back to Czechoslovakia. Almost a year had passed since he had battled the Americans in Rumania. By now, they would certainly be stronger. When he landed at Deutsch Brod, his comrades in I/JG-52 confirmed his apprehensions. American fighters were penetrating into Czechoslovakian skies regularly. Within a few days, the Blond Knight was again tangling with the Mustangs of the USAAF.

A Russian bombing raid was reported headed for Prague. Erich got the order to scramble. He was to take up a *Schwarm* to intercept the bombers. Bimmel had everything ready and Erich was airborne in minutes, heading for Prague and climbing hard. At 21,000 feet he leveled off and began scanning the skies for the enemy.

The Russian force soon hove into view. Erich counted about thirty bombers, a mixed formation of lend-lease A-20 Douglás Bostons and Russian Pe-2's. Flying top cover was a force of about twenty-five fighters, YAK-11's and P-39 Airacobras. The Red fighters were at about 12,000 feet. Erich switched on his R/T.

"Attack in two elements."

With the sun at his back, Erich was ready to push the stick forward and go diving down on the enemy force. He hesitated. His intuition pricked at him. Then from the corner of his eye he caught sight of a line of contrails, a little higher than his element, descending and closing in from the west. His first thought was that more 109's were coming in to join the attack, but a series of silver flashes from the incoming strangers eliminated them as friends. Polished metal surfaces had long ago been done away with on German fighters. All Luftwaffe ships were painted. They didn't flash in the sun. Polished surfaces usually meant one thing—Americans. Soon the strangers could be recognized. Mustangs!

The silvery craft came in about three thousand feet below Erich and his wingman as they held their altitude. The Mustangs began circling slowly three thousand feet above the Russian top cover. The Americans hadn't seen Erich above them. With the sun behind him and an altitude advantage, he was perfectly set up for a classic bounce. Russians and Americans were now obviously watching each other instead of their tails. The timing was perfect. Erich switched on his R/T.

"We'll make one pass only. Down through the Mustangs, on down through the Russian top cover, and down through the bombers."

At full power the two Me-109's went screaming down on the upper circle of Mustangs. Closing like lightning, Erich's fighter shook briefly with a burst of gunfire and the rearmost Mustang never knew what hit him. The P-51 staggered and went down out of control, tumbling and smoking and dumping debris. In a shallow turn Erich found the next Mustang rushing in to fill his windshield at point-blank range. Erich's burst thundered into the P-51's engine compartment and the American ship nosed up suddenly. With a rolling-out movement, the stricken Mustang went diving down beside Erich, out of control, smoking heavily and shedding chunks of its structure as it rushed to final impact.

Erich's engine was screaming and Karaya One was shuddering as he tore on down at full throttle through the Russian fighter cover. No chance to fire on the fighters. Going too fast. Now the Bostons, rushing up like hell. He squeezed his gun buttons and saw pieces blasted away from one bomber. Hits! Hits! Yes, but nothing mortal. On and down through the bombers and then the brain-glazing pull-out.

The awful suck of gravity on his body drew Erich into a momentary gray-out. He released some of the back pressure on the stick to maintain his vision. As the 109 moaned through its pull-out curve and came up near level with the bombers, Erich checked his tail. His wingman was still with him. What of the second element? He searched the sky.

The second element came slashing down through the Allied formation. Another Mustang came down blazing, but its pilot bailed out and Erich saw the silk billow behind the tumbling flyer. Timing his turn, Erich joined up with the second element as it pulled out, and all four 109's went racing away, their camouflaged aircraft all but indiscernible from above.

Looking back, Erich saw an unexpected and savage consequence of his lightning attack. The Russian YAK's and Airacobras were dogfighting with the Mustangs! The Russians were watching the Americans when Erich drove home his attack. The suspicious Red pilots must have thought the Americans had attacked them. Panic gripped the Russian bomber pilots. They jettisoned their bomb loads, blasting a stretch of empty countryside, then swung around on a reverse course. They were abandoning their mission.

The Russo-American dogfight continued at a furious pace. From the milling droves of planes Erich saw three YAK-11's come flaming down, while a Mustang went limping off to the south belching glycol. Erich shook his head with incredulity. As Allies, the Russians and the Americans seemed to have little trust in each other. Hartmann could not restrain a hearty belly laugh as his Me-109 nosed down and streaked for home.

There would be no more battles between Erich and the Mustangs. The end of the war was imminent. The Americans seemed to know they had won the war, and were confident, numerous and sure of themselves. In big gaggles they felt safe as they ranged over Europe at will, pouncing on every enemy they could find. Sometimes their confidence led to diminished vigilance, as in the battles with Erich Hartmann.

Today Erich writes of vigilance in the air on the basis of his better than eight hundred aerial battles:

"In a kind of auto-suggestion, from my own first crash in training until my last landing on 8 May 1945, I never slept in the air. I always had a bad feeling after take-off, because I never had the idea that I was or could be better than any other pilot in the air at this moment. My stomach felt bad during flight to the instant when I recognized my foes. From that moment, I had the feeling of *absolute superiority...*

"I was afraid in the air of the big unknown factors. Clouds and sun were hate and love in my feeling world. Today I am sure that eighty per cent of my kills never knew I was there before I opened fire. My dogfights were fast and simple on that account. But one factor always worked for me more than any other. I found I could spot enemy planes long before my comrades—sometimes minutes before them. This was not experience or skill, but an advantage with which I was born. My rule for airfighting is this:

"THE PILOT WHO SEES THE OTHER FIRST ALREADY HAS HALF THE VICTORY."

In battling the Americans, Erich Hartmann redressed a technical disadvantage by skill and experience, and downed seven of the formidable Mustangs, whose demise was confirmed. When the odds in combat were eight to one against him and the Mustangs had him cold, he triumphed over their best efforts to outfly him and shoot him down. He lived to tell the tale because his American pursuers had not forgotten their sportsmanship, fought fairly, and did not stoop to murder.

CHAPTER THIRTEEN

SURRENDER

We are still savages at heart, and wear our thin uniform of civilization awkwardly.

—*George Bernard Shaw*

BY 8 MAY 1945, operations by I/JG-52 were clearly coming to an end. The German effort in Czechoslovakia had lost all cohesion, and the Russian juggernaut rolled on virtually unopposed. Lieutenant Colonel Hermann Graf and the JG-52 Wing Staff were at Deutsch Brod with Erich's I *Gruppe*, and it was Graf who ordered the Blond Knight's final war operation.

Mission: Find out how far the Russian spearheads were from Deutsch Brod.

Karaya One's instrument panel clock read 0830 as Erich took off with a wingman, and climbing to 12,000 feet, headed east. Using the main road as a line of reference, Erich flew toward the nearby town of Brünn, the closest main center to Deutsch Brod. A smoke pall hung over Brünn like a big black mushroom. The enemy was probably already in the town.

Circling around the smoke cloud, Erich could see heavy fires in the town. The Russians were either bombarding the place or had already begun occupation. On the eastern outskirts, he could see columns of Russian troops and vehicles swarming toward the center of the town. Erich stiffened in his seat. He spotted a loose gaggle of eight YAK-11's flying around the same smoke cloud. The Russians were below him. Intent on the blazing scene in Brünn, the Red pilots did not see Erich and his wingman on the perch, and they were jinking around the sky as if they were taking part in an air show.

Seemingly in a victory salute to the Red Army on the ground, one YAK-11 pulled up into a loop right below Erich. The Blond Knight flicked his wing to signal "attack" to his wingman, pushed his stick forward and sent Karaya One lancing down into firing position just as the Russian reached the top of his loop and hung there inverted. The range came winging down rapidly to two hundred feet. The YAK filled Erich's windshield. He pressed his gun buttons and seconds later broke away in a smoothly coordinated strike. The short burst struck home solidly into the Russian fighter. Snapping over, the YAK began burning and went tumbling down out of control, gushing black smoke. Exploding in a field outside the town, the wrecked Red fighter burned fiercely and added its smoke to the thickening cloud over Brünn. The YAK-11 was Erich Hartmann's 352nd victory.

Erich was in the "See — Decide" phase of another attack on the wheeling YAKs when he caught sight of a flash in the air high above him. Twelve aircraft were flying in tight formation. More flashes from their polished surfaces left no doubt as to their identity—Mustangs. In a potential sandwich between Russians and Americans, Erich put Karaya One's nose down, and with his wingman close beside him plunged into the sanctuary of the smoke pall.

Bursting out of the smoke cloud on the west side and heading for Deutsch Brod at full throttle, Erich looked back immediately to be sure he had eluded the Mustangs. He had lost them, but the Russians were less fortunate. Once again the USAAF and the Red Air Force had mistaken each other's identity. YAKs and Mustangs were whirling in a savage dogfight over Brünn. Erich saw no aircraft go down, but he had no intention of going back to assess the damage the two Allies were doing to each other. The situation was not without humor.

As he set Karaya One down on the improvised airstrip at Deutsch Brod, he knew he had flown his last mission and shot down his last foe. He had downed 261 single-engined fighters, and 91 twin-engined aircraft in slightly over two and a half years of combat. The end of the war was now only hours away for I/JG-52. As Karaya One's engine hissed into silence,

Erich dragged back the canopy to hear bad news from Bimmel.

"The Russians have been shelling the field. We are lucky there are no holes in the runway," said Bimmel.

As Erich swung down from his Me-109 for the last time, the ever faithful Bimmel made ready to refuel and rearm the fighter. Erich caught Bimmel's eye. The Blond Knight shook his head. They both knew Karaya One would never fly again.

Lieutenant Colonel Graf was looking glum and strained when Erich walked into the *Kommodore's* tent to make his mission report.

"The Russians are already occupying Brünn, sir."

Graf nodded.

"I figured that," he said, "but I had to be sure. We're in a pincer here."

Graf's finger pointed to the town of Strakonitz on an area map spread out before him.

"American Army tank units are occupying Strakonitz, one hundred kilometers to the West. Small advanced tank units are reported in villages right up to the demarcation line— that's the Moldau River—between the American and Russian zones. And the Russians are in Brünn. For us, the war is over, Bubi."

"Do you mean we surrender, sir?"

"Yes, I have the order. But first, you and I must make a decision that is for us alone."

Graf handed Erich a radio message.

GRAF AND HARTMANN BOTH FLY IMMEDIATELY TO DORT-MUND AND SURRENDER TO BRITISH FORCES ALL OTHER JG-52 PERSONNEL WILL SURRENDER AT DEUTSCH BROD TO SOVIET FORCES.

GENERAL SEIDEMANN
AIR FLEET COMMANDER

Hermann Graf's face was twisted into a wry grin. He looked directly at Erich.

"The General doesn't want you and me to fall into Russian hands. He knows that things will go hard with two winners of the Diamonds."

Graf flicked the decoration at his throat.

"You and me, Bubi, nearly five hundred and fifty Russian aircraft shot down between us. They'll probably stand us up against a wall and shoot us on sight."

"Then we are going to obey General Seidemann's order?" said Erich.

Graf stepped over and threw back the tent flap.

"Look out there, Bubi. Over two thousand women, children and old people—relatives of wing personnel, refugees fleeing from the Russians—all of them defenseless. Do you think that I can go and jump in a 109 and fly to Dortmund, and just leave them?"

"I agree with you, sir. It would be wrong for us to leave. We can't do it."

"I'm glad you agree. So we can forget the order, and stay with our people. We also forget about surrendering to the Russians."

Graf plunged into details about a convoy with which they would try and reach Pisek in the American zone, where they would surrender to the U.S. Army. He then assigned Erich the responsibility of seeing that the aircraft and munitions were destroyed.

Erich strode out on the field and set about the grim business of burning up what was left of JG-52. There was still fuel and ammunition for the Messerschmitts, but if they took off again the Russian artillery would have the field boresighted and a barrage would kill the hundreds of women and children who were now packing up for their final move. Their safety had to come first.

"Collect all munitions at the armorers' hut. Break open all ammunition boxes ready to destroy munitions. Open all fuel lines of the aircraft and assemble the aircraft as closely together as possible. Collect all fuel. We are going to destroy everything."

Erich rapped out the orders and personnel sprang to comply. The 109's stood with their long noses pointed at the sky. They would fly no more. Airmen slopped gasoline over the once-proud fighters and made ready to put JG-52 to the torch. Twenty-five Messerschmitts would make a hell of a bonfire.

Bimmel opened the pet-cocks on Karaya One. The area reeked of gasoline as the twenty-five aircraft on the field were similarly drained, and drums of gasoline were upended to spill their contents on the ground. Erich checked to be sure that all the women and children were gone. The column of civilians was moving away, shepherded by the personnel of JG-52. The sad moment had come.

Erich jumped into the cockpit of Karaya One.

"Keep back, Bimmel! I'm going to fire the ammunition off into the woods."

Bimmel sprang clear as Erich pressed Karaya One's gun buttons for the last time. Sitting in the cockpit, Erich was astonished by the size of the flashes from the gun muzzles. At high speed in combat they never flared like that. A mighty flash followed as the gasoline vapor was ignited by the gun flashes. In seconds, Karaya One was enveloped in flames and Erich scrambled wildly out of the cockpit. Damn! He could be burned alive on the ground! Out! Out!

Bimmel stood transfixed as the fighter exploded into fire. He made to dash for the ship, but the smoldering figure of the Blond Knight burst out of the flames. Singed hair and two burned hands were Erich's souvenirs of Karaya's fiery farewell. Bimmel ran and jumped aboard a departing truck as soon as he saw his chief was unharmed. That was the last Erich saw of Bimmel.*

As the fire went leaping through the dump of fuel, ammunition and aircraft, it was a hard moment for the fighter pilots of JG-52. Their beloved Me-109's were quickly engulfed in fire. Seeing their trusted mounts burning on the ground by their own hand undermined even some of the tough guys who had ridden them into battle. Defeat had scaly wings.

As Erich piled into a waiting staff car, the ammunition and cannon shells began exploding, punctuated by heavier blasts as drums of fuel detonated. A pillar of smoke swirled up into the morning, and the heavy, black cloud formed an appropriate marker for the pyre of Germany's most successful Fighter Wing. Erich took one last backward glance. Karaya One was sinking to earth on its collapsing undercarriage, and as it hit the ground, the fighter disappeared behind a consuming curtain of fire.

* Sergeant Heinz "Bimmel" Mertens rode the truck to the American lines, and afterward continued hitchhiking westward. He was at home in Kapellan within three weeks, and thus avoided Soviet captivity.

Erich made his way to the head of the strange column. Leading this odd and straggling assemblage was his last act as an officer of the Luftwaffe. He shared this unusual duty with Lt. Col. Hermann Graf and Major Hartmann Grasser, *Kommodore* of JG-210, who had joined them with his wing staff just before the end at Deutsch Brod. Grasser was a steadying professional presence at a difficult time.

A Battle of Britain ace who had flown with distinction on all fronts, Grasser wore the Oak Leaves and was credited with 103 victories. Trained before the war as a professional Luftwaffe officer, Grasser was for a long time adjutant to the immortal Colonel Werner "Daddy" Moelders. As *Kommodore* of JG-210, he had been organizing the flying training of refugee Russians to take the air against the Red Air Force. These Russian air units flying on the German side were envisioned as air support for the Russian rebel forces fighting with the German Army under General Vlasov, one-time hero of the defense of Moscow. At the end of the war, the Americans immediately turned Vlasov over to the Russians and he was hanged, taking with him his intimate knowledge of the men in the Kremlin. Such was the lunacy abroad in the world at that time.

In the late afternoon the column was nearing Pisek. Erich saw a few U.S. Army tanks moving cautiously down the road. The American drivers stopped their vehicles when they saw the Germans streaming toward them across the open fields. Graf and Erich approached the leading tank and saluted the American officer watching the scene from the turret.

"I am Lieutenant Colonel Graf, Commanding Officer of Fighter Wing 52, German Air Force. This is Major Hartmann, Commanding Officer of No. 1 Group of my wing. The people with us are the personnel of that unit, together with German civilian refugees. We surrender to the United States Army."

The American officer plucked a walkie-talkie from inside the turret of his tank and began talking to his HQ in Pisek. Within a few minutes, a truckload of American GI's from the 90th U.S. Infantry Division pulled up beside the tanks. The GI's piled out and began herding the Germans into a field beside the road. The Americans relieved the Germans of their weapons. Officers were permitted to retain their pistols and were charged with maintaining discipline.

German wristwatches were highly regarded as souvenirs by Allied troops, and the captured personnel of JG-52 had to relinquish theirs to their captors. The Americans already had wristwatches of their own, and this puzzled Major Hartmann Grasser. Erich heard the ultra-correct Grasser speak to a fresh-faced American second lieutenant who took his watch.

"Surely you have sufficient wristwatches in a rich country like America?"

The young American grinned and nodded his head.

"Sure we do. But these are souvenirs. That makes them different."

While the Americans were organizing the German captives, Czech civilians and a few American soldiers pounced on the German staff cars and other vehicles. Everything worth taking was seized by the souvenir hunters, and at this time, Erich lost his logbook, photo albums and other records. The fate of these items remains unknown.

The Americans treated some of the German women to admiring glances, but left them alone with their families. Erich felt a profound sense of relief. To lose wristwatches and other personal souvenirs was a small price to pay for the security of being in American hands. In areas of Germany already under Soviet occupation, the Russian troops had indulged in sexual debauchery against the German women hardly paralleled in modern times. Erich gave thanks that his men and their families would be spared this debauchery, as the American officers had given their word that JG-52 would not be turned over to the Soviets.

What Erich did not know was that the U.S. 90th Infantry Division and the U.S. 16th Armored Division working with it, were executing unauthorized reconnaissance thrusts far beyond the eastern limits imposed by their orders. Pilsen was the easternmost objective of the U.S. Third Army. In high Allied councils, Russia had been selected as Czechoslovakia's liberator. This meant that all Germans captured east of Pilsen by the U.S. Army had to be handed over to the advancing Russians.

This doctrine was later extended to cover any German soldiers or airmen who had fought against the Soviet Union, but was aimed primarily at professional German officers. The punishment of these men was a firm Soviet goal. The extermination of fifty thousand professional German officers was joshingly referred to by Stalin and Roosevelt at the Teheran Conference, much to the horror of Winston Churchill.* What was passed off as a joke between Roosevelt and Stalin came perilously close to becoming an active project in the postwar years, when it was not uncommon for professional German officers to be seized in the night at their homes and spirited off to years of slavery in Russian prison camps.

Strangely enough, it was the professional officers of the German forces, forbidden by law to belong to any political party—including the Nazi party—who were largely innocent of political involvement. The idea that prisoners of war should be conveyed to the Soviet Union after legitimate capture by the forces of another Allied power, such conveyance being for the specific purpose of punishment, was a sharp departure from prior procedures. Precedents were established in P.O.W. treatment by these processes that have in latter years brought hardship to many American servicemen captured in Asian conflicts.

Erich's column of refugees and surrendering soldiers was placed in a chicken-wire enclosure near Schüttenhofen in western Bohemia. Thousands more refugees and soldiers from other disbanded German units poured into the compound, which was guarded at each end by an American tank. The open-air camp soon contained over fifty thousand soldiers and civilian refugees of all ages, ranging from children up to old men and women.

Conditions soon became deplorable and sanitation a major problem. The officers were hard put to maintain order at times. The American guards began to close their eyes to the large numbers of "prisoners" who simply drifted off westward, seeking to find their way home as best they could. Many Americans gave advice to the escapees, and assisted many of them with maps and meager handouts of chocolate and GI rations. The action of the Americans was not sanctioned by any military order or decree, but their attitude was essentially the most practical course of humanitarianism open to them. The guards simply figured that the refugees would be better off foraging for themselves and finding their way home, than practically starving to death while they slept on the ground in the Schüttenhofen pen.

* See *Closing the Ring* by Winston S. Churchill, pp. 373–374 (published by Houghton Mifflin Co., Boston, 1951).

The situation at this camp, and in many others in the same general region, accounts for the large numbers of Germans who say today that they were prisoners of the Americans for only a few days. Most of them managed to get home within a few weeks by hitchhiking and foot-slogging. Erich Hartmann was not so lucky.

Rumors went around after about a week in captivity that Hartmann and his men would be moved to the rear. On 16 May 1945, the Americans told Erich, Hermann Graf and Hartmann Grasser that the entire column of prisoners was to be delivered to Regensburg, Germany, for processing. They were told they would be moving out by truck at 4 P.M. that afternoon. For eight days in American hands they had been without food, subsisting on meager dry foodstuffs they had carried with them into captivity and on minor donations of food and chocolate by friendly individual GI's. Erich was glad to be moving out to an area where organization would be better.

The Germans were loaded into trucks and driven away from the Pisek area. After a drive of a few miles, the convoy stopped, and Erich and his companions were ordered to get down. They were in a meadow surrounded by Russian soldiers. As the apprehensive Germans tumbled out of the trucks, the Russians immediately began separating the German women from the men.

Before the Americans could drive away, they were given a glimpse of the fate to which they had unwittingly delivered German civilian women and girls, innocent of any crime save being born in Germany. The Americans found that their Allies were quite capable as individuals of descending to the worst excesses of human savagery. The young GI's from Keokuk and Kokomo got a good close-up of the Bear in action.

The unarmed German men were lined up and a row of half-drunk Red Army soldiers swayingly covered them with rifles and machine guns. Other Russians hurled the women and girls to the ground, and ripping the clothes from their bodies began raping them in front of their Russian comrades, the agonized Germans, and the GI's standing bug-eyed with wonder in the U.S. Army trucks.

The Americans seemed paralyzed by the spectacle. When two young German girls, stripped bare, ran crying to their trucks and clawed their way up the sides in search of sanctuary, the American guards had the presence of mind to haul them into the truck beds. This chivalry did not sit well with the Russians. Firing wildly in the air and shouting at the Americans, the Russians made ominous moves toward the U.S. trucks. The GI's let in their clutches and gunned their vehicles away down the road. The last threat to their full indulgence removed, the Russians fell on the German women.

A young German woman in her early thirties, wife of a sergeant and mother of a twelve-year-old girl, begged on her knees to a Russian corporal, and alternately prayed to her God, that the Soviet soldiers should take her and spare her child. Her prayers went unanswered. Tears pouring down her cheeks, she wept out her appeal while the watching German men stood with gun barrels thrust into their bellies.

The Russian corporal stepped back from the woman, his face contorted by a sneer. One of the four soldiers with him slammed his boot into the woman's stomach with all his force. "You damned Fascist pig!" he yelled. The young mother rolled over gasping. The soldier who had kicked her then killed her with a single rifle shot through the head.

The Russians grabbed every German female in sight, regardless of age. The twelve-year-old daughter of the slain woman was dragged behind a tank by her mother's killer. Other Russians joined him. Half an hour later, crying and croaking, unable to stand and completely nude, the ravaged child came crawling back around the tank. She collapsed like a broken doll.

Against the backdrop of the unspeakable scene in the once peaceful meadow, there was nothing prominent about the crippled child's plight. The powerless Germans urged their Russian guards to let them help the girl. Burp guns at the ready, the Russian let a German medic through to attend to the child. She was dead in an hour, her final whimperings tearing the hearts out of Erich and his men.

Eight- and nine-year-old girls were pitilessly raped time after time by hulking Russian soldiers. They showed no feelings other than hate and lust. As each brute satisfied himself amid the wildly terrified screams and groans of the women, Erich and his men stared into the muzzles of machine guns.

With blood on their uniforms the Russians who had slaked

their lusts came grinning to relieve the machine gunners standing guard over the Luftwaffe men. Mothers who tried to protect infant daughters were clubbed senseless and dragged aside, then raped as they lay unconscious. Hard-case pilots who had survived hundreds of air battles and many wounds broke down and wept unashamedly. Sick to heart in a way he had never known in his life, Erich fought down an overpowering impulse to retch.

A debauch of such violence could not maintain its soulwrenching intensity. Gradually lusts were quenched, and something akin to sanity began to settle over the scene. Sometimes smirking, sometimes stolid, occasionally even a little crestfallen, the Russian soldiers returned the women and girls as they finished with them. Some were driven away in trucks, never to be seen again. Those who came back collapsed in the arms of their distraught husbands and fathers. The full measure of misery and degradation had been meted out to them already, but more was to come.

The Germans were herded into a rough encampment in the meadow. They were allowed to go down to the lake and wash. Then a ring of thirty tanks was drawn up around the meadow and the area secured for the night. Russian soldiers came again and again among the Germans, dragging the women and girls from what little pitiful comfort they had found in the presence of their husbands and fathers. The rape went on throughout the night, abating only in the predawn hours. The women were hurled back like rag dolls when the Russians had finished with them. The soldiers of JG-52 had a hard decision to make that night, and many of them made it.

When the first shafts of dawn rayed into the armor-ringed meadow, a large number of Germans did not stir. Those who awoke found themselves involved in a somber death scene that would burn itself into their memories forever. As Erich awoke, he saw a sergeant and his wife and daughter lying near him in the empty stiffness of death. The sergeant had quietly slashed his wife's wrist artery with an improvised dagger, disposed of his eleven-year-old daughter the same way, and then slit his own wrist artery. Life had quietly drained out of them while Erich slept not far away.

Other men had suffocated their wives and children, and then hung themselves with improvised ropes from the sides of trucks. They chose death as the alternative to a living death. Erich began quietly talking to himself as the emotional impact of the scene bludgeoned at his fighting heart. "You must stay alive, Erich, no matter what happens. You *must* survive to tell others what you hardly believe yourself, now, as you look at it. You will never forget what kind of things men can do when they descend beneath the level of animals."

The debauch ended a day later just as abruptly as it had begun. A Russian general arrived and took in the scene in an instant. He needed no reports to know what had happened. He issued immediate orders forbidding these excesses, in accordance with a new Red Army directive. The plunder and rape of eastern Germany had already become infamous around the world.

The general ordered the German NCOs and enlisted men separated from Erich and the other officers. The women were placed in the custody of the officers and the Russian soldiers were ordered to stay away from this area. When Russian soldiers violated this order by coming to the officers' compound during the night, and kidnaping and raping a girl, Russian punishment proved itself as pitiless to the native son as to the late enemy.

The raped girl was asked to identify her assailants. Three soldiers were picked out of a line-up. There was no court martial, no appeal and no further question that the Russian general's orders were to be obeyed. The hands of the three soldiers were bound behind their backs with telephone wire, and they were promptly hung in full view both of the Germans and of their fellow soldiers. The lesson in discipline went home with singular force.

This, too, was the Russian mentality, as Erich was to understand in the years that lay ahead. Russian literature is full of such arresting barbarism, and hanging became a way of life during and immediately following the 1917 Revolution. For Erich Hartmann, barely twenty-three years old as he stood in the meadow and watched the swinging corpses, it was as shocking as the rape binge.

Combat flyers seldom captured anybody. Rarely did they meet an enemy face to face. On the occasions when they met an enemy pilot on the ground after having shot him down, the fight was over for both of them. Chivalry had survived in an attenuated form among combat pilots, but in the ground war brutality and subhuman conduct of all kinds was the rule. Erich's night with the infantry platoon on the line, after his escape from Russian capture, had given him an unforgettable glimpse of the savage ground war. Now this was more of it, the kind of mentality created by the sheer inhumanity of modern war.

After the hanging of the three soldiers, the situation in the prison compound stabilized. Fear for the welfare of the German women soon changed to a different emotion—shame. The single women and girls in many cases went to the Russian victors for sex play. Mothers went to Soviet officers and sold their bodies for more food for their children. After a week the distraught German men began to feel the effects of starvation and to show it externally, while those German women who had changed their minds about the Russians stayed lively and began growing plump. The emotional consequence was an indescribable inner turmoil in which Erich participated to the full.

Dwelling in his later years in the shadow of the Soviet colossus, even though back in Germany, Erich never forgot the bitter, penetrating lessons of this time. He taught his wife, Usch, the realistic approach to a similar situation should it ever be thrust upon her by events:

"Never hesitate in such circumstances. Go to the highest-ranked officer and do your charming with him. Flatter him and stay with him. He will protect you against all others. In this way, you have to suffer only one man and you can avoid the brutality and dehumanization of belonging to every man. Others will be able to take you only over the dead body of your protector."

And he adds:

"In the kind of age in which we are living, where civilization might well be overturned at a maniac's touch, *every Western wife should be aware of this approach to dealing with people of Eastern mentality*."

That was the lesson that came out of Erich's anguish in the meadow. Conduct alien to everything he had been taught as a German soldier, and to the example set by his humanitarian father, was now to become part of his way of life. He thanked God in his emotional extremity, as he shuddered through the rapings and hangings, that his beloved Usch was safe in Stuttgart.

Erich was only a handful of years removed from a fair-haired Korntal *Hochschule* boy who could not abide a bully, and that made the emotional impact of these events all the more resounding. The resilience of youth had brought him through fourteen hundred combat missions in a heroic career that would never be surpassed, but there was barely enough bounce in him to confront such bestiality in forced silence. Ahead of him lay ten and a half years in Russian prisons, a brutal decade that would leave him with many black memories. From the mass of recollections, good and bad, that he would carry into the evening of his life, one would stand out with ineradicable starkness and vividity—the Dantean nightmare in the meadow.

Authors' Note:
Events described in this chapter have been set down solely to show their shocking effect on Erich Hartmann, exposed for the first time to mass sexual savagery, and not for the purpose of fomenting hatred of the Russian people. The authors are in total agreement with Colonel Hartmann that the basic kindness inside all human beings, including the Russian people, can arrest the endless cycle of war and peace if permitted to become uppermost in human affairs. Colonel Hartmann is adamantly opposed to the fomentation of new hatreds between peoples.

Savage sexual debauchery has been a perennial concomitant of mankind's worst social aberration—war. These pathological mass misuses of the sex function evoke from the uncomprehending individual no more profound reaction than a resigned shrug. Men accept that such things "always" go on and will "always" continue to go on, and thus they evade the clear evidence that frustration of the human love impulse lies at the root of all social sickness that convulses the world. Psychotic leaders, thus aided by human ignorance or indifference, are able to manipulate the colossal energies made available by the frustrations of destitute millions. This little-understood phenomenon lies behind every irrational social movement, including both Red Communism and Black Fascism—antithetical political expressions stemming from an identical power source.

The despots who lead millions of fundamentally kind people again and again to ruin, could not prevail under modern conditions without the services of propagandists—specialists in presenting lie and legend as truth and fact. Goebbels filled this role in Nazi Germany. Ilya Ehrenburg was the Soviet Goebbels. The Red Army was incited to its excesses against the German civil population by Ehrenburg's psychotic exhortations to vengeance.

The Russian troops were urged to kill the Fascists wherever they found them, and to "take the proud German women" so that they might forget the hard battles. The aged were fair game. Even the innocent children of Germany were targets of Ehrenburg's hateful diatribes. "Never forget that every German child you see is the child of a Fascist," he ranted. The mass debauch that ensued sent a wave rolling into the Bohemian meadow where Erich Hartmann saw it break. Red Army orders eventually halted these excesses, but not before Ehrenburg's evil genius had done its work.

Mankind has been plagued throughout its history by such happenings, and therefore lulled into their acceptance. The time is at hand when men will have to confront themselves frankly in the light of new knowledge. The hard-won discoveries of Freud and other pioneers concerning the human psyche and character structure have provided the answers. To date, these findings have been evaded in their application to mass problems.

Especially germane is the work of the late Wilhelm Reich, M.D., onetime first clinical assistant to Freud, who supervised the German workers' psychoanalytic clinics in the critical years preceding Hitler's advent. His 1932 book, *The Mass Psychology of Fascism*, is probably the most significant social work of this century. With scientific psychoanalysis, the psychic plague was identified that throws up and sustains the Hitlers and Stalins and their propagandist lackeys.

The basis of the sexual excesses inseparable from the ultimate human sickness of war, has been well identified by Reich and his followers. The psychic pestilence is international and world-wide. No nation enjoys immunity. As this is written, social massacre at home and war abroad strain the integrity of the American Republic. Machinations to suppress the knowledge capable of eradicating this pestilence work efficiently and beyond the ken of a public that deems itself well informed. A fugitive from the Fascist and Communist terror whose etiology he exposed, Dr. Reich died in a U.S. federal prison in 1957. His books and experimental journals —including *Mass Psychology of Fascism*—were burned by the U.S. government.

The authors considered it mandatory, before presenting the story of Erich Hartmann's decade in Russian jails, to establish that they write with an understanding of the psychological processes that sustain modern dictatorships. The NKVD in Russia, the SD in Nazi Germany, and all other secret police organizations of a kindred order are gathering-grounds for psychopaths, wielders of illegal power over millions. Honest outrage at the existence and activities of such organizations is rational and necessary if this blight is ever to be lifted from struggling mankind.

The authors wish to make clear their unalterable opposition to the oppressors, and their sympathy for the oppressed—a stance with which all free men must surely find themselves in agreement.

CHAPTER FOURTEEN

SOVIET PRISONER

> . . . treat them with humanity, and let them have no
> reason to complain. . . . Provide everything necessary
> for them.
>
> —*General George Washington's instructions to
> Colonel Webb concerning prisoners taken in
> the Battle of Trenton*

AFTER THEIR INTRODUCTION to the Russian soldier in his role
of conqueror, Erich, Hermann Graf and the rest of I
Gruppe's officers were taken with the womenfolk to a transit
camp at Neubistritz. Little more than a barbed-wire stockade,
the camp's purpose was to let Soviet bureaucracy take a
firmer grip on its captives. Commissars and quill-drivers began
the formal cataloguing of the Blond Knight and his men.
Names, ranks, serial numbers and basic military data were
perfunctorily recorded, but the Russians were interested in
something more realistic than the status of their captives in a
Luftwaffe that no longer existed.

Physical examinations were given to the Germans. The
Russians were not concerned with the health of Erich and his
men from any humanitarian motives, but as an evaluation of
their capacity as laborers. Erich's physical capacity to work
was beyond question. He was a lean, tough and strong young
man of twenty-three, physically resilient and highly intelligent.
Bureaucratic formalities at Neubistritz took three weeks to
complete, after which the Germans spent several days awaiting their fate.

Erich found himself musing over the evident Russian intention to make them into forced laborers. The ranting polemic of the Communists about exploitation of one man by another kept running through his mind. Marx and Lenin asserted that this vicious situation lay at the root of all evil in the capitalist world. Now, in their time of triumph, these idolators of Marx and Lenin had no other thought but to enslave their late enemies. A capitalist from the depths of the Industrial Revolution would have saluted their instinct for cheap labor.

A move from Neubistritz was imminent. Erich tried to squelch some of the rumors that were sweeping the camp, but to no avail. Men in suspense will speculate, imagine and even try to manufacture a destiny for themselves. Rumor-mongering halted when Russian guards rudely moved them out of the pen and started marching them southeast along a dusty road.

Erich was assigned to load the effects of the old people in a baggage cart, and directed to ride the cart under the personal surveillance of an armed Red Army master sergeant. In a short time, Erich established contact with the Russian. His name was Sascha. Noncommittal at first, he soon warmed to Erich.

"Where are we going?" said Erich.

"Budweis."

Erich knew the town. Budweis was at least sixty miles distant. Since the Russians obviously intended that the column make the journey on foot, he was grateful to be sitting up with Sascha behind the two horses that pulled the baggage cart. For five dusty days the dispirited prisoners trudged along, and the rumors grew more and more imaginative. The word "Siberia" began whispering its way through the column, but at Budweis a Russian commissar put an end to the rumors.

He spoke soothingly to Erich, Graf and a group of their officers.

"We are not taking you to Russia. That is propaganda, pure propaganda. We are taking you down to Vienna by train, and from there you will go home."

The Russian smiled blandly. Erich noticed that the commissar's face straightened immediately when he thought the Germans had turned away. Erich was skeptical, but he could do nothing but bid the kindly Sascha good-bye and board a rackety train the following day. Spirits brightened as the train kept rattling southward, but this soon changed.

The train screeched to a halt in a country siding. Russian guards and officers went running up and down outside, shouting and gesticulating. Shunted back and forth with much slamming of couplings and jarring of the filthy coaches, the train was obviously being diverted. When they went lurching away from the siding, Erich could see that they were no longer heading for Vienna.

A Russian officer gave them the story in broken German. Big trouble in Vienna. Riots, fighting, looting. A dispute over occupation of the city. The train was being sent instead to Budapest. Erich's hopes of an early return home began fading. Budapest was farther east than Vienna, and closer to Russia. These were bad tidings.

Hours after passing Budapest there was another jarring halt and more shouting and running. They were at the town of Sighet in the Carpathians.* Erich caught the words "plague" and "quarantine" as they were shouted back and forth between Rumanian officials and Russian guards. The train was dragged into a siding and the Germans climbed out stiffly. They were herded into another barbed-wire pen. Erich overheard enough conversation to know that they would not now be going to Budapest, and that their probable destination lay beyond—in Russia.

The Maramures pen was run by the Rumanian Communists. Guards clad in exotic red trousers and armed with long, heavy sticks beat the prisoners unmercifully at the slightest provocation. Erich had to constantly fight down his rage, but the second night the bullies went too far. Two red-trousered sadists caught a young pilot in the latrine during the night, and beat the defenseless man bloody and unconscious. He crawled back into the barracks an hour later on all fours, a whimpering wreck.

Erich's hatred for bullies had lived in him since boyhood. Black rage welled up in him at the sight of the beaten young pilot. A tough old major from the German paratroops was

---

* Sighet/Maramures, a Rumanian town on the border of the Ukrainian SSR, 225 miles east of Budapest.

similarly incensed by the cowardly attack. Two other pilots from Erich's group joined them. At intervals they sauntered out of the barracks toward the latrine. In the gloom of the latrine, the two sadists soon loomed with their clubs, eager to fall on another defenseless German and thrash him.

Erich sprang out of the shadows as one of the bullies raised his club to strike one of the decoys. Smashing his fists into the guard's face and then driving blows into his belly with all his force, Erich felt the man crumple. He saw the paratroop major's elbows pumping wildly in the gloom, and heard the breath go hissing out of the second bully under this assault.

In seconds, both would-be disciplinarians lay unconscious on the ground. Erich nodded to the paratroop major. They picked up the guards and dumped them bodily into the latrine, red trousers and all. The sound of the two bullies wallowing in the muck was music to their ears as they padded back to the barracks. Two of the red-trousered guards were missing the following day. The others appeared without sticks. They nodded and smiled as they quietly patrolled the pen.

A week later, the Germans were ordered to reboard the train. Machine guns bristled now from the rackety coaches, and searchlights had been mounted on top of several cars. The filthy coaches into which Erich and his men had been jammed on the ride to Budapest, were now bulging with heavily-armed Russian guards. Sixty Germans, including Erich, were relegated to second-class status. They were stuffed into a small freight car in almost intolerable discomfort.

The jam-packed baggage car was as hot as a furnace. The air quickly became giddyingly stale. Erich set up a basic routine for lessening the worst aspects of their sardine-can existence. One-third of the men would lie down at a time on the wagon floor. There was no room for sixty of them to lie or even sit at one time. Lying down for two hours and then standing for four, they began the ordeal of Russian confinement.

Hermann Graf and Erich were two of Germany's most famous heroes and winners of the Diamonds, but the leveling effects of their confinement were irresistible. They lay down and stood up in turn with sergeants and second lieutenants. Other senior officers in the car were Colonel Hein Heuer and Major Arthur Riele. Rank and decorations were soon forgot-

where you could get a cup of real coffee for a ruble, was at the bridge. The manager of the cafe was a . . . rather dangerous fellow, who would use his coffee to induce war prisoners to talk.*

"When the stream was iced over in the winter, ice-shooting by the elite of the camp would take place, and in the summer, members of the camp could bathe there when they felt like it. The soccer field was in a meadow outside the barbed wire. In the camp there was a second meadow at our disposal for athletics and gymnastics. In the spring, merely for propaganda purposes, a bowling alley was opened. . . . When the weather was nice, promenade concerts were held in the so-called birchwoods, and on Sunday mornings the dance band played in the cafe.

"One could hardly have wanted anything better if it hadn't been for the fact that everything was merely a front."

When Erich arrived in this environment of relative luxury, fresh from the Kirov swamp camp, it did not take him long to recover his morale. After brief hospitalization to ensure that he had not brought typhus back with him from the swamp, he soon got his spirits up and his bounce back. A job in the kitchen, a relatively easy assignment with access to all the food he needed, further enhanced his new outlook on life.

These were the circumstances under which he was introduced to the strange and divided world of German P.O.W.'s in Russia. Incarcerated Germans, whether officers or not, were far from being a monolithic bloc of determined resisters. In this respect, the outwardly luxurious Gryazovets was a veritable jungle.

The background to the divided loyalties of many imprisoned Germans is to be found in the political make-up of pre-Hitler Germany, when there were millions of convinced Communists and the Communist party was a major factor in elections. Hitler's seizure of power grew out of the Communist threat, to which he and his Nazis were mortally opposed. After Hitler became Chancellor, the Communists were deprived of all possibility of obtaining power, and the movement was suppressed. There is nevertheless no evidence that mil-

* Presumably to report these conversations later to the NKVD in return for favors or later release from Russia.—Authors

lions of Communists who lived in pre-Hitler Germany—whether members of the Communist party or not—relinquished their convictions. Hence it should not be surprising that following the catharsis of Germany's defeat and under the stimulus of Soviet confinement, many Germans became allied with the Soviet cause.

Organizations like the so-called National Committee and the German Officers' League were formed in the Russian prison camps. Politicians like Ulbricht and Pieck were members of such groups before the Russians released them to run the new East German government. Field Marshal von Paulus, who surrendered at Stalingrad, was another notable anti-Fascist, and probably the most notorious was General von Seydlitz, with whom Erich was eventually confined in Novocherkassk jail, many years after the Blond Knight had his first experiences with the bewildering political world of German prisoners of war. Establishing the differences between anti-Fascists and pro-Communists, between German nationalists and masquerading pro-Soviet stool pigeons, would have been a challenge to a learned political scientist.

In late 1945, the twenty-three-year-old and politically naive Erich Hartmann had to find his way among these many factions—all of them representing themselves as devoted to his welfare. Those who seemed to do best in a material sense collected in the Antifa (i.e. anti-Fascist) movement, and the Antifa became the focus of the pro-Soviet forces. Hermann Graf was drawn to this faction, and tried to swing Erich to the same line of thought. Erich was disturbed to find informers and stool pigeons among his countrymen on all sides. Fellow Germans repeatedly asked him to embrace the Communist philosophy, and confess his crimes against the Soviet people. Even his assignment to the kitchen, although he did not know it at the time, was the opening gambit in an NKVD effort to bring him into the service of the Soviets.

A heavy emotional blow came in Gryazovets when Hermann Graf succumbed to an NKVD campaign aimed at his compromise. Graf was a man Erich admired, and his last commanding officer in the Luftwaffe. As outlined in an earlier chapter, Graf was among the greatest popular heroes of the war in Germany, as well as a redoubtable fighting pilot with 212 victories to his credit. As one of the nine fighter aces to win the Diamonds, Hermann Graf was a valuable prize to the NKVD because of his decorations and fame.

Allegations about Graf's conduct in Russia, made in Assi Hahn's book *I Tell the Truth*, have made Hermann Graf something of a pariah among surviving German fighter pilots, although the one-time hero is still alive and resides in Düsseldorf. During the war, he proved himself a capable leader and a brave man, and he was widely admired as a fighter by those he led, including Erich Hartmann. Graf kept on flying combat after he won the Diamonds, when he could have stepped down.

Since Erich Hartmann served under Graf in JG-52, surrendered with him, passed into Russian confinement with him and generally knew him well, his account of Graf's actions in Gryazovets are of significance:

"At the end of the war, Hermann Graf was very famous. Propaganda and publicity concerning him was spread all over Germany. He led the famous football team 'The Red Fighters.' He was always, in my opinion, a nice fellow and a hell of a fighter. But underneath it all, he was a man of essentially simple character. He had not been given the advantages of a long and careful education, as were many of his later critics.*

"After the surrender, he was stripped of his fame and reduced to plodding along from one day to the next at menial jobs. His dissatisfaction with the change was evidently something he could not control.

"One day he came to me and said, 'I've changed my mind about staying here,' and he asked me if I would join him in switching to the Soviet side. I told him I had no such intention. He said, 'All the old regulations are gone, and each of us must choose either the Anglo-American way or the Russian way. There is no Germany any more. I have decided that I want to be on the Russian side.' Soon afterward, he wrote to the Russian administration, offering his services to the Soviet Union, and offering to take one rank lower in the Red Air Force than he had held in the Luftwaffe. He was soon afterward flown out of Gryazovets to a camp near Moscow. He

---

* His critics also forget that Graf's deliberate disobedience of General Seidemann's order to fly to Dortmund and surrender to the British was a courageous act in behalf of several thousand defenseless German civilians.

wrote a laudatory article in the P.O.W. newspaper about the Red Air Force, and told the Russians about his experiences against the Anglo-American air forces during the war. He came back to Germany in 1950."

Graf thus was repatriated five years before Erich Hartmann, but that the onetime *Kommodore* of JG-52 contributed anything of real value to the Russian cause is doubtful. History will say it is unlikely that Hermann Graf could tell the Russians anything they did not already know, or have access to through espionage. Graf's limited abilities—despite his unquestioned combat courage—were of doubtful utility to the Soviets. Nevertheless, the NKVD compromised him, and he has dwelt in the shadows ever since in the German fighter pilot fraternity.

At the time Graf confessed his change of heart to Erich, Soviet prisoners had endured little compared with what lay ahead. The psywar effort of the NKVD had hardly begun. Graf was a lieutenant colonel in his thirties, and considerably more mature than twenty-three-year-old Erich. The two winners of the Diamonds gave each other their word of honor that neither of them would ever surrender surrender his decoration to the Russians. The Brilliants would be thrown away.*

Erich was summoned a few days later to the office of Captain Klingbeil of the NKVD, a renegade German with the inappropriate nickname of "Dad." Hermann Graf's Diamonds were lying on his desk. Erich was shocked. Klingbeil demanded Erich's Diamonds.

"I threw mine in the river," stammered Erich, struggling to retain his composure.

"Dad" Klingbeil's face darkened. Then he gloatingly held out Graf's decoration.

"You should have the good sense of your old *Kommodore*, Colonel Graf. He has turned his Diamonds over to us, and confessed that all he did in wartime was wrong."

Graf had not only been compromised by the NKVD, but

---

* Erich Hartmann's original, authentic Diamonds remained at home in Weil during and after the war, and he has them today. An American soldier took a paste copy from him when he surrendered in Czechoslovakia, and he had a second paste copy with him in Russia. Surrender of the Diamonds to the NKVD was a symbolical act, unrelated to the monetary value of the decoration.

also had gone back on his word of honor to Erich. The effect on Erich was shattering. If a fighter like Graf could go under, Erich thought to himself, then who could be trusted? When he subsequently confronted Graf about breaking his word of honor, his former *Kommodore* was so ashamed as to be almost in agony. Erich told him that henceforth they must go their separate ways, and on that basis they parted. The strange, impenetrable, yet intangible barrier that suddenly appeared between them was a new experience for Erich. Graf's defection was a powerful psychological weapon against young officers, and the NKVD made full use of this asset.

Erich's natural analytical ability soon led him away from the Antifa movement into which Graf had tried to draw him. The men whose views he shared were those branded by the NKVD and its German stooges as "Fascists." They were actually decent German officers determined to maintain their self-respect and not become tools of the NKVD psychopaths. Erich allied himself with this bloc of recalcitrant Germans and began his long struggle with the NKVD. These resistant staff officers were placed in separate quarters and classed as agitators by the prison administration, which consisted of Red-lining Germans under the Stalingrad war-judge Schumann. These renegades announced that Hartmann's group of agitators could have no visitors in their segregated quarters, thereby cutting them off from contact with the rest of the camp.

Erich went over the head of Schumann to the NKVD commander, and demanded that visiting rights be restored. His forceful presentation on behalf of the staff officers resulted in the NKVD overruling their renegade German lackeys. Furthermore, the Politburo's representative in the Hartmann group, Dr. Bauer, was removed following Erich's representations. These dramatic concessions seemed too good to be true. Erich got the old fighter pilot's apprehensive feeling in the backside. Something was afoot.

Summoned soon afterward to the office of the NKVD commander, Erich found Captain Uvarov in a genial mood. A couple of years older than Erich, Uvarov had blond hair and blue eyes just like the Blond Knight. He could have passed anywhere for a typical German boy in appearance. Seated in a comfortable chair, Uvarov offered Erich a cigarette.

"Please sit down, Erich," he said.

Erich definitely felt the same feeling in the backside now that he used to get in the air when a Russian fighter got on his tail. Better watch this fellow, he told himself. He took the proffered cigarette and sat down, nodding his thanks to the Russian officer but remaining deadpan. Uvarov leaned back in his chair and blew smoke in the air.

"Are you satisfied and happy now that Bauer has been removed, Erich?"

The Blond Knight nodded.

"Then you can see how anxious we are to get along with you, Erich. When you want something done, we do our best to oblige."

"That's very kind of you."

"Yes, we are kind even to our biggest enemies, those like you who destroyed hundreds of our aircraft. That is why we assigned you to work in the kitchen, so you can eat as much as you like."

"The kitchen job has been pleasant enough," said Erich.

"Perhaps then, you would care to show some good will toward us—reciprocate the cooperation we have shown you."

Erich knew Uvarov was on his tail now. He waited for him to open fire.

"There are a number of men among the staff officers in your group who are guilty of serious crimes against the Russian people. They have shot civilians, burned villages and destroyed factories. We know that they are secretly Fascists and make propaganda. Here is a list of the names."

Erich ran his eye down the list. Colonel Wolf, Colonel Ackermann, Colonel Van Camp, Colonel von Tempelhof. Lieutenant Colonel Prager, Majors Hahn, Ewald, Ellerbrock and others. Most were professional soldiers, committed since boyhood to honorable conduct in war. Erich looked up from the list at Uvarov.

"What do you want me to do about these men?"

Uvarov took the bait.

"Listen to them. Find out what they did during the war— the war crimes they committeed—shooting civilians, looting, burning." The Russian was speaking faster and faster.

"Report *everything* to us about their past, their families. *Everything*. We know we can rely on you to bring them to justice."

Erich retained his deadpan.

"And what happens to me if I do this work for you?"

Uvarov was sure he had a pigeon now.

"Why, after you've written everything for us, you will go back to Germany on the first train. When can we expect the first report from you, Erich?"

"I cannot ever make such a report." Erich spoke slowly and quietly, in contrast to the Russian's agitated tone.

Uvarov shot forward in his chair.

"What do you mean you won't make such a report?" His voice was shrill.

"I mean I will not do what you ask. First, these are all honorable officers. They would be as outraged and angry as you over wanton killing of civilians. To try and inform on such men for my own gain—to become a *stukatcha**—is unspeakably dirty. I will not do it, now or ever."

Uvarov was obviously fighting down his fury. He thrust a paper across the desk to Erich. The document was written in Russian.

"Sign it," he said.

"This document is not in my language, what does it—"

"The paper says that you certify you were interrogated without being threatened. It is routine."

"Please translate the paper into German and I will be glad to sign it. Otherwise I will not sign. It could be for my own death for all I know."

Uvarov's face was now a savage mask.

"Damn you, Hartmann, I am a Soviet officer. You take my word for that."

"I will not sign unless it is in German."

"You damned Fascist. You will work for us or by God I guarantee that you'll never see Germany again."

Uvarov hammered the last sentence home by pounding on the desk with his fist.

Erich took a final puff on his cigarette and crushed it out on the ashtray beside the Russian's hand.

"You can do what you like about sending me home. I am not able to do anything about that. But I absolutely refuse to be an informer for the NKVD under any circumstances."

Uvarov's face was purple with rage and the veins bulged in his neck.

* Stool pigeon.

"Damned Fascist! You damned Fascist, Hartmann! Your holiday in the kitchen detail is canceled. You hear that! No more easy work and a full belly. You'll go to work on the road-building detail, that'll sweat the insolence out of you."

"Is that all?"

"No, by God, that's not all. You've insulted me, a Soviet officer. For that you get ten days in the bunker. Ten days, you hear? Take him away!"

Erich stood up and extended his hands as though for handcuffs.

"I am ready."

As the guards prodded him out the door with their rifles he marveled inwardly at his own ability to control himself. The impulse to spring across the desk and throttle Uvarov had been overpowering. Somehow he had kept cool and in the process his will had conquered Uvarov. There were no medals for victories like this, and the rewards were different. You were paid off with time in the bunker.

The filthy hole to which he was now consigned was his first encounter with NKVD discipline. Nine feet long, four feet wide and six feet high, the stone-walled chamber had a dirt floor and no heat of any kind. A shaft about three inches in diameter located in one corner of the bunker and screened with wire mesh, provided the dungeon's total resources of light and ventilation. Beneath the shaft stood an open can that served as a latrine. There was no furniture.

Each morning, guards shoved six hundred grams of bread, two liters of water and five grams of sugar into the hellhole. Sleeping on the ground, half-frozen, completely alone, able to tell night from day only by staring up the shaft, Erich knew the bunker was designed to break down the fiercest will. Isolation, stench and chill could melt resolution. Starvation could sap defiance. Without a focus for his thoughts, he might just as well be on the moon. He turned his mind to Usch.

He ran through his memories of their childhood love like old and adored movie films. He recalled every detail of their trysts in the theater in Weil, their days in dancing class, and the happy reunions and tender partings of the war days. He played mental games trying to decide whether their baby was a boy or a girl. The child would be born by now. Perhaps it had fair hair, like him—or maybe the child would be another dark-haired, beautiful girl like Usch. He knew he would like that.

From the time of his first confinement in the wretched bunker at Gryazovets, Erich had a deep feeling of contact with Usch that gave him indescribable inner comfort. The blackness around him became like a friendly ether, through whose medium he could reach out and find his beloved as though time and space did not exist. Something inside him came alive when he turned his thoughts to Usch in these black dungeons, as though he had plugged in a tiny but powerful dynamo that energized his being. The love and harmony of his home life, and his ability to focus on it in confinement, eventually proved stronger than the worst that sick men could do to him.

The ordeal of the first years in Soviet custody is summarized in a letter written by Erich Hartmann to his wife on 30 October 1947, and subsequently smuggled out of Russia by a returning prisoner of war. A few such smuggled letters provided Usch Hartmann with the only uncensored contact she had with Erich during the ten and a half years of his imprisonment. Official communications remained limited to twenty-five words on a postcard—during the times when the NKVD did not capriciously reduce the permitted words to five or ten. This 1947 letter tells its own story of an imprisoned man's bitterness and frustration.

"Camp 7150

"Oct 30, 1947

"My darlingest Uschmutti:

"Tomorrow another transport leaves here—maybe this letter will reach you. Now, shortly, my story: Taken prisoner by the Americans on 8 May 1945, and delivered to the Russians on 14 May. On 25 May 1945 we started out from Budweis, via Vienna, Budapest, the Carpathians, the Ukraine, Kiev, Moscow to Kirov. In a camp in a swamp we met 1,000 infantrymen and approximately 100 officers, all in pretty bad shape, poor food and miserable treatment. In Kirov, I became the leader of the officers' group. Graf was with me and was in charge of all. The infantrymen were worked so hard that they died like flies, two to five of them a day.

"On August 17 we raised the devil with the Russian administration and all officers were loaded and brought to this camp, now called Camp 7150, 60 km south of Vologda. I am still in this officers' camp. Accommodations are in large barracks—one room for each 400 men, with narrow plank beds, the whole arrangement revolting. I am sure that cattle in Germany are better housed than we are. But of course, one gets used to it, even sanitary facilities that are like 1,000 years ago. Medical attention is passable. Food consists of 600 grams of bread, 30 grams of butter (about one ounce), 40 grams of sugar, with two thin soups each day (total of about a pint), and about three-quarters of a pint of porridge.

"One is eternally hungry. There is no bathtub, only small wooden buckets being provided for this. People living under such conditions appear as you might expect, and dystrophy is common. I personally seem to assimilate food well, which helps me see this life through.

"The camp is administered by the NKVD, the Russian secret police, aided by renegade Germans. Among these is a German military judge who is mightily afraid of the Russians, but does his share organization-wise. The others are mostly political swine and traitors and similar types in charge of the camps. They call themselves the 'Antifa.' Looked at closer they are former SS medics, Hitler Youth leaders, SA commanders and similar trash. I don't know what the Russians mean to do with them, yesterday they betrayed us and tomorrow they will change flags again. Such people make imprisonment hell for us.

"Until about nine months ago, there was continual strong political pressure brought to bear on us. Every suspect was put to a political test, and that, of course, had its reaction upon us all. Political attitudes governed the kind of clothing, type of work and general treatment given to the individual prisoner. From their appearance, one could guess where the sympathies of the various prisoners lay.

"I was shocked to see, for once, the German officer corps with its pants down. There is no profession nor rank where one could say they had all resisted successfully. Colonels steal, turn traitor, denounce their comrades and play informers for the NKVD. I can tell you that I have learned to look at people through strong glasses to see if there is anything behind the make-up—the outer façade.

"We get a change of laundry every one or two months, once every three months in summer. Now winter covers this dirty country with its white coat, and bedbugs and fleas are our constant companions in their hundreds of thousands. I do not exaggerate their numbers. So much for exterior circumstances. Now to myself.

"As a German TEPOU [Hero] I am personally rather well treated by the Russians, probably because of the consistency of my behavior. Once I was brought before an NKVD board—a sort of trial—but I was released because I immediately asked to be shot. They did not accept. The other methods they used I will not describe. You have probably already heard about them.

"I did not know anybody when I came to this camp, only Graf was with me. He soon went over to the 'Antifa' and then wanted to influence me constantly. In this area I was entirely ignorant, and let them lead me astray during the first months, up to a point, but I soon saw through their game and went my own way as a 'fascist.'

"Thank God my own countrymen now keep away from me. Informers turned me in to the NKVD, and I suddenly faced this trial in the middle of the night. I was accused of being an archfascist, a saboteur and the instigator of a resistance movement. Here were the Middle Ages with their inquisition methods, but I did not fail to make the proper answers. I was able to refute all accusations, until the Russians themselves recognized what my countrymen had tried to do to me, and the NKVD then punished the informers. After this, I was left in relative peace.

"Graf was sent to Moscow and follows a downward path there. The first year we were forced to work— even the staff officers. Work here is the worst type of slavery imaginable, worse, I believe, than in Roman times. Can you conceive of six or eight civilized, educated human beings strapped into a harness and pull-in a wagon, like horses before a plow? Roadwork is all done with spades, heavy woodcutting with hand-axes —and all work is to meet specified quotas or food was immediately reduced.

"At the end of 1945, a sudden command was issued that staff officers thereafter were only permitted to volunteer for work. Since I felt I was not born to work for the Russians, I ceased work immediately. Threats, exhortations and flattering inducements were all turned down.

"I do not count on being freed until the end of 1948, and also at that time only if pressure is exerted by the West, and if there is no new war. A new war would make the outlook black for us. We are counting on getting home with the assistance of the West.

"Mail is the only thing we have to look forward to in here. The NKVD shows what it is in that respect— 25 words per month. An increase from 10 words per month is true progress, in their eyes, and everything else here reflects the effects of this mentality. A thin layer living well, the rest poor and in rags—their idea of the freest and happiest country. One could write a book on the effects of their born stupidity mingled with their inferiority complexes.

"So here you have a picture of how I am. I can only hope that the last of it passes quickly, and that we can see each other again and lie in each other's arms. Until then, one says in soldier-talk, 'stand it, fight through it, and courage!' Without combat there is no conquest and no bonus without price, and nothing is given to us for free.

"We'll meet again, embrace again, and together we'll soar. In my thoughts I have my arms about you.

> Your
> Erich."

Eight more years of persuasion and pressure would pass before the yoke was lifted from the stout shoulders of Erich Hartmann.

CHAPTER FIFTEEN

PERSUASION AND PRESSURE

Only those who have endured Soviet imprisonment are entitled to valid opinions concerning it.

—Major Hartmann Grasser
Soviet prisoner, 1945–1949

You dirty Fascist pig! Don't you know that you are completely in our power? Don't you know that you Germans are dirt in the eyes of the world? Here in Russia we can do anything we like with you—*anything*. No one cares what happens to you, Hartmann."

The NKVD officer thrust his sallow face close against Erich's.

"What would you say if we brought to you—right in here on a tray—the heads of your wife and baby son?"

Erich felt the blood drain from his face. His stomach felt like jelly. The NKVD man pressed his helpless victim.

"Do you know that we could go right to Stuttgart, with our East German operatives, and spirit your wife right out of Germany? Remember how we reached Trotsky? And General Miller in Paris? We can reach out anywhere in the world to anyone we want."

The Russian officer's blood-chilling threat was hitting Erich literally where he lived. In the solitary-confinement bunkers in total darkness, there was but one focus for his mind, one anchor in the black ocean that threatened to engulf him body and soul—Usch. The bright visions he could conjure up of her in her parents' home in Zuffenhausen, or in the friendly

209

Hartmann home in Weil, could hold at bay the forces of disintegration.

As long as he knew Usch was safe at home, that all was well with her and his loved ones, Erich felt he could somehow endure the NKVD attacks on his mind. The paralyzing fear he felt at this open threat to his main source of strength had to be concealed. He took a grip on himself and looked squarely back at the NKVD officer.

"You can do anything you wish. You have the power. I know that. But I am not going to work for you against my country and my prison comrades."

Erich maintained a steady gaze, right into the Russian's eyes. For a minute, his antagonist returned his gaze. Then the NKVD man slammed his fist into the palm of his hand.

"Damn you, Hartmann! Damn you to hell! Why won't you work for us?"

Scenes such as this were enacted in half a dozen different Soviet prisons, with eighteen or twenty different NKVD persecutors advancing their proposals in every conceivable form. Inducements ranged from savage blackmail threats to a contract to join the East German Air Force. Erich's answer was always the same—NO. If his friends, associates and superior officers find him today a stubborn man, they might well remember how much that quality was called upon in his brutal decade, and how it stood between him and his ruin as a self-respecting individual.

German prisoners in Russia were under the control of the NKVD. This army of ex-servicemen became an army of slaves, and many were starved to death in the initial postwar period. The Russians could have put the skilled German engineers, artisans and technicians to work in rebuilding Russia, but the NKVD indulged itself instead in the irrational degradation of its captives. The secret police later launched a psywar program more effective in Soviet interests than direct physical vengeance.

Pressure to break the will of the individual German prisoner never diminished. Insufficient food was the primary weapon in crumbling the ego, and the NKVD filled the prison environment with hopelessness, suspicion, lies and ceaseless propaganda. Physical torture in the pattern of the Gestapo was strictly forbidden by Soviet regulations as characteristic of capitalist exploiters. Compromise of the individual and destruction of his integrity by NKVD methods proved more potent in serving Soviet ends.

Erich learned of the Russian prohibition against beating prisoners not long after his capture, when the Russian bureaucracy digested the mass of data concerning its captives that it had ingested at the surrender. At Gryazovets, the NKVD intelligence staff matched up Erich's name with *Karaya One* and the dreaded Black Devil of the South. He was summoned to an interview with two NKVD officers. They were poring over his dossier when he was escorted into the room.

One NKVD man was doggedly shaking his head.

"I am sure we have the wrong man," he said in Russian.

The second NKVD officer looked downcast. The first Russian walked over to Erich and pointed at his flaxen thatch.

"Look," said the Russian to his companion, "he has blond hair, golden hair. He cannot be the Black Devil." Erich knew enough Russian to realize they were discussing his hair.*

The second NKVD man banged his hand down on the dossier.

"There is no use your denying, Hartmann, that you shot down three hundred and fifty-two aircraft on the Russian Front. We have that documented here."

Erich nodded noncommittally. They had addressed him in *Deutsch*.

"Then that would make you the top-scoring fighter pilot of Germany!" The Russian was excited now.

Erich shook his head.

"No," he said, "I am not the most successful German fighter pilot."

"But no other pilot in any air force shot down such a large number of aircraft," the Russian argued.

Erich smiled indulgently, like a schoolmaster elucidating a mathematical fact for a dull student.

"Well, I shot down only Russian aircraft, with a few American machines. On the Western Front, we had a pilot named Marseille who shot down over one hundred and fifty British

---

* Hartmann is a natural linguist. He speaks very good English as well as Russian, French and German.

aircraft. In our air force, one British-flown aircraft was considered the equal of three Russian-flown machines. So I am not the leading pilot."

The Russians exploded into puzzled and angry exchanges between themselves. They did not like this downgrading of their flyers. Erich sat deadpan until they settled down and came at him again. The questions came thick and fast as they pumped him for confirmation of the material in the dossier. Finally, Erich could see no further point in his masquerade. These bloodhounds would eventually know the facts no matter what he told them.

"Will you admit that you were the Black Devil?"

"That is what I was called on the Russian radio during the war," said Erich.

"But your hair is golden," protested one of the NKVD men.

"I have always had fair hair," said Erich. "For a couple of months my aircraft was painted with a black pattern and your people gave me the name Black Devil at that time."

The second NKVD man settled back behind the desk and tapped the dossier.

"A price on your head during the war. I would be rich if our government would pay it today."

The Russian looked Erich up and down in his soiled and battered Luftwaffe uniform. He looked like anything but the formidable Black Devil, but there he was, the most feared fighter pilot on the Eastern Front, a common prisoner.

Further grilling over a period of several hours also revealed that Erich had flown the Me-262 jet fighter, the most advanced operational aircraft of the war. The Blond Knight made little of his experience with the jet, which had been confined to a few checkout flights under Heinz Baer at Lechfeld. The NKVD nevertheless felt that this was special knowledge that would be useful.

The Russians had captured several Me-262's intact, and had taken them to Russia for evaluation. Operating these advanced aircraft was a serious problem without the background acquired by the Germans. Erich was accordingly interrogated at length concerning the jet fighter, several days after his identity as the Black Devil had been established.

Erich was able to offer only limited assistance to the

NKVD, even in telling them all he knew about the Me-262. He explained that he had only flown it about ten times. His image as the most successful fighter pilot in the world nevertheless worked against him. The Russians seemed to automatically assume that his eminence as a combat pilot also implied expertise as an aeronautical engineer. The lengthy interview became steadily more acrimonious as a Russian officer kept pressing him for information he did not possess.

"Major Hartmann, you are holding things back. Why will you not tell us all we wish to know? You *must* tell us."

The bullying NKVD lieutenant was not an air force officer, and this made Erich's problem all the more exasperating. He tried again.

"I can tell you how to start the aircraft. I have already told you that. I can tell you how to fly it, and the things the pilot must watch for, in particular the sensitivity of the throttles. I have told you this, too. What I cannot tell you is the kind of parts that are in the aircraft or precisely how they work. I am a pilot and not an engineer."

The Russian scowled, obviously unconvinced. He had been reading questions about jet aircraft from a questionnaire, and it was obvious that he had no real knowledge of aviation. He looked to Erich like a man who might have been raised on a farm. The Blond Knight accordingly tried explaining his situation in terms comprehensible to a peasant.

"With a jet aircraft, I am like a farmer. You know how a farmer couples a horse to a wagon. He is able to do that, and also to drive the combination. But he does not know what goes on inside the horse."

With a shout of fury the NKVD lieutenant sprang to his feet and slashed Erich across the face with his cane. The stinging blow triggered Erich's temper into a savage cloud of red. He leaped across the room, and picking up a chair, hurled himself at his tormentor. Swinging the chair in a high arc, he brought it crashing down on the Russian's head. The officer collapsed on the floor unconscious.

His anger slaked, Erich felt cold fear gripping him. They would beat him for sure, or shoot him. He opened the door of the interrogation room and called the guard. As they shook and patted the NKVD lieutenant conscious, the Russian pointed his finger at Erich accusingly.

"The bunker for you. Take him to the bunker."

Erich spent forty-eight hours in the hellhole, and the isolation, cold and lack of food heightened his anxiety about his fate. When guards came on the third day to hustle him out of the bunker, he was sure he was going to be beaten or shot. Blinking and hiding from the light like a mole, he was ready for the worst. As he was led directly back into the room in which he had assaulted the Russian officer, he had resigned himself to a beating.

He was amazed to find the NKVD lieutenant sitting in the room waiting for him, a smile playing about his slab face. The Russian had a bottle of vodka and some bread on the table.

"Ah, Hartmann, how is everything going, eh?"

The lieutenant gestured toward the food and drink.

"Help yourself, Hartmann. You can probably use some food and drink."

Erich was flabbergasted. This man had been fiercely angry with him. Now he was offering food and drink with a smile on his face. In no mood to evaluate Russian psychology, Erich lunged into the bread and poured down a draught of the fiery vodka. The Russian watched him. As the standing Erich set down the vodka glass, the lieutenant smiled broadly and tapped the chair he was sitting on.

"I am *sitting* on the chair this time, Hartmann, you see. No chair for you. Now I think you should go back with the other prisoners. I am sorry that I struck you with my cane."

Erich nodded his acceptance of the Russian's apology. As the guards took him back to the compound, Erich mulled over the strange action of the NKVD man. Truly the Russians were a people whose oppressors defied rational codes of behavior. Veteran prisoners told Erich that the NKVD man's striking him with the cane was a serious offense against the Russian regulations, involving severe disciplinary penalties for the lieutenant if his superiors ever heard about it.

This proved to be the truth. In ten and a half years of Russian confinement, the blow across the face with the cane was the only direct physical punishment inflicted on Erich Hartmann. His reaction to the Russian's blow was duly entered in his dossier. Years later, at Shakhty prison, a Russian girl interpreter showed him the relevant entry: "Be careful

how you handle this man—he *hits*." Several times through the
years he had heard his guards refer to him as "the Hitter,"
but he had not realized how this minor happening had become a part of his image as a recalcitrant and troublesome
prisoner.

Physical beatings were thus looked upon as an inferior
method of persuasion by the NKVD. Their armory contained
more efficient weapons for breaking a man's will, and these
weapons were multiplied in potency by the pervasive hopelessness in which the Germans led their wretched lives. The
prisoners were politically as well as physically lost, for the
German government had gone down in ruins with the Nazis.
A new civilian government had to be raised under the aegis of
the occupying Allied powers, and a political rupture soon
developed between Russian-occupied East Germany and the
remainder of the country.

The NKVD delightedly reported to the prisoners the details
of their fatherland's postwar convulsions, embellishing every
negative fact, amplifying every adverse report. Anything that
would help convince the prisoner he was forsaken was
brought into full psychological utility. German officer prisoners were often told by the NKVD that their imprisonment and
loss of rights had been approved by the Allies at Teheran.

Stripped of any means of having their plight redressed,
many Germans simply gave up hope. As the struggle of the
infant German Federal Rpublic to find its feet spread over the
years, German soldiers rotted and died in Russian prisons by
the thousands. Pontifications about justice resonating around
the halls of Nuremberg raised only empty echoes in the
barbed-wire pens on the Steppes.

The Russians flatly told their victims that the NKVD would
take all the time it needed to break them down. The NKVD
proceeded on the basis that as omnipotent captors they had all
the resources necessary to make the Germans do or become
whatever they wished. Protracted punishment of surrendered
soldiers is new to relations between civilized states, but the
basis was firmly laid for it in Russia after the Second World
War. Inordinate punishments are part of the warp and woof
of Soviet psychology, and since such punishments were meted
out to internal opponents of the regime, the invading Ger-

mans could hardly have expected better. The tacit approval of the Allies with this project, however, will long remain a stain on the Western escutcheon.

Exacerbating the misery of German prisoners was the impossibility of escape. Russian society in the time of Erich Hartmann's confinement was organized so as to virtually preclude escape from inside the Soviet Union proper. Russian people were confined to their own village area, traveling beyond its boundaries only with official permission. Village children were trained from infancy to report the presence of strangers to their schoolteachers, who then reported the interlopers to the police.

A border escape zone, thirty miles wide, was settled with reliable Communists and heavily sprinkled with military posts, from which complete surveillance was maintained. Belts of buried metal-detection grids covered vast areas of the border, giving instant warning of the passage of metal across the ground above. Border guards on the ground and helicopter and light aircraft patrols overhead sealed the border effectively.

The Iron Curtain was a reality, not a figure of speech. Russian political prisoners incarcerated at various times with Erich Hartmann asserted that without this reverse border defense, the Soviet Union would lose at least a million citizens as refugees to the West. Any German fortunate enough to reach this border zone and in a position to bribe the villagers for aid had to reckon on the NKVD counter tactic, which was to double the German bribe and let the Russian informer keep all the money.

Crossing the Steppes from the Urals and then crashing the iron border to the West was a challenge to discourage the boldest lionheart. In Erich Hartmann's words:

"I don't know of one honest case where a P.O.W. has come out from inside Russia. There are stories on TV about this, but if you try to find out who the man is that actually did it, nobody can tell you. Perhaps it was possible from camps in Poland or the Baltic States, or East Germany, but I never heard of one authentic case where a German P.O.W. got back home from inside Russia."

The pressure applied with such consistency by the NKVD —largely through dehumanization—was almost a solid physi-

cal presence. To ease or escape the pressure on his will to
resist, a German could give up something of himself in return
for an NKVD favor. He might inform on a fellow prisoner,
becoming a *stukatcha*. He might confess to an alleged war
crime. The humblest things became glittering prizes to these
embattled souls. An easier job, a chance to read a letter from
home—common activities to which a free man in a free
country pays no thought—became the fulcrums with which
the NKVD separated the individual from his self-respect.

The most odious and intolerable technique used by the
NKVD against its captives was the interception of mail. Right
from the earliest postwar days, all mail from Germany was
intercepted by the secret police, scrutinized for ammunition
that could be used against the individual's psychological
armor, and then either destroyed or used for blackmail and
persuasion. This blackguardly tactic makes a physical beating
administered to a helpless man appear almost humane by
comparison. The consequences of interrupted contact with
home on the inner life of the individual were devastating.

Erich Hartmann was not permitted to write his first postcard home until Christmas Eve, 1945, nearly eight months
after his capture. Usch received the missive in January 1946.

> My Usch—
> I can tell you that I am alive. I wish you all a nice
> Christmas and a good New Year. Fear not for me. For
> which do I congratulate you, a daughter or a son? All
> my thoughts are with you. With a lot of kisses
>
> > Your
> > Erich.

Every month thereafter, Erich was permitted to write twenty-five words to Germany, until 1947. With the war over for
two years, the Russians reduced the quota to five words once
a month. Usch wrote steadily, sending between 350 and 400
letters to Erich in the ten years of his imprisonment. He
received less than 40 of these.

He did not learn until May of 1946 that a son, Peter Erich,
had been born to him and Usch on 21 May 1945. The little
boy did not survive the grim postwar years, and after he died
at two years and nine months, it was a further year before

Erich learned of the loss. When his beloved father died in 1952, Erich did not find out for more than a year.

The grinding process thus went on, year in and year out. Americans got limited exposure to this form of warfare when a small number of American servicemen were illegally detained by the Chinese Reds following the Korean War. Among these Americans was one of the USAF's most famous fighter aces, Colonel Walker M. "Bud" Mahurin, a hero of both World War II and the Korean War.

A literate and analytical man, Mahurin set down his experiences with brainwashing in a first-class book, *Honest John*, which ought to be required reading for Americans in these troubled times.* Mahurin later met with Erich Hartmann in Germany, and the two aces compared notes on Communist confinement. Both agree that judgment of prisoners of war by people at home is wrong, since the average inhabitant of a civilized Western country can have no real understanding of Communist prisons and the methods employed to break men.

Hartmann and Mahurin both agree that given the time and the power, *any* individual can be broken by Communist tactics. There is no question of courage, loyalty or patriotism providing sufficient armor against such an assault. They do not. Influential Americans exposed to no more serious event than a television gunfight have nevertheless seen fit to draw up weighty codes of conduct for U.S. servicemen totally in the power of an unscrupulous enemy. Beyond any direct aid from their own government and often completely cut off from contact with their families, such men may do things that will make them the targets of home-front criticism.

Prisoners of war may be motivated, under some circumstances, to write letters, sign papers, tape radio broadcasts or give television interviews of a damning nature. These acts are not prima facie evidence of weakness or disloyalty. They may have become involved in such things for fear of their lives, the lives of loved ones, or for something as seemingly rudimentary as food to stave off starvation.

* The story of U.S. Navy Commander Lloyd M. Bucher and his captive ship, U.S.S. *Pueblo*, is perhaps the beginning of another chapter in the history of brainwashing. Captured by the North Korean Navy, Bucher and his crew were tortured from the day of capture, 23 January 1968, to their release eleven months later.

No tactic is forbidden to the oppressor, no threat to his powerless captive is considered beyond the rules, and no ethical impulse or fundamental decency governs the captor's conduct. From armchairs in safe lands nevertheless, the defenseless prisoner is exhorted to resist or face ostracism on his return to his homeland, and possibly even a trial as a traitor. With more Americans in Red power as this is written, some rethinking of popular notions on brainwashing is overdue.

The only contact with human kindness experienced by most Germans in Russia was with ordinary villagers from communities near the prison camps. These human exchanges were a nettlesome nuisance to the NKVD sadists, who could not bear to see any manifestations of human feeling, either in the Germans or in their fellow Russians.

Camps located in areas of the Soviet Union occupied in wartime by the Germans were a major source of difficulty for the NKVD. Russian villagers in these regions, on the basis of their experience, were kindly disposed toward the Germans, Ilya Ehrenburg's propaganda notwithstanding. The villagers bitterly resented the imprisonment of their former enemies, and constantly made friends with the Germans. Trading and bartering between P.O.W.'s and villagers was carried on through the guards, many of whom were former front-line soldiers sympathetic to the plight of their ex-enemies.

Red Cross packages reaching the Germans were often a disappointment. The NKVD delays imposed on shipments resulted in stale foodstuffs. The NKVD restrictions reduced other Red Cross activities in behalf of the prisoners to ineffectuality. By some special magic, the evangelist Bishop Haeckel* in Munich was able to provide a reasonable package service to P.O.W.'s despite capricious NKVD supervision. The contents of these packages sustained a brisk barter between P.O.W.'s and Russian villagers, brightening the lives of all concerned. Good relations stemming from barter and friendship between Russian civilians and German P.O.W.'s infuriated the NKVD.

* Bishop Haeckel polled the wives and families of P.O.W.'s to determine the needs of the incarcerated men. He circulated a newsletter in which reports of camp conditions and transfers were consolidated, and his services in general were practical Christianity of the highest order.

The guards were given intensive propagandist indoctrination against the Germans to rekindle old hatreds. The shabby prisoners were depicted as "the men who killed your wives, sisters, fathers and brothers . . . they are the Fascist murderers." With these ideas driven into their subconscious minds by the NKVD psychopaths, the guards came to their duties fairly bristling with hostility.

Only a few days were required to break away the armor in which the propagandists had clad the guards. Friendship and common humanity won the day over bigotry and falsehood. Resistant spirits among the guards felt the villagers' wrath. The villagers taunted the guards, told them their captives were only soldiers "just like you," and that they had wives and families at home "just like you."

Erich Hartmann recounts that some of the younger guards often broke down emotionally:

"The inner conflict between the rubbish the propagandist had taught them and what their contacts with us awakened in their feeling world would literally bring them to tears. There they would be, standing on the other side of the wire, tommy gun in hand, breaking down because of the untruth they were being forced to live.

"Often I would say to such a soldier, 'Why are you crying? Just one hour of propaganda and now we are enemies again. You are silly.' Sometimes, that would snap them back the way they were, and they would forget the propaganda. You cannot hate such people. Often, I am expected to hate the Russian people, as though no other emotion could possibly be open to me, but *my ten years in Russian prisons taught me the difference between the Russian people and their secret police.*"

The efforts of the German prisoners to establish contact with the villagers were so successful that the NKVD was forced to change the guard completely at the camps every four weeks. Later the camps were moved from the former German-occupied zones back into the Ural areas. The villagers in these regions were well-fueled with Red propaganda about the Fascist beasts, and half-expected to see horns on the heads of the prisoners when they arrived. Nevertheless, contact was eventually established, and common humanity again won out over propagandist distortions.

Occasional contact with Russian civilians was nevertheless

insufficient to overcome the NKVD's remorseless program of dehumanization through constant pressure. Once men began to crack, the NKVD could use them—up to a point. The utility of a given German prisoner depended on what he could contribute to NKVD projects, and was largely a function of his knowledge and character and his status among his fellows.

The "war criminals" psychosis of the postwar period saw this conception, originally intended to punish premeditated crimes against humanity, applied to nearly every German soldier in Russian power. When prisoners cracked under the pressures of their environment, the NKVD pumped them relentlessly for information on alleged war crimes that they may have witnessed. They were persuaded by threats or favors, or both, to disclose the names, places and dates involved in these alleged crimes. Then the long and vengeful arm of the NKVD could reach out for the perpetrators. Prisoners were persuaded to confess to their own war crimes. A German drafted into the army and sent to fight in Russia was guilty of a war crime in the NKVD version of history.

The NKVD could break down men of ordinary character and background with relative ease under Russian prison conditions. Most men years removed from their families could hardly be blamed for doing anything either to alleviate their hardships or to promote their freedom. Offering freedom to individuals in exchange for damning information on fellow prisoners proved a temptation to some men beyond their powers of resistance. The stool pigeons became part of prison life, and the German officer corps contributed its share to their numbers.

Germans who survived the Soviet prisons are generally tolerant toward men whose breakdown point came earlier than others. All of them know that everyone has a border beyond which resistance ceases, and most of them went to or beyond that border in Russia. This attitude contrasts sharply with the unrealistic home-front viewpoint that only the weak succumb. The noisiest views in this connection have been expressed by men who have never had to face the problem as prisoners of war.

For extraordinary tasks in West Germany and other sensitive areas, the NKVD needed extraordinary men, and the process of bringing such individuals into Soviet service was invariably difficult. Men with ability, courage and will power were ideally suited to espionage assignments outside Russia, but these were the very individuals whose character made them resistant to NKVD pressure. Natural leaders like Erich Hartmann were prime targets of the Soviet persuaders.

Brainwashing has been fictionalized and misrepresented. Erich Hartmann writes of this technique, after more than ten years' experience with it, in these terms:

"The main pressure on a Communist prisoner and the real force in brainwashing is *hunger*. Starve a man, and in the ensuing egocentric fight of the individual for his own life all else is rapidly obliterated. The unavoidable, self-preservational choice 'him or me?' sunders all bonds of comradeship.

"Surrounded by a mass of his fellows, the individual yet becomes isolated within the limits of his own shriveling personality. Helpless and fearful, cut off from even the faintest glimmer of hope, he functions within ever-diminishing boundaries. Ethical connections to his fellow men and to the culture that produced him, all teachings, laws, rules and regulations dissolve under the acid of self-preservation.

"Thus divested of his resources of resistance, the bereft individual is pitted against a remorseless and inhuman regime. Collapse was virtually unavoidable. This was how the NKVD reached the masses of the prisoners and made them instruments of the Soviet will.

"This is the reality of brainwashing."

Erich Hartmann confronted the reality of brainwashing and felt its lash in the depths of his being. He fought a mercilessly unequal two-year battle with the NKVD, a struggle with the political equivalent of the Forces of Darkness that might one day also be ours. His ordeal in this struggle will now be related, and it may give all free men cause to wonder how they would fare in a similar encounter.

Erich Hartmann
Weil im Schönbuch
Kreis Böblingen Wvtbg

Die Kriegsflugzeuge der Feindmächte

Teil II:

Sowjet-Union

Bilder und Leistungen

(einschließlich brit. u. USA. Lieferungen)

Stand: 1. 10. 1943

8.	1 J. G. 52
Eing.:	— 5. DEZ 1943
Brief Nr.	4651 Ant.
tried.gt:	

Sonderausgabe des „Frontnachrichtenblattes der Luftwaffe"
B/1/43

43. *Pilots' Handbook of Enemy Strength.* Title page of handbook issued to Hartmann in Jan., 1943, on the Soviet Front. The booklet contained photos of Soviet, British, and American Aircraft most likely to be encountered in aerial combat. Detail drawings showing the locations of armament and vulnerable fuel tanks of several types of aircraft follow.

IL-2 = ИЛ-2

Schlachtflugzeug

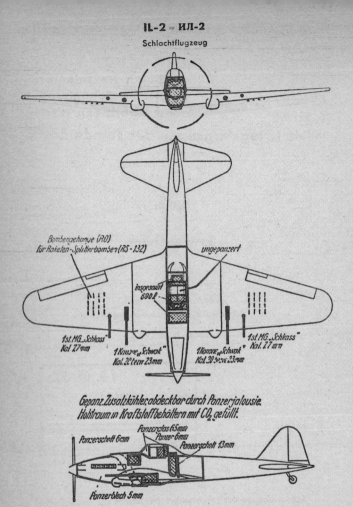

Bombengehäuse (RO)
für Raketen-Splitterbomben (RS-132)

ungepanzert

insgesamt
690 l

1st MG „Schkass"
Kal. 7,7 mm

1 Kanone „Schwak"
Kal. 20 bezw. 23 mm

1 Kanone „Schwak"
Kal. 20 bezw. 23 mm

1st MG „Schkass"
Kal. 7,7 mm

Gepanz. Zusatzkühler abdeckbar durch Panzerjalousie.
Hohlraum in Kraftstoffbehältern mit CO_2 gefüllt.

Panzerglas 65mm
Panzer 6mm

Panzerschott 6mm

Panzerschott 13mm

Panzerblech 5mm

44. Stormovik, the Soviet answer to the Luftwaffe's Stuka dive-bomber. The Ilyushin Il-2 was a highly effective close-support bomber and the heavy armor-plating protection of its vitals made it an almost impossible aircraft to shoot down. Hartmann's first victory was an Il-2 on Nov. 1942. Between then and May 7, 1945, Hartmann shot down 62 Il-2 aircraft, this score including a number of later models of Il-2 known in some circles as the Il-7.

SB-2 CB-2 (SB-2 M-100)
Kampf- und Aufklärungsflugzeug

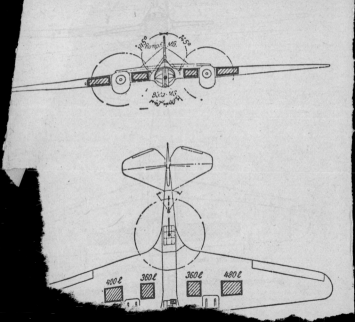

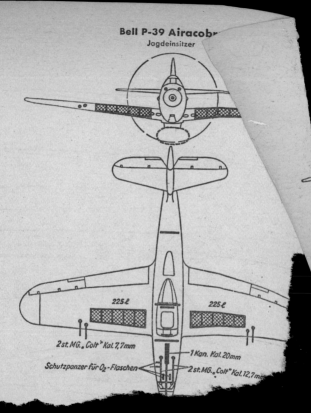

Bell P-39 Airacobra
Jagdeinsitzer

225 ℓ   225 ℓ

2 st. MG. „Colt" Kal. 7,7mm

1 Kan. Kal. 20mm

Schutzpanzer für O₂-Flaschen

2 st. MG. „Colt" Kal. 12,7mm

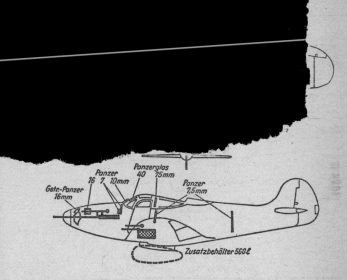

Getr-Panzer
16mm

Panzer
16 7 10mm

Panzerglas
40 75mm

Panzer
7,5mm

Zusatzbehälter 560ℓ

45. Over Russia the call "Airacobra!" was heard and dreaded by the Luftwaffe because the Soviets equipped a group made up of the best fighter aces with this type of aircraft. They painted their planes red and called themselves "Red Guards." Hartmann shot down 18 Airacobras up to Oct., 1943, and estimates another 15 fell victim before the war ended.

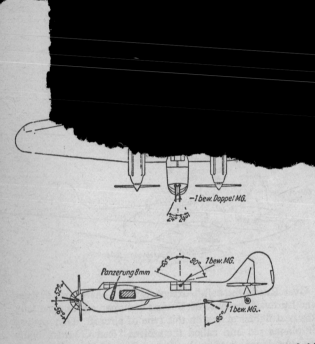

— 1 bew. Doppel MG.

24° 24°

65° 80° 1 bew. MG.

Panzerung 8mm

57°

65°

85° 1 bew. MG..

46. SB-2. Hartmann shot down approximately 40 of this type of Soviet twin-engine aircraft.

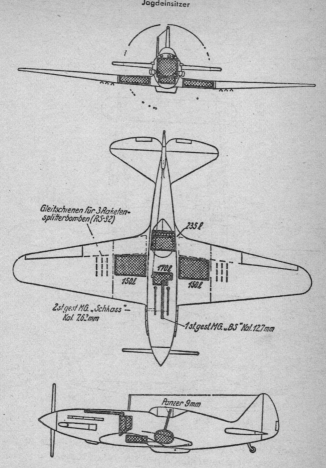

Gleitschienen für 3 Raketen-
splitterbomben (RS-82)

235 l

170 l

150 l

150 l

2 st gest MG. „Schkass"-
Kal. 7,62 mm

1 st gest MG. „BS" Kal. 12,7 mm

Panzer 9mm

47. MIG-3. The Mikoyan-Gurevich-designed Soviet Fighter used early in the war against Germany. Hartmann scored only 1 victory over the MIG-3, that on Jan. 27, 1943, over Amavir in the Caucasus. The MIG-1 and MIG-3 aircraft were being phased out at this time. Maximum speed was about 390 mph, but it lacked maneuverability necessary for aerial combat.

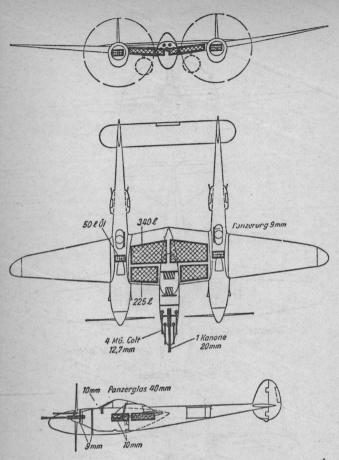

50 ℓ Öl · 340 ℓ · Panzerung 9mm · 225 ℓ

4 MG. Colt 12,7mm · 1 Kanone 20mm

10mm · Panzerglas 40mm · 9mm · 10mm

48. Lockheed P-38 was furnished through lend-lease to the Soviet forces. Hartmann shot down several of these.

49. Lagg-3. With a top speed of about 350 mph and lacking maneuverability, this fighter seemed doomed from the beginning. However, it could absorb a tremendous amount of lead; German bullets made toothpicks out of its Siberian birch frame fuselage and it still kept flying. Hartmann shot down 27 Lagg-3 aircraft in 1943.

LAGG-3 ЛАГГ-3
Jagdeinsitzer

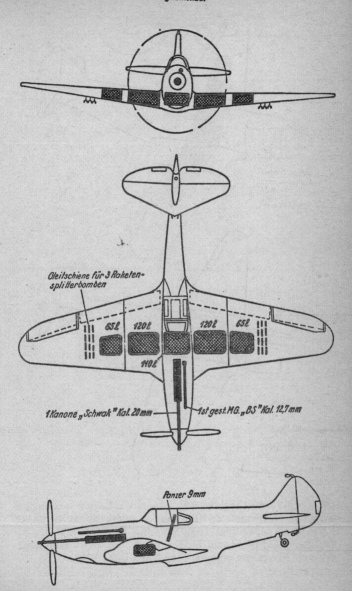

Gleitschiene für 3 Raketen-
splitterbomben

65ℓ 120ℓ 120ℓ 65ℓ

110ℓ

1 Kanone „Schwak" Kal. 20 mm —— 1st gest. M.G. „BS" Kal. 12,7 mm

Panzer 9 mm

LA-5 = ЛА-5
Jagdeinsitzer

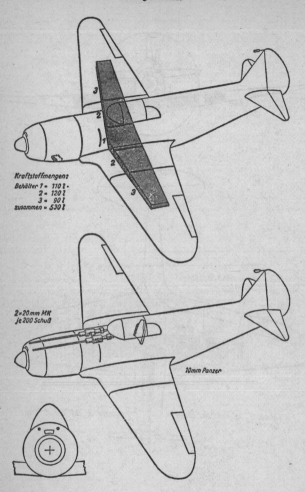

Kraftstoffmenge:
Behälter 1 = 110 l
         2 = 120 l
         3 = 90 l
zusammen = 530 l

2 × 20mm MK
je 200 Schuß

10mm Panzer

50. **Lagg-5 Soviet Fighter.** This later model Lagg was equipped with a radical engine and the Russian pilots capitalized on its low altitude capabilities. Lagg-5 top speed was 402 mph and its successor, Lagg-7, could buzz along at 413 mph. Hartmann downed 70 of them between May 7 and Dec., 1943.

Hawker Hurricane II C

Jagdeinsitzer
Herkunft: GB.

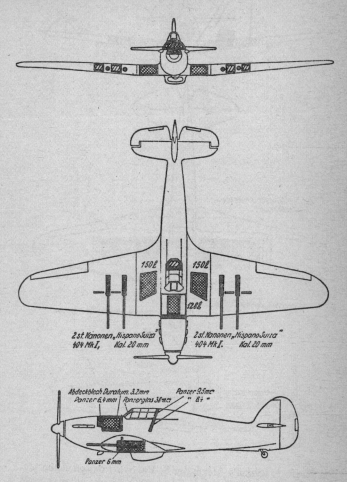

2 st. Kanonen „Hispano Suiza"
404 Mk I.   Kal. 20 mm

2 st. Kanonen „Hispano Suiza"
404 Mk I.   Kal. 20 mm

Abdeckblech Duralum. 3.2 mm
Panzer 6.4 mm   Panzerglas 38 mm
Panzer 9.5 mm
„ 6 "

Panzer 6 mm

51. British Hawker Hurricane. Hartmann occasionally encountered lend-lea e, Russian-flown aircraft. He remembers com-
bating the Hurricane, but since his second logbook is still
missing he is reluctant to say how many fell before his guns.

JAK-1 ЯК-1
Jagdeinsitzer

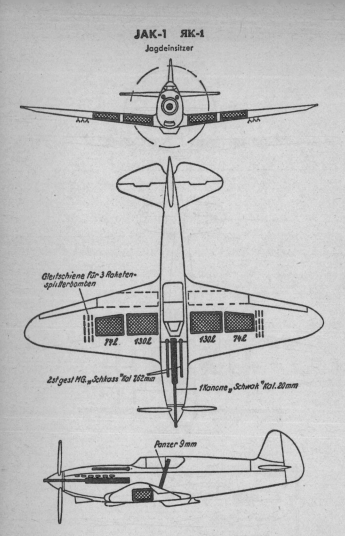

Gleitschiene für 3 Raketen-splitterbomben

74L   130L   130L   74L

2st gest.MG. „Schkass"Kal.7,62mm

1Kanone „Schwak" Kal.20mm

Panzer 9mm

52. YAK-1. Russia's Alexander S. Yakovlev designed the plywood and metal "Krasavec" (Beauty) YAK-1 fighter, known early in the war as the I-26. A later improved model was known as the YAK-7. Hartmann shot down 16 YAK-1 and YAK-7 aircraft between Aug. 1 and Aug. 9, 1943.

Supermarine Spitfire V
Jagdflugzeug
Herkunft: GB.

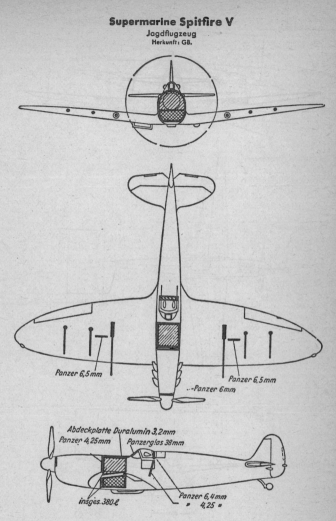

Panzer 6,5mm

Panzer 6,5mm

--Panzer 6mm

Abdeckplatte Duralumin 3,2mm
Panzer 4,25mm   Panzerglas 38mm

insges. 380 ℓ

Panzer 6,4mm
 "   4,25 "

53. Spitfire. Russia received approximately 14,700 lend-lease aircraft of which over 6,000 were from Great Britain. Of the total, 8,200 were fighters and, in order of numbers delivered, they included P-39 Airacobra, Spitfire, Hurricane, Curtiss P-40, North American P-51 "Mustangs."

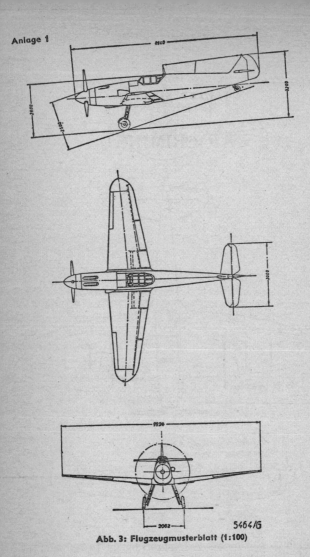

Anlage 1

Abb. 3: Flugzeugmusterblatt (1:100)

54. Three views of the **BF-109G-5 (ME-109G)**. Hartmann flew all of his combat in various models of the 109, including Bf-109G-7, G-10, G-14, G-**16,** and Bf-109R-4. In addition. he has flown the Bf-109-B, C, **D, E, F,** and all G models listed above.

CHAPTER SIXTEEN

WAR CRIMINAL

Perhaps man's history is simpler than we think. It is
summed up in proclaiming the right and doing the
wrong.

—*Clemenceau*

IN A CAMPAIGN to break Erich Hartmann, launched in 1947,
the NKVD interrupted his mail both ways as a primary tactic.
Scraps of news taken from Usch's steady stream of letters to
Erich, were fed to him in a heartless, Pavlovian effort to make
him obey. He was given just enough information from home
to arouse almost unendurable cravings for human contact.
Everything else was withheld. This cruel campaign lasted two
years.

The NKVD wanted Erich Hartmann to sign written state-
ments confessing to a range of war crimes. The NKVD had,
of course, itself composed these "confessions" and manufactured all the details. The irrelevancy of Erich's forced confes-
sion to such fictional crimes never impressed itself on his
tormentors. Obsessed as all bureaucrats are by signed, completed forms and perfect documentation, validity or truth of
their content was of no significance to the NKVD. Irrational
like all psychopaths, they preferred to have him sign a lie
than to hear him tell the truth.

All possible pressure was exerted on Erich, but he fought
back and managed to keep his cowardly foes at bay for two
years. The man who tries to meet irrational individuals with
rational argument is doomed to fail in his quest for reason.
The perverse world they inhabit is upside down and back-to-

235

front—a negative of the world of normal men. In Erich Hartmann's own words:

"The Russians—by which I mean the NKVD psychopaths —have a mentality that no rational Western-educated individual can comprehend. You can kill your father there, and confess it to the police, and they may confine you for two years. If you steal something, that is inconsequential. The Russians laugh if you *don't* steal something. But if you say that the American Chevrolet is better than the Russian Ziss car, then you will get *twenty-five years in jail.* If you say Stalin, or Khrushchev, or Brezhnev is a bad leader—whichever one of them happens to be leading Russia at the time— then they will hang you or give you life imprisonment. Many of our prison mates were Russian citizens who had violated current Red dogma. They were men with gumption and reason, but the NKVD ensured that they stayed out of circulation."

The final nine months of the NKVD's campaign to break him saw him spending most of his time in the bunker. He was at Camp Kuteynikovo in the Donets Basin, less than a mile from the airstrip from which the 7th Squadron of III/JG-52 had operated in the summer of 1943. He had taken off from the Kuteynikovo Airfield on the morning that he fell into the hands of the Russians and later made good his escape. In 1949, there would be no escape. He was willing to die in Kuteynikovo if necessary, rather than surrender. He crowned his resistance with a hunger strike, rejecting even the handful of bread necessary each day to sustain life. He fully intended to commit suicide in this way if he was forced to, and while he was not yet twenty-eight years old, his physical power was at an end. The Russians let him go three full days without food or water.

On the fourth morning, the door of the bunker burst open and two hulking guards hustled him out of the dungeon and into the office of the camp doctor. In his bare surgery, the Russian medic was waiting with an array of bottles and tubes on a table. The doctor nodded to the guards.

Massive muscles seized the emaciated Erich and pinned his arms to his sides. He was dragged to a cot on one side of the surgery. Kicking his legs from under him, the guards pinioned his limbs as he lay prostrate. He was powerless. The doctor walked over impassively, and forcing a tube into Erich's mouth, connected the other end to a plastic bladder full of yellow liquid.

The doctor squeezed the bladder, and Erich felt a sweet and sickly flood in his mouth. Spitting and gulping he tried to get rid of the tube. Overpowered at every move by the guards, Erich began swallowing the mixture to avoid strangulation. The doctor kept pressing the bladder.

"Eggs and sugar, Hartmann," said the doctor. "You must eat. The Commissar has ordered it."

The ruthless cycle of force-feeding and confinement in the bunker continued for a further twenty-seven days. At the end of this time, Erich felt a hopeless, moribund wreck. He had abandoned struggling with the guards, but they continued to pinion him solidly at every feeding. On the twenty-seventh day, the NKVD Commissar visited him in his dank hole.

"Erich, Erich, what are you doing?" he cajoled. "You are such a young man. Don't starve here. If we get the order from Moscow, we will kill you—just shoot you down—understand? But we have the order that you are to live, and so you will live, even if we have to force you to live as we have been doing."

Erich stared groggily into the face of the Russian. His body felt wasted to a wraith. Malevolent and heavy, the Commissar's countenance swam before him in a fog. The coaxing voice came floating again through the cloying mist of unconsciousness, and this time his tormentor was applying the ultimate pressure.

"Look, Erich, *look!* I have five letters from your wife, Usch. Five of them. They will be full of interest for you, with all kinds of news about your home and family. All you have to do is stop this starving and you will get these letters."

Erich peered at the array of letters the Commissar was holding in his hand like a royal flush in a poker game. Erich could see the Stuttgart postmark. Yes, and that was the handwriting of his beloved Usch. For two years he had heard nothing, now here were five more links with the human world being dangled before him.

In the dank and wretched bunker at Kuteynikovo, which thousands of Germans had cursed a thousand different ways, Erich felt a consuming void inside himself grow and swell and pulsate until it burst over him in a black tide. There at that moment, in that hellhole in the earth, forsaken by all but his Usch, Erich knew he had come to the end of his rope.

His tortured soul ached in his wasted body. Resistance was ended and he knew it. He had to have those letters no matter what the cost. Two years—God in Heaven, was there no mercy? He resolved that beaten as he was he would deny the Commissar the pleasure of seeing him crack. Summoning all his remaining strength, he spat out his answer.

"I will not sign your damned paper, and I will not eat!"

Gaping in disbelief at the shriveled skeleton still snarling defiance, the Commissar straightened up. Stuffing Usch's letters in his pocket, he turned and stumped out, cursing. But the brave man in the bunker knew that he had shot his bolt.

Erich sank back on the cold ground in the bunker, his energy and spirit spent. He found himself sobbing softly in the darkness. If he needed any confirmation that he had reached the end, the involuntary sobbing was proof enough. Yet, through the blackness of his despair, the spirit still struggled bravely.

For two more nights and days he continued to resist the now ever present impulse to surrender. He found himself inwardly glad when they dragged him out for oral injections of milk, sugar and eggs. In the blackness of the bunker, the Commissar's malignant face swam before his mind's eye, standing out among a covey of taunting phantoms that came hurtling up from his subconscious.

Every NKVD bully, persuader or persecutor that he had ever resisted in Russia took part in the parade of images that crossed his mind. He relived the horror of the rape pogrom in the meadow. The humid death-stench of the Kirov swamp camp seemed again to pervade his being in nauseating waves. Time after time in his mind he smashed the chair down on the head of the bullying Russian lieutenant. Commissars and faceless phantoms in NKVD uniforms swirled before him and with accusing fingers bawled, "Bunker!" "Bunker!" "Bunker!" "Twenty-one days, forty days, sixty days . . . bunker, bunker, bunker."

When at length the phantasmagoria dissolved and departed, he found his brain strangely purged and his thinking quick, quiet and cool. He knew now that he must eat to save himself. His prior resolve to kill himself by starvation was an aberration. He must not die in Russia and leave his beloved Usch alone in the world. She was waiting. He must not fail her. Somehow, by some means divine or human, he would return home. He realized that if he died he would be of no use to anyone, but alive he could keep hope burning for others, as well as for himself.

As in his combat days, he began quietly talking to himself. "Erich, you first must conquer your main enemy—hunger. Get something to eat, no matter what you have to do. Then, by God, you get your hands on those letters and read them, before you die of curiosity. Then you will see life differently."

As though responding telepathically to the trend of Erich's thoughts, the bunker door swung open. The two hulking guards again stood ready to escort him to the surgery. With a Herculean effort, he stood up and walked shakily out of the bunker. His legs felt like rubber. The guards shoved him into the surgery ready for another pinioning prior to force-feeding him. Weakly, he waved the guards away.

"I will eat. I will eat on my own. I . . . I . . . give up my hunger strike."

The Soviet doctor looked at him in surprise. Then an oily smile of satisfaction spread over the Russian's face. He offered Erich a cigarette.

"Good. You will eat. I will tell the Commissar. The guards will take you now to the Commissar's office."

The doctor picked up the feeding tube and bladder, looked at them wryly, then let them fall back on the desk.

"This is a hell of a way to eat, Hartmann," he said. "I am glad you have finally decided to listen to reason."

Erich went stumbling shakily out of the surgery, guards at his elbows, and made his way to the Commissar's room. The seventy-yard walk pushed him to his absolute physical limit. Sweating profusely, trembling violently and near collapse, he went reeling into the Commissar's office and slumped down in a chair. A guard went to the kitchen and brought him back some bread on a tin plate.

Lunging into the stale bread, Erich clawed it into lumps and ate voraciously. A long draught from a cup of soup washed down the bread, although his hands were trembling so much he could hardly hold the mug. Never had food tasted so good, even if it was little more than hog fodder. A feeling of increasing solidity in his belly acted like an anchor, and soon his head stopped spinning and the trembling abated in his limbs. Strength came seeping back. He quietly swore to himself that he would never again embark on such a damned fool thing as a hunger strike. A bullet in the heart would be better.

The Commissar brought him his five letters from Usch. He ripped the envelopes open and fell on the pages of writing as avidly as he had fallen on the dry bread. Usch was well. Wonderful! Details of home surged into him like adrenalin. "Flowers in bloom . . . a band concert in town . . . Erich's mother and father were well . . . a new dress. . . ." The trivia of everyday German life throbbed with interest. He pored over the letters like an archaeologist absorbed with writings exhumed from some ancient pyramid. Life could be bearable again, now that he knew Usch was safe and the home front was secure. The news put more vitality into him than the food. He felt like a new man—ready for anything.

As Erich finished reading the five letters for the third time, a shadow came between the paper and the small window. The Commissar's somber bulk intruded on his paradise. The Russian drew a paper from his pocket and set it in front of Erich together with a pen.

"Here is what you have to sign," he said.

Erich glanced at the usual juvenile summary of alleged charges to which he would be pleading guilty by signing the document. He had murdered women and children, destroyed property and inflicted grievous matériel losses on the Soviet Union. The Blond Knight had recovered enough of his fire to fight again. If he knew Usch was fine, he could stand anything. He pushed the paper back at the NKVD man.

"I have read my letters, and therefore it is not now necessary for me to confess to these lies," he said.

The Russian's face dropped.

"You mean you now refuse to sign, after we have fed you and saved you from suicide?"

"I mean only that I will not sign your paper. It is not even written in my language. Besides, I have never killed women and children in my life, not even in the war. I am not ashamed of having been a soldier of my country."

"I warn you, Hartmann. This will mean severe punishment for you. You will never be released."

Erich looked directly into the NKVD man's shifty eyes.

"You have been saying the same thing to me for years. You violate even the commandments of your own god-hero, Lenin. He said that any nation retaining war prisoners more than six months after a war was uncivilized. You keep me here in Russia as a slave for five years, and want me to confess to crimes that your NKVD propagandists have invented. No. I will not sign your damned paper."

Bulging with fury, the Commissar snatched up the paper.

"You will pay for this dishonor," he barked, and flung out of the room red with rage.

Erich read his letters again and basked in the sweetness of news from home. He didn't care if they shot him down. Let them. Today the letters were his world, and it sang with vitalizing harmony.

In the ensuing days it was obvious that the Russians were glad he had quit his hunger strike. Erich kept after the food and began to regain a little of the weight he had lost. He began feeling stronger, and could soon walk around without fear of collapse. The NKVD left him alone until he was clearly out of danger, then they began another approach.

Guards took him to the Commissar's office, then left him alone with his adversary. The Russian offered him a cigarette. Erich took the cigarette, lit it and sat down in a stiff-backed chair to which the Commissar waved him.

"Erich, we have been reviewing your case. Yes, we have reviewed it quite thoroughly, and as a result we have reached some new opinions about you."

Erich dragged quietly on his cigarette and looked back evenly at the Commissar, at his wavering eyes and fidgety hands. When these NKVD types called him "Erich" he always got a bad feeling in his backside, like having an enemy on his tail during the war. He waited for the Russian to commit himself.

"We are exceedingly sorry, of course, to know that your young son died in Germany. Bad luck. Very bad luck indeed, Erich."

"Perhaps if the Russian government had allowed his father to go home and take care of him he would be alive today."

Erich's reply was quietly spoken, but the Commissar's obvious and immediate discomfort told Erich that the Russian knew he had used the wrong ploy in attempting to gain his prisoner's confidence. The Commissar took another tack.

"Erich, you are barely twenty-eight years old. You are so young. Really, you were much too young in wartime to have been a Fascist. You were caught up in the war and forced to fight. . . ."

"I did my duty as a soldier, nothing more."

"Of course, of course. And now we have another soldier's job for you, one that would help you blot out the past. It would allow you to go home to your family."

Erich's heart leaped. "Home"—that magnificent, incomparable word.

"What kind of job do you have in mind for me?" said Erich.

The Commissar leaned forward, encouraged by this arousal of his prisoner's interest.

"The Soviet Union is supporting the development of a modern air force for the East German People's Republic. We are supplying the latest Soviet jet fighters, but we have many difficulties."

"Where do I fit in with all this?"

"Erich, our major difficulty is in finding experienced leaders around whom this new air force can be built. You follow me?"

Erich nodded.

"We know your record as a fighter pilot, of course. And we know from your prison history that you are a leader . . . even if in here you were a ringleader, eh?"

The Russian laughed nervously as his clumsy attempt at humor failed to evoke a response from Erich. The Blond Knight's face remained expressionless, his gaze steady.

"We need you for the East German Air Force, Erich. We will prepare you for this job immediately, take you out of this prison and up to Moscow for schooling. You'd like that. Then you can decide what you want to do—whether to work in the East German Air Force as an officer or on the political side of the air force organization. But you must work for us."

Ending his pitch with hope in his eyes and anticipation written all over his face, the Russian officer looked at Erich. The Blond Knight slowly shook his head. The Commissar's face straightened.

"You don't like this proposal?" he said.

"Before we can talk about any kind of job at all, flying, consulting, political or whatever, you must first send me out as a free man to my family in the West."

The Russian looked downcast. Erich further depressed him.

"After I am at home in the West, you can make me a normal contract offer—a business deal such as people sign every day all over the world. If I like your offer, and if I choose to accept, then I will come back and work with you in accordance with the contract. But if you put me to work—or try to put me to work—under coercion of any kind, then I will resist to my dying gasp."

The Commissar shook his head sadly.

"I am sorry you feel this way, Erich, because it means that you can never again see your family."

The Commissar's mournful expression was almost too good to be true. Erich half-expected the Russian to burst into tears, his hopes of winning Erich over had obviously been so high. The Russian pressed a button on his desk and two guards came clumping into the room. In Russian he ordered the prisoner taken back to barracks. As Erich was walking out through the door, the Commissar ended the interview more typically of the NKVD—with a threat.

"This time, you Fascist bandit, you are really going to regret not working with us."

Erich immediately felt more comfortable. When the NKVD called him a "Fascist bandit" or a "capitalist murderer" he knew he was on the right track. That was the NKVD in its true form. When they told him he was a nice young fellow, and called him Erich and offered him cigarettes, he had learned to beware.

Shortly afterward, massive shipments of German prisoners for home were begun. There were fourteen hundred German soldiers in Kuteynikovo with Erich, and within a few weeks more than two-thirds of them were repatriated. True to their threat, the NKVD excluded Erich from the repatriation groups. Glad outwardly to see many men going home, he ached inwardly that he was not among them. He soon found out why.

A few days after the last big draft of prisoners was moved out, the Commissar stalked into the barracks with a detach-

ment of armed guards. A sergeant bawled for silence. The
Commissar stood up on a bench and began reading a Soviet
government proclamation. There were reams of polemic, allegations concerning the brutal murder of Russian women and
children, destruction of Soviet property and other familiar
Ehrenburg-style rantings of the propagandists. Then the Commissar began reeling off a long list of names. "Erich Hartmann, Major, German Air Force" was among them. Then
came the bomb.

". . . all the above-mentioned German prisoners of war are
as of this date, by order of the Soviet government and the
verdict of its judiciary, convicted as *war criminals*. As *war
criminals*, these prisoners will hereinafter be deprived of the
protection of the Geneva Convention and the International
Red Cross, and will henceforth be treated as criminals under
Soviet law. All the above war criminals are hereby sentenced
to twenty-five years at hard labor."

A roar of dismay went up from the prisoners. A menacing
movement toward the Commissar was arrested by the cocked
rifles of the guards. The sergeant bellowed for silence. The
Commissar resumed.

"War criminals will receive formal documentation of
charges against them on an individual basis in the next few
days. That's all."

The Commissar's threat to Erich had not been empty.

In the ensuing weeks, the prisoners were paraded before a
Soviet war judge and presented with lists of the charges
against them. Erich's name was called and he was marched
with four other "war criminals" to a ramshackle wooden
building outside the camp gates. A huge Soviet flag hung
limply over the doorway, and a sentry went through the
business of inspecting the passes of the guards and prisoners.

In the so-called courtroom, behind a rough wooden desk sat
the Russian war judge, a slab-faced man with thinning hair
and a fat belly. Erich was given his charge sheet, which
already had his "twenty-five years at hard labor" sentence
written on it and signed by the judge. A group of perhaps
fifty Russian civilians sat in the courtroom watching Soviet
legal apparatus in action. When he heard his name called,
Erich stepped up to the bench.

"I want to know why I am charged with war crimes, and the specific nature of the charges," said Erich.

The judge looked at him beadily.

"Yes, you are Hartmann, the Black Devil. The great pilot, yes? The big war criminal, yes?"

"The great pilot, yes, perhaps. War criminal, no."

The judge opened Erich's dossier and ran a blunt forefinger down an index.

"From this," he said, "it is quite obvious that you are a war criminal."

He went leafing through the dossier until he found what he was looking for. He looked up at Erich triumphantly.

"Charge One. You participated in the illegal, brutal and unprovoked attack on the Soviet Union, and destroyed a great quantity of Soviet war matériel, including at least three hundred and forty-five expensive Russian aircraft."

The judge was warming to his administration of justice.

"Charge Two. In the central sector of the Russian Front on 23 May 1943, you attacked a bread factory. Before your attack, the bakery was producing sixteen tons of bread daily for the Soviet people. After your attack, the factory was able to produce only one ton of bread."

The judge paused briefly to glare at Erich.

"Charge Three. In a village near Briansk, you killed seven hundred and eighty Russian civilians, including women and children. . . ."

Erich could no longer contain himself.

"Am I permitted to defend myself against these charges?"

The judge smiled icily.

"Of course. We are not Fascists in Russia. We have justice here."

"I shot down Russian aircraft, just as your pilots shot down German aircraft, as a soldier of Germany. It was my duty. That is not a war crime."

"And what about the destruction of the bakery?"

The judge was gouging away abstractedly at his fingernails. Erich shook his head in incredulity, but continued his defense.

"I never shot at or in any way attacked any bread factory. Where was the building located?"

The judge gave a bored sigh. He scrabbled briefly in the dossier.

"In a village near Smolensk," he said.

"But that is nowhere near where I served. That was in the area defended by Fighter Wing 54. I was with Fighter Wing 52 on the southern sector of the front."

The judge nodded knowingly.

"Yes, oh yes. All the war criminals were somewhere else when the crimes were committed. Or so they say."

Erich stubbornly continued his defense.

"Charge Three is absolutely false. I never killed any Russian civilians, let alone children. How can you be so sure of the exact number anyway? I was never near Briansk. How can you possibly accuse me of slaughtering Russian civilians on such a scale?"

The slab-faced judge plunged again into the dossier.

"We don't just *accuse* you, Hartmann. We *prove* you did it. We have justice here. Under the Soviet system of justice there are no innocent people in our jails."

"Well, then, prove to me how I killed seven hundred and eighty civilians. I engaged only in aerial combat, against other armed aircraft manned by your soldiers."

The judge twisted a little in his seat. He picked up his gavel and waved it at the Russian civilians sitting in the room.

"Take these people out. Clear the court. They have seen enough of these war criminals."

The judge pored over the dossier again while the guards herded the Russian spectators out the door. When they had left, the judge looked up, ready to proceed.

"Now, Hartmann. Do you know how many rounds of Ammunition your Me-109 fighter carried?"

"No, not exactly. About three hundred rounds for each of the two machine guns and about one hundred and fifty rounds for the twenty-millimeter cannon . . ."

The judge was reading now from the dossier.

". . . with the eleven hundred and twenty rounds of ammunition carried in his aircraft, Major Hartmann did therefore brutally murder seven hundred and eighty innocent Russian civilians—"

Erich broke in on the absurd recital.

"But I fired only at Russian aircraft in the air. Don't you understand that?"

The judge nodded.

"I do understand that. I understand perfectly. But you don't seem to understand that when you fired your guns all the bullets did not go into the other aircraft. They fell to the ground. There they killed our innocent civilian people. Seven hundred and eighty of them. You see how easy it is to prove that you are a war criminal?"

Erich smiled resignedly at the sheer nonsense of the proceeding. The judge burst out laughing. He threw his head back and roared, his double chin jumping like jelly. Suddenly sobering, he pointed a finger at the Blond Knight.

"Don't you know this whole thing is *political*, Hartmann? Why do you think I sent those people out of the court? You are trying to defend yourself in a situation that is impossible. Now then, you are an intelligent man. We have orders here from Moscow concerning you. You sign the papers we give you and you can go out to the West, now, to your family."

"Then what?"

"We will help you to advance very quickly in West Germany. Later on, we will contact you, but we will do this only if we have you in the right position. Our influence in the West German government is very substantial."

"And if I don't?"

"If you don't work with us, then you will never get out of here."

"You offer me a strange alternative. If I sign your paper, you have the means in your hands to get me jailed or shot in my own country by my own people. If I don't sign you keep me in jail here."

"You understand completely."

The judge drummed on the desk with his stubby fingers, waiting for his answer.

"I will not sign your paper now or ever. I demand that you shoot me down now. I am not afraid to die and I want a bullet."

The judge's face went as dark as that of an Inquisitor turning a thumbscrew. He crashed his gavel down savagely.

"War criminal! Twenty-five years' hard labor. Take him away."

And with that, the Blond Knight sank further into the power of his tormentors.

Weeks later, local newspapers in the Stuttgart area carried reports of Erich Hartmann's sentencing as a war criminal. Usch's mother found her dark-haired daughter brooding over a newspaper. A wartime photograph of Erich in his flying jacket, with his Diamonds decoration neatly airbrushed out, smiled out from amongst the black type. Frau Paetsch had been dreading the moment when Usch would read the story.

Putting her arm tenderly around her daughter, Frau Paetsch sought to comfort her. Usch gave a sad, Madonna-like smile.

"I'll wait for him, Mother. I'll wait."

"But Usch, twenty-five years, my dear. Your Erich will be more than sixty years old."

"If they keep him that long, that's how old he will be. They may keep him until he is seventy. But when he comes home I will be waiting."

Such was the love that reached out to Erich in bondage.

CHAPTER SEVENTEEN

THE SHAKHTY REVOLT

If a man cannot look evil in the face without illusion he will never know what it really is, or combat it effectually.

—*George Bernard Shaw*

WAR CRIMINAL STATUS deprived Erich of what vestigial rights he possessed under the Geneva Convention. While this international agreement was largely ignored and often blatantly flouted by the NKVD, it was the only source of rights to which German prisoners of the Russians could cling. Erich's fate was shared by other recalcitrant Germans who refused to work for the Soviets against their own country and their prison comrades. In the eyes of the Russian law—the only law valid now for Erich Hartmann—he was no longer a soldier and a prisoner of war. Confinement henceforth would be with German "war criminals" like himself, and with common Russian criminals and felons. The sentence was twenty-five years' hard labor.

Erich resolved that whatever the consequences he would not knuckle under to the illegal Soviet classification of himself as a criminal. As the train carrying him to the slave labor camp at Shakhty rattled southward, he was quietly talking to himself as he did during his aerial battles and times of deep trial.

"No one will defend your rights except *you*, Erich. This is how these people try to beat you under. They make you into an island, isolate you, so you crack up under the pressure from inside as well as outside. You must resist, Erich, no matter if it costs you your life."

In this frame of mind, Erich marched with the others from the train into the Shakhty labor camp, a depressing vista of ugly stone houses, barracks and the inevitable wire and guards. Underground work in the coal mines a couple of miles away was to be the opening punishment of his hard labor sentence. As the prisoners shuffled through the camp gates, Erich looked up and saw a banner that made every fiber of his being harden.

"OUR LABOR MAKES THE SOVIET UNION STRONG."

If he helped make the Soviet Union strong, Erich thought to himself, he would never get out of their grip. That thought braced his will to resist. If they tried to make a slave of him, he would starve himself to death. The NKVD would have to force-feed him to keep him alive, but he would never be a Soviet slave.

In recent years in the United States, and despite the ordeals of U.S. servicemen captured by the Reds in Korea and Vietnam, the confinement of men as prisoners of war has actually become a source of commercial humor. As George Bernard Shaw once pointed out, the imprisonment of a man is an act of diabolical cruelty, yet the life of P.O.W.'s is depicted in one vacuous television series as a continuous fun game.

Treatment of P.O.W.'s has varied from country to country. American prisoners in Germany generally received good treatment, while American P.O.W.'s in Japan were often nearly starved to death. German P.O.W.'s in the U.S. and Canada were not coddled, but they were adequately fed and clothed, many of them returning after the war to take up permanent residence in North America.

For the Germans in Russia, by contrast, there was no way out except by sale of the soul. Escape was impossible, discipline so strict and control so complete that the prisoners were literally isolated from the rest of the human race. Revolt under such conditions as those prevailing at Shakhty therefore required tremendous stimulus.

The first day in Shakhty, the prisoners were rousted from their dingy barracks and lined up outside. They would march to work in the coal mines. When the rest moved out, Erich stood fast.

"Good luck, Bubi . . . ," someone called to him from the line of shambling prisoners as they moved away to face twelve hours of backbreaking labor underground.

In a few seconds, Erich's lithe blond figure stood alone in front of the barracks. The guards called the column to a halt. A beefy Russian walked up to Erich and shoved a rifle in his stomach. The blue eyes looked back evenly into the guard's face.

"Move!" barked the guard.

Erich spoke quietly.

"I am a German staff officer and under the Geneva Convention I am not required to work. Therefore I will not work."

"You'll work," said the Russian, digging the barrel into Erich's belly.

"I demand to see the camp commandant."

The guard bawled for the sergeant. He came stumping up, a thick-bodied Slavic type with short legs and a cannonball head.

"What's going on here?" he said.

"This prisoner says he won't work, Sergeant."

The sergeant stared incredulously at Erich, then walked up to him with his jaw thrust out.

"*Why* won't you work? Are you sick?"

"No. Because I am a major, a staff officer, and under the Geneva Convention I do not have to work. I want to see the camp commandant."

The sergeant pulled back a little.

"You'll find that fancy rules don't mean much around here. We *all* work, to make the Soviet Union strong."

The cool blue eyes looked steadily back.

"I know that. That's why I am not going to work. I have two left hands."

The sergeant swallowed hard. The blond man had somehow made him bend.

"All right then. I'll take you to the commandant. But you'll be sorry you started this. Come on."

As the guards moved the other prisoners off to the mines, the sergeant led Erich across the dusty camp grounds to the commandant's office. Ther sergeant went over to the commandant's aide and whispered in the officer's ear. The aide looked hard at Erich as the sergeant related the scene in front of the barracks. The aide set down a file he was holding, knocked gently on the commandant's door and disappeared inside.

Snatches of agitated talk were audible through the closed door. Erich knew he was in for another confrontation with the NKVD mentality. He consoled himself with the thought that there wasn't a thing they could say, a dialectic gimmick they could employ, that he had not already encountered. They thought in straight lines, and had no real human contact. The commandant's door swung open and the aide beckoned to Erich.

The commandant was a colonel, a roly-poly administrative type. He had a face from which kindness had not been completely erased, but he regarded Erich stonily.

"What in hell is this about refusing to work, Hartmann?"

"Under the Geneva Convention, I am a staff officer and—"

"For *you*, the Geneva Convention does not exist. You have been convicted of war crimes. I've seen your dossier. Soviet justice has mercifully left you alive. You should be glad to work, glad to be alive."

"Your country won the war, Colonel—more than five years ago. I am an officer in the air force of a defeated country, and not a criminal of any kind. Your own Lenin says that any country that keeps prisoners of war longer than six months is imperialist and degenerate."

The colonel's eyebrows shot up in surprise.

"You know Lenin's writings, Hartmann?"

"Yes, I do. I have read all of them. He also says that a nation that puts prisoners of war to work is a parasite on those prisoners."

The colonel stood up quickly. He had obviously had enough Lenin for one day.

"You refuse to work?"

"I refuse absolutely. I insist that an international tribunal be appointed to investigate these camp conditions. If not, then I ask that you shoot me down. I wish to be executed, because I will *not* work."

The colonel pressed a button on his desk, and the aide appeared.

"This prisoner is to be put in solitary confinement until he agrees to work. Take him to the bunker."

The colonel watched impassively as an armed guard came in and escorted Erich out of his office.

The bunker at Shakhty was a small room in the rear of the guardhouse at the camp gates. Access to it was through a heavy door inside the wire. As the blackness of solitary confinement closed over him once more, Erich fought down the desperate tide that welled up inside him. Darkness and solitude gave only one solace, the chance to focus his thoughts on Usch. By concentrating on her, he could project himself back to Weil im Schönbuch to happy days in which he was surrounded by decency and love. Visions of home put power in his will, and as the days rolled by he knew that somehow he would survive here as he had in all the other bunkers into which he had been cast.

The other German "war criminals" who had come to Shakhty with Erich were in a black mood after a day of slavery in the mines. The labor was murderously hard, the working conditions and equipment primitive, and food was barely sufficient to sustain life, let alone a day's work. When they crawled back exhausted into their dismal mass dormitory, Erich was missing. The sergeant of the guard told them that the Blond Knight was in the bunker.

News of Erich's punishment acted like gasoline on a campfire. The prisoners' already ragged tempers flared out of control. Shouting and yelling in the barracks brought out the guards to subdue the prisoners. There were mutterings about a revolt. As the days went by and Erich failed to return to the barracks, the rage of the prisoners—intensified by the backbreaking slavery in the mines—began building up to flash point.

At the end of the fifth day, on their way back to barracks from the mines, prisoners trudging past the guardhouse saw the bunker door ajar. Inside they could see Erich Hartmann, his hands and feet tied to a chair. Two bulky guards stood over him, and while one pulled Erich's head back by the hair and forced open his mouth, the other crammed food down his throat. This degrading spectacle applied the ultimate strain to the bone-weary but already fuming prisoners.

The following morning when assembly sounded an angry roar bellowed from a hundred throats. Before any of them really knew what they were doing, the infuriated prisoners burst out of the barracks and overpowered their guards. A wild mob went streaming across the prison yard to the commandant's office. The Russian colonel's eyes bulged with terror as his office door crashed open and the scruffy mob seized him roughly.

Sitting tied to the chair in black silence, Erich's first inkling of the revolt came when he heard a heavy pounding at the bunker door. Someone yelled, "We'll get you out," and an ax blade smashed a hole in the door. More ax blows opened a hole large enough for a hand. A scrawny arm came through and tripped the lock.

Two sweating and excited prisoners burst into the bunker, breathing heavily and hardly able to talk.

"We've got the whole camp staff under guard. You're free, Bubi. It's a revolt."

They cut his bonds, and Erich stood up, rubbing circulation into his legs and arms. The daylight hurt his eyes. The two other prisoners led him out of the bunker. As they stepped outside they passed the bunker guard, a Rumanian prisoner, who was being thrust into the cell by two grinning P.O.W.'s. They tied the guard quickly to the chair.

"See how *you* like the bunker," one of them yelled.

Erich heard the heavy door slam shut, and quietly gave thanks amid the tumult that he was free of the black hole.

When Erich got back to the commandant's office, an excited horde of prisoners was milling around outside the building. A colonel and two majors made up the command structure of the camp, together with sixteen guards and a lady doctor. Two German officers, Colonel Wolf and Lieutenant Colonel Prager, had played a large role in raising the revolt, but the prisoners all looked to Erich for leadership now. They had done this for him. He was expected to take charge.

The colonel commandant and his two majors and the lady doctor looked somewhat surprised. They obviously expected to have their lives snuffed out by the man for whom the prisoners had revolted. They were to be disappointed.

"Let them all go. Don't hurt any of them in any way," said Erich.

The prisoners in the flush of their triumph had released other prisoners, Russians. They had also caught and beaten a few of the hated stool pigeons. The ruckus inside the camp and the freeing of the Russian prisoners had brought part of the populace of Shakhty town to the prison gates. The Russian prisoners managed to get out of the gates, but the Germans hesitated.

An elderly Russian woman with a babushka around her head beckoned to the hesitant Germans from outside.

"Come out! Come out now while you can. We'll take you away from here. Come out!"

A couple of eager P.O.W.'s started to move slowly toward the gates. Erich sprinted across from the commandant's office and headed them off, standing in front of them with his hands raised.

"Stop! Stay here! Nobody among us goes outside."

"Why, Bubi, why?" The prisoners were a little shaken.

"If you go out, you're escaping. The Russians have regulations about that, and guns. They'll shoot you down like dogs before you get five miles."

"What do we do then? Tell us what to do."

"We're going to stay right here in the camp," said Erich firmly. "Someone must come when we contact higher headquarters. We'll tell them what's wrong, maybe get things put right or made better. *But don't go out or they'll kill you.*"

Muttering among the P.O.W.'s now replaced the shouting. They stopped their movement toward the gates. The freedom beckoning beyond the gates was enough to torment a man to death. They teetered on the knife-edge of decision. A voice back in the mob shouted, "Erich's right. They'll kill us if we go out." The rumble of agreement that followed told Erich he had prevented a catastrophe.

"Come on," he said, "we'll get the commandant and make him call his headquarters."

A roar of approval went up from the prisoners, and they all shambled off toward the commandant's office. The place was jammed with prisoners who hadn't joined the rush for the gates. Erich shouldered his way in.

The commandant was brought to his own office, incredulity and alarm written on his fat face. The Russian officer sat down at his desk with stubble-chinned scarecrows on either side of him, and facing him was the Hartmann grin.

"Colonel," Erich said, "please sit down. We want you to call your higher headquarters and tell them what has gone on here."

The colonel shrugged. "They'll send soldiers and probably shoot the lot of you," he said.

The blue eyes were cool and level.

"I don't think so, Colonel. Now please call them and tell them what has happened. Where is higher headquarters located?"

"Rostov," said the colonel, as he picked up the phone.

He asked to be put through to the commanding general. Erich heard the general come on the line with a querying "Yes?"

"General, this is the commandant at Camp Shakhty. The German prisoners have made a revolution here—"

A squawk on the other end of the phone was followed by a torrent of questions. Finally the commandant managed to get in another word.

"No, General, I am being held by the prisoners with all my officers and staff. . . . No, we have not been harmed, General. The prisoner Hartmann wishes to speak with you."

Erich took the phone. His command of Russian was useful in such encounters.

"General, we have exceedingly bad conditions at this camp. I am responsible mainly for this revolt, because I refuse to work as a criminal and a slave. Our barracks arrangements are vile and the food is not fit for pigs. Underground labor twelve hours a day under such conditions will kill these men."

"What do you want *me* to do about it?" The general's voice was harsh.

"We want a government man from Moscow to come and inspect this place, and an international tribunal to see these conditions. We want something done to improve things."

"We'll see about that, Hartmann. Meantime I hold you personally responsible if anything happens to the commandant and the other personnel."

Erich grinned at his comrades.

"Don't worry about them, General. We're all gentlemen here."

Erich set down the phone and turned to his revolutionaries.

"Something will happen very soon," he said.

Within twenty minutes a tumult of voices and the roar of revving truck engines heralded the arrival of the Red Army at the camp gates. A company of soldiers, perhaps two hundred men all told, armed to the teeth with tommy guns and with cannons mounted on their trucks, pulled up outside the entrance. The tumult came from the Russian civil populace, who booed, hissed and hurled abuse at the Red soldiers—their own people.

"Why do you hold these men here?"

"Let them go home to their own people. They all have families."

"Shame!"

Sentimentally, the Russian people were on the side of the prisoners, and they let the Red Army know it.

Erich and his comrades ambled out and watched the Red infantry getting ready for action. Walking within hailing distance of the gate, Erich shouted at the nervous-looking Russian troops as they rallied their firepower to face the scruffy scarecrows behind the wire.

"You Russian soldiers!" Erich shouted. "We are on this side of the wire because we were once soldiers, just like you are today. We fought a war under orders, and we lost. We are soldier prisoners."

The Russian civilians turned into a cheering section for the Blond Knight, egging him on.

"Maybe you Russian soldiers will one day be inside a fence, too," Erich shouted. "Why do you do this now to other soldiers?"

He took a few steps forward and let his shabby prison jacket fall open, exposing his chest. He spread his arms wide.

"Shoot!" he yelled. "I can't shoot back."

The later arrival of a general from Rostov was the signal for the nervous infantrymen to ease through the gates in squads and herd the Germans back into their barracks. The Russians cooled down the revolt by suspending all work at Shakhty for five days, and the rumor was put about that a commissar was coming from Moscow. On the sixth day, the Russians made their intentions toward Erich clear.

Guards with rifles came to escort Erich outside the wire to the commandant's office. Colonel Wolf and Lieutenant Colonel Prager were also taken from their barracks. The commandant was back at his desk in full uniform.

"We will not be having any more revolts here, Hartmann," he said.

"Why have you sent for me, Colonel?"

"The political people have investigated your revolution.

They think you have too much influence over the other prisoners to remain here. You are not only a Fascist and a ringleader, but also a revolutionary."

"Then what do you propose to do?" said Erich.

"We are going to break up this association between you and the other prisoners. We know who the leaders are and they'll be sent to other camps. You and Wolf and Prager are going to Novocherkassk as part of that plan."

"What about the conditions in this camp, and the tribunal?"

"Some things are going to be changed, Hartmann. But you won't be here to see them. You won't see anything in fact, because at Novocherkassk you are going into the bunker again as punishment for this revolution. Your comrades here will be told that you are going to be shot, and you'll disappear. That'll put the fear of hell into them. That's all, Hartmann."

Five of the ensuing nine months at Novocherkassk jail Erich spent in the bunker, during which time his mail was again interrupted. In response to his incessant requests, the Russians let him appear before a tribunal specially set up for consideration of his case. A general came down from Moscow, and with four colonels and two majors plus a secretary, the kangaroo proceeding was convened.

In the back and forth of his confrontation with the tribunal, the Russians returned again and again to something that Erich considered a side issue at best. They accused him of having incited the civilian populace of Shakhty to revolt against the Soviet government. This unfounded contention clearly obsessed the tribunal. Erich could see that he was involved in another vain deadlock with the irrational Communist mentality. His final statement summed up his experiences with the Soviet judicial machinery:

"Your government convicted me of war crimes without any credible evidence, in fact, with evidence that in any truly civilized country would be considered insupportable. You have flouted the Geneva Convention and all other decencies that prevent men from becoming savages. You try to strip me of the humblest rights and sentence me to twenty-five years as a slave for things that never happened.

"When I resist and ask only for an international tribunal to investigate—I am not afraid that the world should know about anything you claim I have done—you put me in solitary confinement for months and let the word go about that I am dead. In the world today, your government talks and seeks peace, but with sixty thousand or more German soldiers in your power, you refuse to end the last war. Someday you may be treated the same way, Soviet officers.

"You are at war with the world through your inferiority complexes and stupidity. Perhaps you are right about the civil revolt at Shakhty. I never said a word to the Russian people to raise them against their government, but someday all of you will have to face what is in their hearts. Were it up to them, I would be free today. You should be afraid of your own people, for one day they will be done with you and what you call justice. God help you then."

The tribunal shuffled uneasily under this quiet rebuke, but when he was done they looked at each other and nodded. The verdict had been reached—long before the tribunal ever sat in its mockery of fair play.

"Twenty-five years' hard labor. Clearly a member of the international bourgeoisie."

Erich's ordeal had its counterpart in what his wife and parents endured in Germany. His mother made a series of pathetically desperate attempts to secure Erich's release by writing to high Soviet officials. Part of her letter to Generalissimo Stalin is reproduced here to convey something of the heartbreak felt by a mother under such conditions.

To
Generalissimus Stalin   28 April 1951
Excellency:

Excuse me and please understand, Generalissimo Stalin, if I herewith address myself, a mother of a prisoner of war, to you the highest personage of the USSR.

For your information I beg to state the following: My son, Erich Hartmann, born on 19 April 1922 in Weissach near Stuttgart, Württemberg, Germany, active member of the air forces (fighter), was serving at the end of the war in 1945 near Prague, when he was taken prisoner by the Americans. Fourteen days thereafter, he was, together with 7,000 men, put under Russian mandate and has been in Russian captivity since then.

My son is said to have been condemned, in December 1949, to 25 years of forced labor because he had been a staff officer. I cannot believe this condemnation, for my son has, like every Russian, done nothing but his duty of soldier toward his country, did he not?

This cannot, I believe, be considered as a punishable crime and entail such a severe condemnation.

Excellency: In this time of the many endeavors for world peace, I appeal to your sense of justice and beg you to relieve a mother from her greatest and so consuming grief, a mother who yearns toward her son and has not received any notice from him since December 1949. I beg you to have pity and to set my son, prisoner of war Erich Hartmann, free, and to have him sent back to his native country, i.e. to Weil im Schönbuch, Kreis Böblingen, Württemberg, Germany.

Should you have any objections against such a measure, I herewith assure you that my son, when again at home, will never again participate in activities against you and your nation, but will quite *peacefully* and in entire *neutrality* lead his further life. I promise you this, and as his mother I shall cause him to do so. I shall exact this promise from my son immediately after his return, and I know that he keeps unconditionally what he promises. Therefore please be kind and hear my supplications. And let six years of captivity be penance enough.

Hoping very much not to meet with hard-heartedness, I am, Excellency,

Yours very truly,
Mrs. Elisabeth Hartmann

Generalissimo Stalin, the Soviet Union's "Man of Steel," proved in this as in so many other instances to have a heart of stone. No reply of any kind was made to this or to a similar plea directed in desperation to V. M. Molotov, at that time Soviet foreign minister. In typical fashion, the Soviet Union was unable to take advantage of the measureless opportunities for international good will that the prisoner-of-war situation opened to their country. An insane vengeance binge was their only response.

As an intelligent NKVD colonel once said to Erich Hartmann at Cherepovets prison camp:

"I do not understand our government, or the people who run it. With the war over, they should have taken you fellows down to the Black Sea for a sixty-day vacation, filled you up with vodka and stuffed your bellies with the best food in Russia. Then they should have sent you home. We'd be sitting on the Atlantic today if they had done that."

When Erich left Novocherkassk in 1953 and was sent up to Diaterka in the Urals, the story of the Shakhty Revolt had already become part of the prison legends. Other ringleaders from Shakhty had been sent to Diaterka after the revolt, when Erich was sent down to Novocherkassk. At Diaterka, Erich got a rousing welcome from the prisoners, and an immediate interview with the Diaterka commandant.

Erich anticipated another frustrating duel with a typical NKVD man, but he knew things were different the moment he stepped into the commandant's office. The man was a pudgy little Russian with nervous hands and a smile to match. He was obviously apprehensive and he began the interview by greeting his prisoner as Erich.

"Erich, I hope you will find Camp Diaterka satisfactory."

"It is a camp. Nothing more from what I can see, except perhaps more wire and fences."

"Well, Erich, please . . . *please*, I don't want that you should make a revolution in my camp, like in Shakhty."

"The revolt in Shakhty came about, commandant, because the administration said I must work at hard labor, and I say I am a staff officer and do not have to work. And so I would not work and there was a revolt when they punished me."

The Russian smiled widely.

"But Erich, then we have no troubles in Diaterka. I agree you shouldn't have to work. That is right for a staff officer. I agree with you."

"Then, commandant, we will not have a revolution."

"Fine, Erich, fine. We understand each other."

The seemingly good beginning at Diaterka was not destined to last long. Erich was assigned to a maximum security pen constructed within the confines of the Diaterka camp itself. The camp was typical of many in the Soviet Union in which German prisoners were incarcerated.

Rows of large barracks buildings, each accommodating

from two hundred to four hundred prisoners, provided crude shelter for perhaps four thousand men. The inmates were jammed into three-tier bunks to maximize the capacity of the buildings. Crude latrines were outside, with zero privacy. Prisoners in Russia had no secrets from each other concerning any of their bodily functions.

Around the buildings, but inside the inner high fence, was a "dead zone" with watchdogs on each side. The inner fence was a ten-footer, crowned with barbed wire. A few yards beyond this was a stockade-type, high wooden fence, with guard points equipped with machine guns at each corner. Beyond the wooden stockade was a barrier of electrified wire. If a man touched it he could be fried on the spot. Beyond the electrified wire was a final, eight-foot, chain-link fence topped with barbed wire. There were no escapees from Diaterka. No one thought it even worth-while to try.

The maximum security pen for problem prisoners, to which Erich was assigned, was a prison within a prison. His new home was like a second, smaller prison built within the general perimeter of Diaterka just described. This special barracks stood inside another high wooden stockade and yet another high wire barrier. Inside were confined some of the Soviet Union's most prized prisoners, to whose society Erich Hartmann was now admitted.

There were Otto Gunsche, Hitler's adjutant for the last two years of the Third Reich; Major Count Siegfried von der Schulenburg, of the same aristocratic family that provided Germany's prewar ambassador to the Soviet Union; Harald von Bohlen und Halbach, brother of munitions maker Alfred Krupp; Richard Seyss-Inquart, son of the infamous Dr. Seyss-Inquart; and others whose roles in Hitler Germany, or whose family names, made them special objects of Soviet suspicion and antagonism. In the pen with them were common East German and Russian felons, as well as Russians who had made the mistake of opposing the regime. About forty-five men in all shared the joys of the maximum security pen.

The close confinement and mixed character of the inmates led to frequent brawls. Erich found himself allied most often with Otto Gunsche and "Sigi" Graf von der Schulenburg. Otto in particular proved himself a formidable bruiser if attacked, although otherwise he was a mild and gentle giant.

Big, fair-haired and heavy, with brawler's arms and immense strength, Hitler's ex-adjutant was a man of quiet and kindly temperament—the reverse of what might have been expected. Otto's last assignment in Hitler Germany was to burn the Führer's body after his suicide.

Otto told Erich the same story many times during their year together, always with the same consistent details and without embellishment or elaboration. After Hitler's suicide, Otto carried the Führer's body, rolled in a rug, behind the *Führerbunker* in Berlin. Six or seven twenty-liter cans of fuel were poured over the wrapped corpse, saturating the rug, the corpse and the surrounding ground. Otto struck a match and the Führer's body was thus crudely cremated.

Sigi Graf von der Schulenburg was another man whose character enabled him to resist Soviet pressure, and led him to the super-pen at Diaterka. The Schulenburg family had served the fatherland for generations. Service in the military and in the civil government was a family tradition.

The Russians captured Sigi Graf von der Schulenburg near Bromberg in January 1945. He was a professional German Army officer, and had served with the 1st Cossack Division, a unit organized from Cossack refugees anxious to fight against the U.S.S.R. Von der Schulenburg also had a famous name. His value was immediately recognized by the Russians, and he was asked by a commissar to go to Berlin and help identify important leaders in the German government. When he refused, he began a long grind under the Soviet heel that brought him to Diaterka.

Erich's friendship with Otto Gunsche, von der Schulenburg and Harald von Bohlen Halbach helped sweat away the months in the super-pen. They slept on the floor and fought their battles shoulder to shoulder. As 1954 rolled away, Erich got the inner feeling, despite the oppressive maximum security conditions, that his prison ordeal was coming to an end. Otto and Sigi shared this feeling and they helped buoy up each other's spirit, until Erich was transferred back to Novocherkassk in July of 1954. This second period in the infamous Novocherkassk prison camp was to complete ten and a half years of confinement.

The brutal decade left Erich Hartmann with definite views concerning the handling of prisoners of war. Characteristically, he is concerned that the kind of catastrophe that befell him should not descend on other young men of any nationality. Since the probability of future wars stands far higher than the strongest hopes for peace, the possibility of further clashes with the Red world cannot be discounted.

The following request to the governments of the world from Erich Hartmann is presented in this book where it stands squarely amid the experiences that led to its formulation. The United Nations could serve as the agency through which such a necessary reform of prisoner-or-war codes might be effected. The merit of Erich Hartmann's request is self-evident.

CONCERNING PRISONERS OF WAR

My Request to the Governments of the World.

1. No nation engaging in hostilities, anywhere in the world, should keep in its own territories the prisoners of war it captures.

2. All nations of the world should agree that during wartime a neutral nation should keep all the prisoners of war captured by both warring powers or warring combinations of powers.

3. The neutral nation holding the prisoners of war should retain all prisoners of both sides until the conflict is ended.

4. Upon the termination of hostilities, all prisoners should be returned to their homes as soon as possible.

This request is made by me because practical experience involving tens of thousands of men has demonstrated that the P.O.W. provisions of the Geneva Convention are under actual conditions nonsense.

(SIGNED)
ERICH HARTMANN
Ten Years Prisoner of War in the U.S.S.R.

CHAPTER EIGHTEEN

RELEASE

Life is a whole, and good and ill must be accepted together.

—Winston Churchill

ERICH'S INTUITION DURING the last year of his confinement that the ordeal was coming to an end had a foundation in real events that lay outside his direct knowledge. Moves were afoot in his behalf back in Germany. His mother's letters to Stalin and Molotov went unanswered and unacknowledged, extinguishing all hope of help from that direction, but conditions in 1954 were changing radically for the better in Germany. This enabled Elisabeth Hartmann to approach another significant personality, and this time to evoke a human response.

Nine years after the end of the war, the recovery of Germany was well advanced. With her people working industriously to rebuild shattered cities and erect new factories, with German industry going full blast and export markets expanding, the country was creating an economic miracle and taking its place again in the human family. Recovery brought with it a strengthening and revitalizing of the body politic, and these processes saw the emergence of the most significant figure in postwar Germany—Chancellor Konrad Adenauer.

Frau Elisabeth Hartmann wrote to the leader of her country and asked his assistance in securing the release of her son. Chancellor Adenauer received her letter and replied personally. He held out the hope that positive steps in winning

Erich's freedom might be taken in the coming months, and stated that the German government was deeply concerned about the prisoners. This kind letter did much to alleviate a mother's grief, made all the more acute by her widowhood. Thereafter, Adenauer became something of a hero in her eyes.

"Der Alte" was as good as his word. When he went to Moscow to reach a general settlement and trade agreement with the Soviet Union, the question of P.O.W.'s still in Russia was in the forefront of his mind. At least sixteen thousand men were still imprisoned to the certain knowledge of the Bonn government, and unofficial estimates ranged as high as a hundred thousand men illegally detained. A traditionalist and a decent man, Dr. Adenauer felt that the return of ex-soldiers held for a decade was a mandatory Russian concession. Eager for a *rapprochement* with resurgent Germany, the Russians saw that the time had come to use the prisoners as a bargaining fulcrum. As part of the general settlement, the Soviet Union agreed to release prisoners of war held since 1945.

Erich Hartmann's name was cited as one of the individuals whose return was desired by the German government. Guards at the Novocherkassk jail told the prisoners about Adenauer's visit, and scraps of news that appeared about the role of P.O.W.'s in negotiations led to wild rumors among the prisoners. The Russian bureaucracy began to move after the agreements were signed in Moscow. Chancellor Adenauer's request for his release was eventually transmuted into an order Erich received from a Russian guard.

"Report to Building Five for clothing issue."

He was given some new clothes, roughly tailored and baggy, but infinitely superior to prison garb. Years of dashed hopes and shattered dreams had conditioned Erich against thinking too strongly about his release. This was something different. New clothes were of no use in prison. When the Russian camp commandant invited Erich and other prisoners to enjoy the camp cinema, the whole thing seemed too good to be true, and they declined his offer. Despite his suspicions, Erich allowed himself the luxury of thinking that release was imminent. Back in Germany, Usch was having similar thoughts.

Her hopes for Erich's early return had been fortified first

by Dr. Adenauer's letter to Erich's mother, and then by the German leader's Moscow visit. Newspapers in the Federal Republic extolled Adenauer's achievements in the Moscow meeting, and Germany was assured that its long-lost sons were coming home. A *Pravda* release, published in Germany, said that the prisoners had been granted a general amnesty. Then came formal notification from the Bonn government that Erich would be released.

The days flitted by and Usch's hopes became interlaced with occasional disquieting doubts. A returning prisoner who had been briefly with Erich told Usch that he would not be released because he was a war criminal. The man went on his way after making Usch miserable. She waited on, hardly able to bear the mounting tension.

Two days after drawing his new clothes, Erich was told to pack his few belongings and prepare to leave the camp. The prisoners were lined up outside the barracks and the commandant shook hands and wished them luck, expressing the hope that there would be no more wars. A grubby bus took Erich to Rostov where he transferred to a train that would carry him home.

Boarding the train, he went wild with excitement inside. Home . . . Usch . . . the family . . . it was almost too much to believe. There was a lump in his throat, but outside he stayed unruffled, even if obviously happy. With fifty other prisoners he sat back contentedly on the hard seats, and as the train rumbled away from Rostov his thoughts turned momentarily from home to a rail journey of ten years ago. He still could hardly believe that he was finally reversing the journey in the jam-packed cattle-car that took him to the swamp hell at Kirov.

As the train rolled through Voronezh, Stalinogorsk, Moscow and Briansk and kept rattling westward, the reality of the experience began to take hold. All week long his heart sang as the Russian countryside passed in flat panorama. As they lurched across eastern Poland to Brest-Litovsk and then entered the new state of East Germany, the click-clack of the wheels sounded like the music of deliverance. The train crossed the border into the Federal Republic of West Germany and Erich saw the station sign.

HERLESHAUSEN

He was free!

With border formalities quickly completed, Erich got out of the train and pushed his way through the platform crowd to a specially established Red Cross office. To a pretty German girl behind the counter he dictated his first free telegram in nearly eleven years.

DEAR USCH——I HAVE CROSSED THE BORDER TODAY INTO
GERMANY WAIT AT HOME UNTIL I COME LOVE
YOUR ERICH

Two hours later, Usch was reading the wire, her eyes filled with tears. The unprepossessing yellow telegraph form held the most wonderful message she had ever received. He was free and he was coming home. Usch's mother shared her tears of joy. They telephoned Erich's mother in Weil and there were more happy tears. Word of Erich's release and imminent arrival home soon spread all over Weil and Stuttgart.

The P.O.W. welcoming committee on the station platform at Herleshausen had warm words for everyone. The *Bürgermeister* of the town gave a short address of welcome. Newspapermen were running back and forth recalling half-forgotten names like "Erich Hartmann" and those of other prominent soldiers due for repatriation. In pathetic counterpoint to the joy were the plaintive and searching inquiries after missing men. Sad-faced women waved photographs and asked the prisoners if they knew anything about husbands and fathers swallowed into the Soviet prison system a decade ago.

The P.O.W. organization had planned a big reception for Erich Hartmann on his return to Stuttgart. Almost a thousand people were expected to attend, including high figures in public life. The representatives rattled on about the arrangements for the celebration. Erich held up his hand to still the flood of talk.

"Please," he said, "there must be no reception. I cannot agree to any kind of celebration."

Newspapermen clustered around the Blond Knight, sensing a story. They all wanted to know why he would decline a reception in his honor after almost eleven years away from his country.

"Because the Russians view life differently from us. They

might decide, on hearing or reading of such a celebration, not to release any more German prisoners. I know the Russian secret police well enough to be fearful on this account for the continued imprisonment of my countrymen in the Soviet Union. When they are *all* home—then we will have the celebration. Meanwhile, we must not rest until all German soldiers imprisoned in Russia are repatriated."

He thanked the *Bürgermeister* and the P.O.W. committee for their kindness and stepped aboard a bus for the final leg of the trip, which would end with clearance through the P.O.W. center at Friedland. As the countryside rolled past the bus windows he reflected with alternating contentment and awe on his return to his native land. That was *Germany* out there. He had to keep assuring himself that he wasn't in a dream about paradise.

How green and vitally alive his country looked. People appeared markedly different from what he remembered. Clothing shapes and styles were completely changed. The hundreds of shiny cars he saw along the roads were like glittering artifacts from another planet. Times had changed. Germany was a new land. He felt a keen and living affinity with the legend of Rip Van Winkle, except that while the mythical figure slept, he had lived a nightmare.

At Friedland a familiar, smiling face appeared out of the crowd—Hans "Assi" Hahn, a fellow prisoner from Gryazovets days. Assi had got word of Erich's return. Fat and prosperous, Assi pumped Erich's hand and insisted that he must come to his nearby home. He could telephone Usch from there, and then Assi would personally drive him home to Stuttgart.

This impromptu arrangement cut across family plans to get Erich home to Usch with minimum delay. Even as Assi Hahn collected him at Friedland, Erich's brother Alfred and a boyhood friend named Helmut Woerner were speeding northward in another car to drive the Blond Knight home. His telephone call to Usch from Assi Hahn's place was almost a disaster. After he told her where he was, Usch, who had been waiting for him nearly eleven years, got a little excited.

"At Assi Hahn's place? What in the world are you doing *there* when I'm *here*?"

In a few hours, Erich was racing on to Stuttgart with

Helmut Woerner and Alfred, after they collected him from the celebrant atmosphere at Hahn's place. Every glance out the car window brought something new to Erich's mind. Germany was like a new civilization. The drabness of the war years had gone. Colors on signs and colored clothing on the people seemed nothing short of dazzling after ten years of jails. They drove on all through the night, and the commonest neon sign seemed to Erich as though it had been transported direct from fairyland.

Usch had gone to bed on Saturday night knowing that Erich would be home the next day, although the time of his arrival was indefinite and dependent on road conditions. Already she had forgiven him for his digression to Assi Hahn's. She was in a fever of anticipation. Fitful snatches of sleep were interspersed with constant clock-watching. She was dozing around 4 A.M. when the telephone bell shattered the silence. Usch leaped two feet clear off the bed and grabbed the instrument.

"Usch?"

"Erich! Where are you?"

"We're in Frankfurt. We've stopped here for coffee. Should be there in a couple of hours or so."

The tension of the ensuing hours was almost unendurable for Usch. She got up and lay down in innumerable restless cycles. The hands of the clock moved with tortuous slowness as dawn came. She had dropped into a light doze when she heard a gentle knocking. When she sat up, the knocking stopped. For a moment, she thought she was hearing things. Then the knock sounded again.

Usch ran to the window, flung it open and leaned out, craning over to see the front door below. Someone was there, not fully visible.

"Erich?" she called softly.

The figure moved into full view, looking up at her. The hair was as blond as ever, the eyes looked even bluer than she remembered. The face was gaunt and the wiry body incredibly thin. He smiled and her heart leaped. Her Erich had come home.

For a tender, numbing instant they looked at each other without speaking. Usch broke the silence.

"Erich, our love is as though you had never been away."

Erich's tongue came free a moment later.

"You look good," he said. He was at a loss for words.

Usch dashed to the front door and in a moment they were in each other's arms. Love, faith and trust had won through. The great challenge had been met and conquered. For both of them it was an unforgettable moment as they clung together in a mutual outpouring of joy that took away their breath and speech.

Usch's parents joined briefly in the reunion, overwhelmed that their daughter's long vigil had not been in vain, and tearfully happy that Erich had survived to take up life again. Erich telephoned his mother, and then there was the supernal luxury of a hot bath. After that, the lovers were left alone. The flooding sweetness of physical love, lost to their lives for a decade, inundated and swept away their bitter yearnings on a rolling tide of fulfillment. If nirvana has ever come among the earthly, it came that morning to Erich and Usch.

Their bliss remained undisturbed for a little over two hours. Then a procession of well-wishers, friends and relatives began passing through the Paetsch home. Happy men pumped Erich's arm, and their wives embraced him. Friends' children who had grown almost to adolescence without his seeing them were introduced to the heroic blond man. Flowers, gifts and tokens of esteem jammed the living room and had to be stacked in adjoining rooms. Between three and four hundred people milled into the house during the day, so that those closest to Erich had to be content with little more than snatches of conversation. Erich and Usch did not see each other alone again until after 10 P.M.

In the next few days Erich began to recover from the immediate exhaustion caused by his long trip out of Russia, and the emotional excitement of reunion with his loved ones. After he had talked himself out with Alfred, his mother, Usch and her parents and many friends who came to welcome him back, he was inwardly appalled by the way in which the last ten years had evaporated. The warmth of hearth and home was like a healing balm that seemed to have annihilated the brutal decade.

"Now that I'm home," he said to Usch, "it seems incredible that I was gone ten and a half years. What has happened to all that time . . . *all those years?*"

"I feel the same way, Erich. Just as though you had been gone a couple of weeks."

The brutal decade had vanished into the limbo, gone forever into the labyrinths of time, but it had left its marks on Erich. His brother Alfred had qualified as a medical doctor while Erich was in prison, and had set up his practice in the same home and office on Bismarckstrasse in Weil that their father had built on his return from China. When Alfred first saw Erich's physical condition, he blanched.

The rugged, muscular, athlete's body that Alfred knew so well had shriveled to barely a hundred pounds. Erich's drawn face fairly reflected the ordeals of prison and the fight he had made to preserve his sanity and self-respect. Conversation quickly demonstrated to Alfred that his brother's mind and outlook were unimpaired. Said Dr. Alfred Hartmann of this time:

"His physical condition gave me a bad jolt initially. To what I saw in Erich on his return and as a doctor, I was able to add my knowledge of him since childhood. The main thing to me was that he was unimpaired in mind. I well knew the strength of his constitution and his excellent recuperative powers. I knew that he would make a good recovery."

The top priority task for Erich and Usch in rebuilding their lives together was to get Erich's bodily health and strength restored. He was in no condition to take up any commercial activity, so they decided to reverse the roles of husband and wife in the meantime. Usch kept her job at the Post Office in Stuttgart, and Erich put on an apron and shouldered the burdens of running the home. This decision helped phase him back into normal life after ten years of total severance from ordinary civilized living.

The most successful fighter pilot in the world describes his introduction to domesticity thus:

"Every morning I would get up and fix the breakfast. After Usch left for work on the 8 A.M. commuter train, I would wash the dishes, sweep the floor, make the beds, do the laundry and generally straighten up the house. All of this I did just like a girl! Then I would go outside and work a while in the garden, tending the flowers and cutting the lawn, doing a little painting and other odd jobs, including building a wall.

"I learned to appreciate the wide range of chores our wives

must do when we men go away to work. I would go shopping in the village and set a nice table, and at night I would wait at the door for Usch to come home. This period confirmed for me what I firmly believe to be the truth—that without Usch I am nothing."

The simplest daily happenings were, for him, invested with magnetic charm. Like a child at Christmas time he gawked into store windows. The sheer novelty of window shopping took weeks to lose its attraction. The glitter and color of beautiful new goods of all kinds fascinated and absorbed him. The taste of home-cooked food seemed more delicious than he could ever remember—even in his prison-camp dreams of the outside world.

He read voraciously, catching up on the world. The oldest magazines he found full of new information. He slept and dozed when not handling his household chores, and in barely perceptible increments the strength seeped back into his muscles, and firm flesh began to erase the main stigmata of the prisons. The restoration of a full and satisfying marital relationship after ten years in an emotional desert brought him indescribable inner comfort. The psychic wounds were deeper than the emaciation of his body but soon even these began to yield to a mode of living that had love at its core.

The prison psychology—the behavioral habits forced on him during the prison decade—gave him many difficult moments in the first weeks at home. He was actually afraid to talk to people when he went shopping in the village, or in other casual contacts. People in peacetime Germany thought differently from when he had last been home, and compared with P.O.W.'s their thought processes were wider and more versatile. The German people were also differently occupied from ten years previously. These impressions united to give him the feeling at times that he had been reincarnated on another planet.

The feeling that he was being watched persisted for several weeks. For more than ten years he had done everything under the scrutiny either of Russian guards or of his fellow prisoners. There was a strong psychological barrier now to doing the most normal, everyday things, because of this sense of presence and of all normal action being forbidden.

One evening he was walking with Usch in Stuttgart, and

they strolled past a ballroom. Music came floating out on the evening air, and couples with smiling faces were going in to dance. Dancing was something Erich and Usch had loved since the days of their 1939 dancing-class trysts. Usch caught the mood and the memories in an instant.

"Let's go in and dance, Erich."

He wanted to go in, but something stopped him. He was physically blocked. The sensation was akin to being tongue-tied. He felt awkward, silly and hung up. He could not force himself to go inside to dance, despite his overpowering desire to enjoy this pleasure with Usch. Since men of today captured in today's wars may come home similarly burdened, Erich Hartmann's experience of this post-prison adjustment period merits attention. His words also enjoin understanding treatment of those who may have been decisively changed by their prison ordeals.

"This feeling that someone is watching you from behind, that you are denied and forbidden everything pleasant or human is a haunting ordeal that not every ex-prisoner is able to conquer. With me, it lasted about two months. I believe I was lucky to throw it off, because it is basically a habit of mind that the years of prison routine literally build into your mental make-up.

"Other prisoners who were with me in Russia were not so lucky. I know this from meeting and talking with them. They are still in the grip of this prison psychology today, and because of it, cannot find a new beginning for themselves. These men are finished. I wish that some attention could be given to the tragic plight of some of these psychically disfigured individuals.

"At night comes the real horror. They are transported back in their dreams to those soul-crushing camps. They will never be free."

Erich's recovery continued as warmth, kindness and love worked their wonders. In November 1955, he and Usch took care of a long-delayed marriage detail. They added a church wedding ceremony to the courthouse proceeding of September 1944 in Bad Wiessee. Erich's uncle, Protestant pastor at Bopfingen, performed the ceremony. The wedding was a tender moment, made all the more touching by the strength of the love that waited ten years and won.

Body and mind, Erich kept responding positively to the human warmth of Weil. His thoughts started turning increasingly to the question of his future. He began asking himself, in his thirty-fourth year, questions that men in ordinary times ask themselves before they are twenty. He had to earn a living for himself and Usch and there was a larger challenge involved. He had to provide for the family they had decided to have in rebuilding their lives together.

Had the war not intervened, Erich knew that he would in all probability have become a doctor like his father. He felt his father's death acutely as he pondered the problems of the future. His understanding counsel would have been welcome. Erich would have still liked to be a doctor after his return from prison, but he could add and he was above all else a realist. At thirty-three, a demanding modern medical course would be a formidable undertaking even if all conditions were favorable. In his case, the reverse was true. He had been cut off from all academic pursuits for over ten years, and even his high-school chemistry and physics had grown dim in his memory. To think of being a doctor now was unrealistic.

He felt the gaping void of the prison decade opening in him when he considered other things. Thirty-three was late to start at any profession. For almost one-third of his total time on earth he had been in jail. His lack of business experience would handicap him not only in working for others, but also in setting up an enterprise of his own. He needed time to get in touch with commercial thinking, to feel its trends, grasp its substance, understand something of its methods. Meanwhile, the need to make a living was unrelentingly present.

This critical period for Erich coincided with the active rebuilding of the German Air Force. Groundwork had begun several years previously in Chancellor Adenauer's office, with old JG-52 aces Macky Steinhoff and Dieter Hrabak, among others, doing the planning. The new force was gradually being built up around Germany's leading pilots and personalities from the Second World War. Barely three weeks after his return home, Erich got a taste of what was to come. The phone rang. Usch answered and handed the phone to Erich.

"Walter Krupinski," she said.

"Hi, Bubi," boomed the irrepressible Count Punski. "Gerd Barkhorn and I are leaving for a jet refresher course in

England next week. Why don't you come with us? By the way, Bubi, how *are* you?"

Erich put his hand over the mouthpiece and looked up at Usch with an expression of incredulity on his face.

"God in Heaven, Usch. He wants me to go on a flying course with him to England next week. He must be crazy."

Krupinski was bellowing into the phone.

"Bubi, where in hell have you gone? . . ."

"Kruppi, damn it, I've been away in prison nearly eleven years and I haven't been home three weeks yet. I can't go to England or anywhere else until I feel better."

"The hell you can't, Bubi. Just take off. You'll feel better when you fly again. Like in the old days."

Krupinski was bubbling with enthusiasm, but it aroused none in Erich.

"Kruppi, call me when you get back. Tell me how flying was and about the new jets then, O.K.?"

Krupinski hung up. He did telephone when he returned from England. So did other pilots who had joined or who were about to join the new air force. Krupinski's suggestion, originally outlandish, again crossed Erich's mind as the weeks went past. He also thought about old comrades who were flying again.

None of these pilots like Kruppi, Gerd Barkhorn or Guenther Rall had been doing any flying while he was away in prison. They hadn't been in the military, either, because there was no military. They had been forced into other things in the interim. The new air force was giving them a chance to use once more the skills, technical knowledge, experience and training that they had acquired as young men. They were fundamentally in the same spot as Erich, except that they were mostly prewar professional officers and were older than he. One day Erich found that he was quietly talking to himself as he used to in a tight spot in combat, or when under pressure in prison.

"Erich, fighter piloting is all you know, the thing you're good at and do best. Maybe you should forget now that you don't like military life, just as you forgot it in 1940 when you had the chance to learn to be a pilot." This line of thought got some powerful reinforcement in the ensuing months.

Persuasive and trusted people began urging Erich to rejoin

the air force. His old *Kommodore* from JG-52, Dieter Hrabak, came to his home to make a personal appeal. Hrabak had worked with Steinhoff on air force organization, and had been to the U.S.A. for refresher training on jets. He outlined the air force in bright but realistic terms. There was a place for Erich, and security as well.

Hard on Hrabak's heels came the Minister of Culture in the Adenauer government, Erich's onetime schoolteacher, Herr Simpfendörfer. With him came Herr Bänsch, a high official in the Defense Ministry in Bonn. This time, the pressure was heavier.

"You have to come back, Erich. We need you in the air force." Herr Bänsch was sincere and serious. "You are the most successful fighter pilot in the world, you have the Diamonds and you are an important personality in the eyes of the young pilots we are going to train. You simply must come back to the service."

Krupinski, Gerd Barkhorn and Guenther Rall all periodically telephoned or called to see him. Macky Steinhoff met Erich at Echterdingen Airport and used his considerable powers of persuasion. Paradise was never promised, but a good career and security could be offered with some certainty. As a sharply disappointing contrast to all these urgings, which emphasized his importance and value, nothing encouraging materialized from the world of commerce. As the months slid past, Erich felt he had to act, and the air force was offering him something familiar in which he had excelled. Life had to go on.

Usch said nothing during these critical months to sway him one way or the other. He knew the decision was his alone, and that Usch would let it be a free decision. When he decided to rejoin the air force in late 1956, she accepted his judgment. She was disquieted nevertheless that Adolf Galland and the other living aces who had won the Diamonds stayed out of the new air force. So did Hans-Ulrich Rudel, the famous Stuka pilot. When Erich went back into the service he was the only officer in the new armed forces who had won the Diamonds in the Second World War. Usch was not the only one who felt uneasy about Erich's decision.

His brother Alfred had abiding regrets. Concerning this time he says today: "I was sorry to see him continue in the military because I knew it was basically against his temperament. But the years of prison had exacted a terrible price. He was unable, at that time, to resume life adequately except in the military."

Erich Hartmann's rebirth would take place in the air force, where in his youth he had won immortality as a fighter. In this next phase of his life, as in his youth and in the prison years, the Blond Knight would need his fighter's heart for the new kind of jousting that lay ahead.

CHAPTER NINETEEN

REBIRTH

No man is any good who has no enemies.
                    —*Major-General Sir Percy Hobart*

ALMOST IMMEDIATELY AFTER Erich Hartmann's decision to rejoin the service, there was disagreement within the German Air Force regarding his status. This minor yet significant controversy was to be typical of many subsequent problems that arose bearing adversely on Erich's new career and progress. The character of these difficulties stemmed from the origins and basic philosophy of the new German armed forces, a brief background of which is germane.

In the Federal Republic of West Germany, the backlash from the Hitler period heavily influenced the organization of the new armed forces. The German people were apathetic toward the *Bundeswehr*, because they had been given their fill of militarism less than a decade before. Organizers of the new services were at pains to ensure the authority of the civil power over the military, as in the British and American establishments. Because of the differences between German political psychology and that of other countries, her new military forces tended to become political in character rather than strictly nonpolitical as in the past. The old system of a professional military caste owing loyalty to the head of state was supplanted with something quite new to German affairs.

Officers remained aloof from electoral politics in accordance with tradition and usage, but they could now belong to political parties. Over-organization in the direction of civilian

279

control accordingly had its consequences in the officer corps. The appointments, promotions and the success of officers have tended to be determined by politics as much as by professional merit.

Damaging things have happened to the new German Air Force through politics and the service being too close. These errors are all too well known to serving officers and they are discussed with some vehemence with trusted outsiders. In the formative years of the German Air Force the officer corps suffered badly from political cronyism. An officer who was well connected politically and in favor in high places could hardly go wrong during the first years, while reasons were found to keep out men of merit or sidetrack them once they were in. These measures were necessary to protect the careers of the favored, when such careers rested on a foundation other than ability.

From the beginning of his second military career Erich Hartmann stayed clear of the political wire-pullers. He was nobody's marionette. He was half-expected to join the Christian Democrats on his return to the air force. This arrangement appears to have been implicit in the promise made to Erich that he would command the first of the new jet fighter wings, although never directly stated. In his forthright fashion, he made it quite clear when questions were asked that he had no intention of joining any political party. He had never belonged to a political party in the past and politics had already cost him more than ten years of his life. This was an unpopular stance in certain quarters.

A proposal was then made by the personnel office that Erich Hartmann come back in as a captain, "since he had been a major for less than two months when the war ended." His ten years in prison as Major Hartmann, exemplifying the correct conduct of an officer, were deemed secondary to contemporary convenience. Officers like Guenther Rall, who knew about his proposed induction as a captain, were horrified. The political people were told it was unthinkable that the world's top fighter ace, and the only Diamonds holder in the new armed forces, should come in at a lower rank than he had held in the Second World War.

Erich's friends won this little skirmish, although he knew nothing about it at the time. The idea of downgrading him might not have seemed so strange had a penetrating glance been directed behind the scenes. A dominant influence in the personnel section of the German Air Force at this time was an ex-major in the Luftwaffe. He had served as a reconnaissance pilot on the Eastern Front during the war. He knew Erich Hartmann—perhaps a little too well for his own peace of mind.

In January 1943, Erich flew fighter protection for this officer on a reconnaissance mission out of Krasnodar, to verify the presence of the Soviet Black Sea Fleet in the port of Batum. Soon after they crossed the lines, the Russian flak opened up, and the major flying the reconnaissance aircraft immediately turned his kite around and headed back to base. The fighters completed the Batum mission, which did not end with their report that the Russian ships were still in harbor. A war judge arrived soon afterward to investigate the major's aborted mission. He was relieved of his command and sent back to Germany. He surfaced in the 1950s ruling on ranks, promotions and appointments in the postwar German Air Force.

Erich rejoined as a major, but this was the beginning of a long *sub rosa* effort to make his way hard. Jealousy and pettiness are natural attributes of the incompetent and fearful, but individuals motivated by these base qualities are not drawn to the open challenge of those they hate and fear. The barriers put in Erich's way were none the less real on that account. Often he was the victim of his own frustrated reaction to the machinations of nasty little men.

Before actually re-entering the service, Erich traced down his old crew chief, Heinz "Bimmel" Mertens, in Düsseldorf. Bimmel nearly dropped the phone when Erich's familiar, drawling voice reached him from out of the past. They had not spoken to each other for over eleven years, although they had been as close as twins throughout Erich's combat service. Their last words to each other had been as they put the remnants of JG-52 to the torch at Deutsch Brod in May of 1945. There was only one crew chief in the world as far as Erich was concerned, and he wanted Bimmel with him again if it was possible. He had previously made up his mind not to upset Bimmel's life if his old crew chief had come upon good times.

Erich found Bimmel doing well as a civilian. He had a good job with the Düsseldorf waterworks, and two children. Joining the air force would obviously be a bad move for such a well-established, secure and happy family man, and consequently Erich never broached to Bimmel the question of rejoining the service. The Blond Knight knew he would have to find another crew chief. A week later Bimmel and all Germany saw the newspaper headlines:

HARTMANN REJOINS THE LUFTWAFFE

Within a few days of these headlines, Erich had passed his personnel and medical tests. The doctors confirmed that he had recovered well from his prison ordeal. An eight-week language course under U.S. direction gave him basic fluency in English, and he was then ordered to Landsberg for refresher training under USAF instructors.

The German armed forces had been actively expanding ever since May 1955, when West Germany officially accepted the October 1954 invitation of the signatory powers to join NATO. The North Atlantic Treaty Organization had been established after the Berlin blockade of 1948 demonstrated the need for concerted defense measures in Western Europe. Germany was a crucial and central element in any such defense system. Flying training for the new German Air Force began at several bases in Germany using American and British aircraft and instructors, while advanced jet training for several hundred German officers was established at Luke AFB near Phoenix, Arizona, by the USAF.

During his months of recovery Erich had flown in a two-seat Piper Cub owned by a friend, to requalify for his Light Airplane Pilot's License. Eleven years had passed since his last contact with an aircraft when he approached the little ship, but when he opened the tiny cabin door and looked inside he had the strange feeling of having flown only the previous day. The little Piper was similar in size and handling to the Storch he had flown so often in wartime. The feel of the controls returned to him immediately. Nothing was missing from his skills as he took her aloft. The glorious roar of the engine was like listening to the voice of a friend previously presumed dead. With this experience behind him, he was eager to recommence military flying when he reported to Landsberg late in 1956.

The phenomenon of the lost years, which had struck him so sharply in flying the Piper Cub, also had its impact on his USAF instructors at Landsberg. Fighter pilots in general are vivaciously cocky and they frequently look younger than other men in the same age group. When Erich Hartmann quietly reported at Landsberg his American instructors could hardly believe their eyes. The most successful fighter pilot in the world looked no more than twenty-five years old, despite fourteen hundred combat missions and ten and a half years in Russian prisons.

Under the guidance of a friendly Texan of the USAF, Captain James Mangum, Erich checked out in fine style in the T-6 and T-33. The North American T-6 trainer, with its 600 hp radial engine and two-bladed propeller, was used as an advanced trainer. The aircraft was a big step up from the Piper but still far short of the Me-109 in which Erich had spent so many hundreds of hours. The T-33 was a two-seat jet made by Lockheed, but even jet propulsion was not new to Erich, for he had flown the twin-engined Me-262 in 1945.

The sensation of being aloft again in a powerful aircraft was one of liberation. He felt as though he was being reborn, but his was not the only birth in the offing. Usch became pregnant in the summer of 1956, and as Erich tackled the challenge of reorienting himself to military flying his world was filled with a warming glow of anticipation. The death of the baby son he never saw while he was in prison had been a heavy blow, and a new family now was therefore a part of a new life.

When a charming little blonde daughter was born to Usch and Erich at Tübingen near Weil on 23 February 1957, their joy was boundless. Ursula Isabel soon became "Little Usch" and helped her parents forget the past in the joy of a fulfilling present. Erich's re-entry into the brotherhood of fatherhood was one of the happiest days of his life.

In 1957 Erich was assigned to advanced training on jet fighters at Luke AFB, near Phoenix, Arizona. The good-byes to Usch and Little Usch were hard, but the new environment at Luke AFB made Arizona Erich's second home. He trained on the T-33 and F-84 in gunnery, strafing, bombing and skip-bombing in near-perfect weather that permitted flying practically every day.

His social contacts with Americans were broadened when

his old friend Colonel Raymond Toliver USAF, coauthor of this book, arranged from England for Erich to be invited to the reunion of combat crews from the U.S. 20th Tactical Fighter Wing then being held at Luke AFB. The Blond Knight had previously been made an Honorary Member of the 20th when the American unit was stationed at RAF Weathersfield in Essex, England. The American pilots at Luke took the world champion of their profession into their fraternity. The friendly social whirl hardly left him time to ponder on the irony that he was shoulder to shoulder with former enemies, seven of whose aircraft he had shot down in far-off Europe.

When USAAF gun camera film from the Second World War was screened at Luke, Erich pointed out convincingly to the young American pilots that the films verified what he had told them about his own combat tactics. "Get in close, if you want to get him down," he had told them repeatedly. "Two hundred and fifty yards? You are still too far out." Some young pilots were skeptical, but the combat films proved him right.

When the pursued aircraft filled the camera lens and the pursuing pilot fired, the explosion of the target aircraft followed almost invariably as the plane took point-blank hits and disintegrated. Long-distance gun camera footage, by contrast, showed mostly the curving and decelerating bullets scoring occasional hits. Rarely was the other aircraft actually seen to go down, except in the case of some spectacular downings in which inflammable Japanese aircraft blew up under even these minor strikes. Few of the long-range films showed anything like the devastation of the point-blank attack.

The young American pilots were intrigued by Erich Hartmann, and admired his modesty and frankness. They also profited by his almost incredible store of experience, the harvest of more than eight hundred aerial battles. The USAF in turn, impressed and surprised the Blond Knight with its spirit and morale, which he found reminiscent of the old Luftwaffe. The German Air Force of 1957 lacked such inner strength, and Erich felt its absence keenly.

Fresh from the political atmosphere of the German service in 1957, Erich found the USAF admirably equipped with the morale that encourages men to excel themselves.

On the personal side of his visit to the U.S., Erich found warm friendship. Major Frank Buzze USAF, and his wife Wylene, invited him to share their home in Phoenix. He found it hard to believe that a regular military officer could live as well as did the Buzzes. They had a pleasant home with all modern conveniences, drove a handsome sports car and were relaxed and happy people.

The Arizona experience, in all its aspects, was such a fairy tale to Erich after the brutal decade that he wanted to share it with Usch. The Buzzes promptly invited the German couple to live with them as long as Erich was at Luke. He scraped up the necessary air fare and Usch flew to Arizona, while Little Usch stayed in the care of her grandparents at the Paetsch home in Stuttgart.

Arizona became an unforgettable experience for Usch as well. The expansive, endless, empty countryside and raw desert terrain were unlike anything the German couple had ever seen. Camping trips amid the magnificence of Grand Canyon fascinated them no less than the vast supermarkets and handsome stores in Phoenix. When they went back to Germany it was the end of an idyl, of which Usch wistfully says today:

"It was the nicest time we ever had in our lives. There was not the slightest resentment of us as Germans, and everyone was kind and helpful. We felt completely at home, and it is the only country outside Germany where I would like to live. Frank and Wylene Buzze are the best people we ever met, uncomplicated friends to whom you could feel kinship as to your father and mother. Sometimes, after we returned to Germany, I was homesick for Phoenix, Wylene, and everything and everybody there."

Erich's adventures in America were intensely professional as well as having a light side. The F-104* naturally intrigued him, as the most advanced weapons system of its kind in the world. He went up to Nellis AFB near Las Vegas, Nevada, where there was an F-104 training squadron, and found out what made the aircraft tick. The American pilots were full of the machine, its speed, performance, climb, weapons—when

---

* The F-104 "Starfighter," a Mach 2-plus air superiority fighter built by the Lockheed Aircraft Corp. of Burbank, California. It is a fighter pilots' dream and is considered the hot rod of all fighters. Over 2550 have been produced and fourteen nations of the world are using them.

they were on the base. When Erich talked to the same young pilots around the bar off duty, the story was a little different.

He asked them why the serviceability ratio was so low and they told him about some of the difficulties with the F-104. Engine troubles, nose wheel problems, nozzle difficulties and other matters were cited as sources of low serviceability. When Erich tackled the maintenance people about the F-104, they told him of the practical problems they had in keeping it serviceable and ready to fly. The catalog of spare-parts troubles, equipment defects and maintenance problems was not a bright record.

Erich had not been sent to America to evaluate the F-104, but he was deeply interested, as a professional military pilot and soon-to-be wing commander, in an aircraft he knew would probably be used by the NATO forces in due course. A young USAF captain whom Erich befriended gave him a large volume containing the findings on the F-104 accidents up to that time. Erich carefully sifted this technical evidence, and his conclusion at the end of his probe was firm and unequivocal. The German Air Force would need much more experience and know-how before it could handle such an aircraft. This view would later hurt him, even as it proved truthful and accurate.

When he returned to Germany, he was offered command of a fighter-bomber wing. He declined this appointment because he did not regard the fighter-bomber role as his job, and he told the authorities he would rather wait for the first all-jet fighter wing. In the spring of 1958 he served for a time at Oldenburg as deputy C.O.* of the Fighter Pilots' School, and in June made a little rendezvous with history.

The first jet fighter wing in the new air force was to be formed at Ahlhorn, and would carry the designation JG-71 Richthofen. The wing would preserve the tradition of Germany's greatest First World War ace, and of JG-2 Richthofen in the Luftwaffe of the Second World War. The wing would appropriately have as its *Kommodore* the Richthofen of the second conflict—Major Erich Hartmann. A rebuilding party and a speech by General Kammhuber, Inspector of the German Air Force, started Erich Hartmann on what was probably his greatest adventure as an air force officer.

* Thirty-six-victory ace *Oberst* Herbert Wehnelt was the commander.

This appointment showed that the German Air Force was capable of good decisions as well as mistakes. The decision to give Erich command of JG-71 seemed to be almost a stroke of genius, because of the way it brought man and task together, matching each to the other. Germany honored Erich Hartmann by making him commander of the Richthofen Wing. The air force was also extending a *challenge* to the Blond Knight, because the task of raising Germany's first modern jet fighter wing from a row of F-86 Mark VI aircraft was a hairy mass of problems. The situation was tantamount to saying, "Blond Knight, let's see if there is something more to you than ace pilot and marksman."

With his combative juices roiling and his competitive spirit aroused, Erich threw himself into his job with all his energy. The young pilots assigned to the wing held their C.O. initially in awe. Erich turned their awe into spirit and *élan* with the quality of his leadership, setting a standard for morale in the new German Air Force. Only in the Second World War, under the great *Kommodores* like Galland, Moelders, Hrabak, Trautloft and Priller were fighter wings invested with the same kind of spirit.

Erich conducted classes, flew continually in the wing's U.S.-built F-86's and became a leading figure in the Ahlhorn Soaring Club on weekends. He taught the young pilots from the Richthofen Wing all that his mother had taught him about gliding years before, plus all that he had learned on his own.

He located Sigi Graf von der Schulenburg, his old prison mate from Diaterka, in an officers' training school in Hamburg and arranged for his transfer to JG-71 as its executive officer. Erich flew about in a little Dornier consulting with NATO officers and expediting matériel for his wing. Everyone was inspired to work like the devil for something they felt was bigger than themselves.

He built up new squadrons and pounded endlessly on the need for flying experience, flying experience and more flying experience. Erich knew the F-104's were eventually coming and he knew how hot they were. The important thing in his mind was to get as much flying experience as quickly as possible, leaving the more mundane aspects of organization for detailed attention later. He knew that the lives of his young pilots would ultimately depend on how much experience they had when the ultra-sophisticated F-104 came to hand.

A superb human element would be needed for handling the F-104G, and he concentrated on the human element—endless training on one side, and spirit and morale on the other. He painted JG-71 aircraft with the same spreading black tulip pattern over the spinner that Karaya One had worn on the Russian Front, and with which he had terrorized the Red Air Force. As JG-71 aircraft were overhauled, they were painted with the tulip pattern. The pilots loved this salty link with the past. A visiting general was appalled. He was not a flyer but a flak officer.

"That's *paint* on those aircraft?" sputtered the flak general.*

"Yes, *mein General*," said Erich.

"But only half the planes are painted, the wing looks a mess."

"We paint them while they are in for overhaul, and that maintains our serviceability ratio. They'll all be painted soon."

"Paint costs money, Major Hartmann."

"That is perfectly all right, sir. I will pay for the paint myself. The paint marking makes for strong spirit in the wing."

Like Krupinski in Russia during World War II he set up squadron bars for JG-71. After each day's flying the pilots retired to bars on the base. There they could relax and talk shop. The new German Air Force wasn't ready, though. Erich's superiors had the bars eliminated under orders. In the German Air Force of today, however, every squadron has a bar and it is encouraged as a morale builder.

Incidents like these, involving high officers, led to circulation of the theme that "Hartmann is not a good officer." Most of the high officers and personnel personages had never flown combat. In some ways, Erich Hartmann might not have been a "good officer," but it depended on the viewpoint and background of the critic. Having seen the German officer corps with its pants down in the Russian prisons, Erich knew the normal conceptions of what makes a good officer have no ultimate validity.

An old JG-52 comrade was assigned to the Richthofen Wing under Erich's command. He was not a man to whom

---

* A flak general is one who has been an antiaircraft artillery commander and is not a rated pilot.

Erich had ever been close, but they had been in Russian prisons together as well as war comrades, and Erich knew that this officer had been badly knocked about in combat. Head injuries had made him something less than he was in the prime of life.

This officer occasionally tattled to Erich's superiors about minor infractions of regulations at Ahlhorn, and was far from loyal to his C.O. In a fashion typical of Erich's outlook on life, the Blond Knight made allowances for all that his old comrade had endured. When this officer got drunk frequently, and had fist fights with enlisted men, Erich declined to punish him. The general to whom the officer had tattled heard about these things, and insisted that Erich punish the battered veteran.

The blond man who had withstood ten years of NKVD bludgeoning could not be made to relinquish as a free man what he felt to be an inviolable ethical principle. Punishing a highly decorated officer who had been a hero in war was in itself repugnant, but to punish a man who needed a doctor rather than discipline was to Erich Hartmann absolutely unthinkable. He refused to depart from this stance and punish his decorated comrade. This was deemed further evidence that he was not a good officer.

Erich Hartmann's critics were in many cases living a long way from reality, for the German Air Force, like most other military organizations, has its roots in an outmoded concept of what is fitting, right and efficient. In the atomic age, military leaders still differentiate between peacetime and wartime, and efficiency is all too often everything in neat rows, pressed trousers, saluting and other frills meaningless and even dangerous in the supersonic era.

As a wing commander, Erich Hartmann took advantage of his experience. He ran JG-71 as though the war was on, "so we don't develop bad habits." He had little use for the parade-ground concept of aircraft drawn up in neat rows, with lines of men standing with their thumbs abaft their seams while peacock officers with no flying experience made ostentatious inspections. Operational readiness, in his view, is made of sterner stuff.

Erich Hartmann believes that future wars will grant no time for "working up" to operational readiness. His approach is therefore operational readiness and dispersal at all times.

The German Air Force more than any other has good reason to function in no other fashion. When the Luftwaffe smashed the Red Air Force on the ground in June 1941, it was the most complete destruction of an air weapon in history.* The Russian planes were lined up parade-ground style on fields close to the front. Erich's view was that the German Air Force should not be set up for a similar, but far more rapid and destructive stroke, in the supersonic age that arrived with the jet and rocket.

His refusal to be content with half-measures in operational readiness brought him into collision with his immediate leadership—not with generals like Kammhuber who knew their business—but with the professionally inadequate and politically potent officers with whom the air force had become loaded. Many of them had been army officers in the war, some had been in the Luftwaffe, but few had flown since 1945 and they were in all respects obsolescent in mind and outlook.

The Hartmann psychology was shaped in the fires of Soviet confinement, forged by its rigors and hardened by relentless processes that never touched those who now said that Hartmann was not a good officer. When the NKVD spent a decade trying to destroy a young man who exemplified decent German character, they turned Erich Hartmann in his maturity into a man who defends an honest view bluntly. For ten years he had clung to truth in the gloom of innumerable bunkers, and no man could now, in the pure air of freedom, extort from him a political "yes" when the military truth was "no."

High officers who were living a lie through political pull understandably recoiled from the blunt blond man. Structurally incapable of bending to meet political expediencies—his legacy from a decade of resisting assaults on his character—he was a threat to the emotional security poseurs enjoyed on the neurotic plane. Thus it became politically fashionable to repeat that Erich Hartmann was not a good officer—and promotional suicide to defend him.

An officer who knew him in his glory days and was incar-

---

* The Israel destruction of the Arab air forces in the six-day war of 1967 is quite insignificant in comparison to the mass destruction of 22 June 1941.

cerated with him in Russia, explained Erich's approach to incompetent superiors—colonels, generals or whatever—with this graphic description.

"He doesn't understand tact. He talks to them as if they were NKVD officers, whose thinking processes have been addled by politics."

To the young men of his Richthofen Wing, he was just the opposite of what he was held to be by those who controlled the chessboard. Like most young people who have grown up since the war, the young pilots had a good nose for a fake and a strong feeling for truth. The Blond Knight was a leader who could push their buttons and turn them on—no mean feat in an age and profession where anyone over thirty is considered burnt out.

When he told them about gunnery and air fighting, there was no question of their confidence in his truthfulness. He was the most successful fighter pilot ever to strap an airplane on his back. When he told them about Soviet psychology and the NKVD methods of character disintegration, they listened and learned. One day, these young Germans knew, they might have to defend themselves against such processes, and they knew they were hearing the living truth.

Barely six months after Erich went to work in creating the formation, JG-71 Richthofen was assigned to NATO in October 1958. The magnitude of his achievement in preparing his wing may be measured by the normal time required by most fighter wings to reach a level of efficiency qualifying them for NATO—usually at least a year. For a leader who was "not a good officer" it was a stellar performance, not equaled even ten years later.

They were his boys and he watched over them like a father. In September of 1960 he proudly wrote the authors about his boys:

"During the last year we reached an air gunnery average in the wing of 24 per cent. I am happy about this, as I think it is the highest score in the German Air Force. My boys are great! I have six sharpshooters with 60 per cent score *average*—young boys of twenty-four—so I have made them section leaders. The boys are better now than the tired old tomcat of a wing commander."

Men who served in JG-71 in those swaddling days of the

German Air Force worshiped their tough, blond *Kommodore*. They still do. They would have followed him through the gates of hell. Today, many of them command wings, and a number of them have been promoted past Erich Hartmann, whose continued unpopularity with the political people retarded his progress. His upbeat achievements seemed to find their counterpart in an opposing conspiracy of events.

The decision of the German Air Force to buy the F-104 hurt Erich's career, although it should have had the opposite result. His rapport with higher leaders who were thorough and competent professionals was excellent. He liked and admired General Kammhuber, the first Inspector of the *Bundesluftwaffe,* and respected his abilities and achievements. The same is true of his relationship with General Steinhoff, the present head of the German Air Force. Frank views could be expressed to such men.

On one occasion, the subject of the F-104 was raised in conversation with Kammhuber. Basing his views on his investigation of the F-104 while in the U.S., Erich said he did not believe that the F-104 would be a good aircraft for the German Air Force *at that time*. He was probably the first to hold this view and express it to his superiors. He felt acquisition of the F-104 should have been delayed.

"My thinking was that I was a good pilot. A normal, average pilot without special expertise, but with lots of luck, nothing more. You must have luck, no matter what your practical experience, as any businessman will tell you. Through my good luck I had gained a lot of experience. This experience told me, when combined with what I learned about the F-104 in the U.S.A., that our young pilots did not then have the experience to change to such a complex weapons system.

"I did not believe that the F-104 was a bad weapons system, but rather that a human problem on our side would cause us grave troubles."

Erich expressed his views frankly to General Kammhuber. He pointed out to his leader that for a decade or more a gap had existed in German aviation, during which no pilots were trained, no technicians gained experience and no organization existed. He reviewed for Kammhuber his investigation of the F-104 in the U.S.—conducted in a way that kept the facts free of political coloring. He emphasized the youth and inexperience of the German pilots and the lack of experience in handling jets on the part of Germany's top leaders.

"I believe, sir, that buying the F-104 is the wrong decision for us at this time, that we should not buy an aircraft we cannot handle."

General Kammhuber, who liked Erich, kept listening.

"Sometimes I think, sir, that this is why Germans are hated in the world. We say 'We are Germans, we can handle it.' Because we are Germans we think we can handle a complex aircraft like this *at once*."

Kammhuber asked him what he thought should be done.

"Let us take from the Americans next their F-100 and F-102. This is the next generation of aircraft, on which we can gain experience with afterburners and other technical advances. Then we can phase in the F-104 on a proper basis of knowledge and experience. But we should not buy an aircraft we cannot handle."

Kammhuber said nothing concerning the content of Erich's remarks. His noncommittal but friendly reply was obviously intended as advice.

"Erich, *never talk about this*," he said. "We are happy to buy this aircraft. The political people have decided that we can buy this aircraft."

Had Erich been the kind of well-adjusted officer that did well in those times in the German Air Force, he would have held his peace. Unfortunately for him, people who asked him straight questions got straight answers reaffirming his view that the F-104 should come later. Through the channels of whisper and hearsay his views on the F-104 filtered back to the political areas and there reinforced the popular concept that he was not a good officer.

The disastrous experience that ensued with the F-104 in the German Air Force verified tragically and expensively that Erich Hartmann's practical analysis had been accurate. The F-104 crashes continued until command of the German Air Force passed, almost in desperation, to Johannes "Macky" Steinhoff in 1966. One of the Me-262 jet aces from the Second World War, Steinhoff also had his share of problems with politicians in Germany. Despite a brilliant war record in combat and command and his demonstrated organizational gifts, political opposition to him arose ostensibly because of his badly burned face—a souvenir of his 1945 jet crash.

The real reason his appointments were resisted was that he was and is a general who knows his profession right through. Good sense and logic eventually prevailed when he was given his first major assignment, as Germany's representative on the NATO Standing Committee in Washington. He made an indelible impression on everyone who met him, and his burned face proved no impediment to the exercise of his dynamic personality and intelligence in Germany's behalf. When the political powers were compelled by conditions to turn to him in the fall of 1966 to take over as *Inspekteur** it was due largely to his leadership—and to his insistence on authority to go with his responsibility—that the Starfighter crisis was overcome.

Significant steps in the reform of the F-104 program undertaken by Steinhoff† included heavy emphasis on training and flying experience, the course that Erich Hartmann had followed to his own professional detriment during the raising of JG-71. In a slashing vindication of the Blond Knight's foresight, the first sixteen pilots he trained in the Richthofen Wing are all alive today save one. The boy who was lost was an F-104 test pilot. He was caught in a heavy ground wind on take-off, and his death was due neither to pilot error nor to a defective machine. The other fifteen are not only still alive, but most of them have between eight hundred and one thousand flying hours in the F-104.

Between Erich's warnings concerning the F-104 and the vindication of his analysis, he became the target of an incredibly petty vendetta by a general who is best left nameless. He was not an officer who had flown in wartime. Military flying officers in Germany hold pilot's licenses, which are routinely

---

* *Inspekteur* of the German Air Force is a position as commander in chief.

† Thousands were involved in the conquest of F-104 problems, but leadership was the key element, just as executive know-how makes or breaks a business enterprise.

GAF F-104 loss rate per 100,000 flying hours in 1965: 41.9

GAF F-104 loss rate per 100,000 flying hours in 1967: 10.7

The 1967 loss rate is the lowest rate recorded by any major nation using the F-104.—Authors

renewed when they are on active duty. The procedure is little
more than filling out the necessary documents and submitting
them with the license for validation.

During the hard-driving days at Ahlhorn, when the Richthofen Wing was being built, Erich overlooked the annual re-
validation of his pilot's license. Later he could not locate the
document. A general used this chink in the Blond Knight's
armor to drive home what he hoped would be a professionally
mortal thrust. A fatuous proceeding was launched against
Erich akin to a court-martial. His prospects looked bleak, but
the maneuver backfired.

Word of Erich's difficulties had spread to America. General
Panitzki, who had replaced General Kammhuber as Inspector
of the German Air Force, was in Washington at the time. A
retired American fighter officer asked him point-blank if the
Bundesluftwaffe was really serious in proceeding against Hartmann, who had stood up for Germany for ten years in Soviet
jails. The embarrassed Panitzki merely replied with the stock
phrase, "Erich is a good pilot but not a good officer." Soon
afterward military judges ruled on the matter, and Erich
Hartmann was absolved of blame. The damage had nevertheless been done through a sort of character defamation. Too
many people had heard the first part of the story but never
heard how it ended. He was relieved of his command of
JG-71 Richthofen and transferred to a staff headquarters at
Porz Wahn, near Cologne.

Forthrightness and honesty placed Erich Hartmann outside
the political mainstream that carried many lesser but more
diplomatic men to high rank. He lived for years in relative
obscurity as a tactical evaluation specialist, and watched
young men he had trained in JG-71 promoted to colonel
ahead of him. He got great satisfaction from the success of
any of "his boys." His allies have always included senior
officers who admired him and valued his work, but their
efforts to get him promoted to colonel were consistently
turned down until mid-1968. By that time he had been nearly
eight years a lieutenant colonel, and his retention in that
grade, as the most highly decorated officer in the German
armed forces, had become more than a little unseemly.

Although sometimes discouraged and occasionally bitter, he
never lost his sense of humor or his overriding philosophy

that all men's doings are kismet. Politicians he continues to view without rancor as a sort of essential nuisance. "Politics makes strange bedfellows," he told the authors in 1966, "if you get into bed with them." His analytical faculty and ability to write good reports found scope in the tactical evaluation job, which he now heads for the German Air Force as Colonel Erich Hartmann.

Those who know him and his scene generally agree that the German Air Force does not quite know what to do with him, how to turn his world status to good account, and above all, how to harness the tigerish energy that still burns within the old tomcat. An incorrigible individualist, he has ennobled his life with an inborn sense of fairness, justice and honesty. He is a heroic man whose faults, if they be understood aright, are but manifestations of a surpassingly positive personality.

The Blond Knight's hair is beginning to turn brown, and heavy lines are working their way into his handsome features. His face is his escutcheon, like the emblazoned shields borne by his medieval predecessors. The record of all his battles in life is etched there—his victories and defeats, his triumphs and tragedies. He has emerged the victor from his jousts in the tournament of life more often than not, but he also knows the experience of being knocked from the saddle, and of being trampled when prostrate by an unchivalrous foe.

He has lived a romance with his lady that must surely warm the spirit of every human being who has ever been in love. His life and love story intertwine tenderness and valor in a living legend. He will not change now, to meet what is called the new world, for he is already old in his mode of attack on life. Wiser than of yore, he listens as his evening approaches for the sound of a thrown-down gauntlet. A bigger challenge may yet lie ahead than any in his past—perhaps a challenge great enough to rouse and rally all his formidable spirit and will. May Heaven help the jouster tilting with him then.

APPENDIX

EXCERPTS OF ERICH HARTMANN'S
VICTORY CREDITS RECORD

Vic.	Sortie	Date	Time	Type A/C	Location
1	19	5 Nov. 1942	1120–1225	IL-2	Digora (Caucasas)
2	41	27 Jan. 1943	1040–1145	MIG-1	Armavir
3	52	9 Feb. 1943	0650–0755	Lagg-3	Slavyanskaya (Kuban)
4	54	10 Feb. 1943	0600–0625	Boston	Slavyanskaya
5	68	24 Mar. 1943	1200–1306	U-2	Kerch (Crimea)
6	75	27 Mar. 1943	1110–1230	I-16 Rata	Anapa
7	91	15 Apr. 1943	1455–1555	Airacobra	Taman
8	113	26 Apr. 1943	1047–1155	R-5	Taman
9	117	28 Apr. 1943	0822–0945	Lagg-3	Taman
10	120	30 Apr. 1943	1554–1638	Lagg-3	Taman
11	120	30 Apr. 1943	1554–1638	Lagg-3	Taman
12	130	7 May 1943	0730–0825	Lagg-3	Taman
13	131	7 May 1943	1620–1725	Lagg-5	Taman
14	143	11 May 1943	0453–0603		Taman
15	153	15 May 1943	1540–1650	U-2	Taman
16	157	16 May 1943	1415–1515	Lagg-3	Taman
17	158	18 May 1943	1725–1840	Lagg-5	Taman
18	182	5 July 1943	0323–0420	Airacobra	Ugrim
19	183	5 July 1943	0648–0744	Airacobra	Ugrim
20	184	5 July 1943	1345–1445	Airacobra	Ugrim
21	185	5 July 1943	1735–1845	Lagg-5	Ugrim
22	191	7 July 1943	0306–0405	IL-2	Ugrim
23	191	7 July 1943	0306–0405	IL-2	Ugrim
24	192	7 July 1943	0545–0645	IL-2	Ugrim
25	192	7 July 1943	0545–0645	Lagg-5	Ugrim
26	194	7 July 1943	1707–1805	Lagg-5	Ugrim
27	194	7 July 1943	1707–1805	Lagg-5	Ugrim
28	194	7 July 1943		Lagg-5	Ugrim
29	195	8 July 1943	1820–0932	Lagg-5	Ugrim
30	195	8 July 1943	1820–0932	Lagg-5	Ugrim
31	198	8 July 1943	1742–1845	Lagg-5	Ugrim
32	198	8 July 1943	1742–1845	Lagg-5	Ugrim
33	204	10 July 1943	0633–0730	Lagg-5	Ugrim
34	206	11 July 1943	1620–1718	Lagg-5	Ugrim
35	213	15 July 1943	1334–1436	Lagg-5	Ugrim
36	214	15 July 1943	1704–1745	Lagg-5	Ugrim

37	216	16 July 1943	0646–0736	Lagg-5	Ugrim
38	217	16 July 1943	1400–1434	Lagg-5	Ugrim
39	233	17 July 1943	1845–1945	Lagg-5	Ugrim
40	240	31 July 1943	0930–1040	Lagg-5	Ivanowka (Donets)
41	241	31 July 1943	1637–1733	Lagg-5	Ivanowka
42	242	1 Aug. 1943	1110–1215	Lagg-5	Ivanowka
43	243	1 Aug. 1943	1355–1500	Lagg-5	Ivanowka
44	244	1 Aug. 1943	1629–1732	YAK-7	Ivanowka
45	245	1 Aug. 1943	1903–1950	YAK-7	Ivanowka
46	245	1 Aug. 1943	1903–1950	YAK-7	Ivanowka
47	250	3 Aug. 1943	1107–1155	Lagg-5	Varvarovka (Kharkov)
48	250	3 Aug. 1943	1107–1155	YAK-7	Varvarovka
49	250	3 Aug. 1943	1107–1155	YAK-7	Varvarovka
50	251	3 Aug. 1943	1730–1830	Lagg-5	Varvarovka
51	253	4 Aug. 1943	1009–1102	Lagg-5	Varvarovka
52	253	4 Aug. 1943	1009–1102	Lagg-5	Varvarovka
53	253	4 Aug. 1943		Lagg-5	Varvarovka
54	254	4 Aug. 1943	1304–1405	YAK-7	Varvarovka
55	255	4 Aug. 1943	1520–1610	Lagg-5	Varvarovka
56	256	5 Aug. 1943	0812–0915	Lagg-5	Varvarovka
57	257	5 Aug. 1943	1117–1215	YAK-7	Varvarovka
58	257	5 Aug. 1943	1117–1215	YAK-7	Varvarovka
59	258	5 Aug. 1943	1647–1748	Lagg-5	Varvarovka
60	258	5 Aug. 1943	1647–1748	Lagg-5	Varvarovka
61	262	6 Aug. 1943	1530–1620	YAK-1	Kharkov
62	263	7 Aug. 1943	0810–0910	YAK-1	Kharkov
63	263	7 Aug. 1943	0810–0910	YAK-1	Kharkov
64	264	7 Aug. 1943	1140–1235	Pe-2	Kharkov
65	264	7 Aug. 1943	1140–1235	Pe-2	Kharkov
66	264	7 Aug. 1943	1140–1235	YAK-1	Kharkov
67	265	7 Aug. 1943	1930–2025	Lagg-5	Kharkov
68	265	7 Aug. 1943	1930–2025	Lagg-5	Kharkov
69	266	8 Aug. 1943	0657–0755	YAK-1	Kharkov
70	267	8 Aug. 1943	1244–1340	Lagg-5	Kharkov
71	269	9 Aug. 1943	0604–0604	Lagg-5	Kharkov
72	270	9 Aug. 1943	0835–0950	YAK-1	Kharkov
73	271	9 Aug. 1943	1615–1654	YAK-1	Kharkov
74	271	9 Aug. 1943	1615–1654	YAK-1	Kharkov
75	277	12 Aug. 1943	0810–0910	Lagg-5	Kharkov
76	280	15 Aug. 1943	0830–0935	Pe-2	Perechepino
77	281	15 Aug. 1943	1745–1805	Lagg-5	Perechepino
78	281	15 Aug. 1943	1745–1805	Lagg-5	Perechepino
79	283	17 Aug. 1943	0455–0550	Lagg-5	Barwenkovo
80	285	17 Aug. 1943	1215–1315	Airacobra	Barwenkovo
81	285	17 Aug. 1943	1215–1315	Airacobra	Barwenkovo
82	286	17 Aug. 1943	1700–1805	Airacobra	Perechepino
83	288	18 Aug. 1943	0930–1030	Lagg-5	Perechepino
84	288	18 Aug. 1943	0930–1030	Lagg-5	Perechepino
85	289	18 Aug. 1943	1230–1330	Lagg-5	Perechepino
86	292	19 Aug. 1943	1000–1105	Lagg-5	Kutanikowo
87	292	19 Aug. 1943	1000–1105	Lagg-5	Kutanikowo
88	294	19 Aug. 1943	1555–1645	Airacobra	Kutanikowo
89	295	20 Aug. 1943	0530–0615	IL-2	Kutanikowo
90	295	20 Aug. 1943	0530–0615	IL-2	Kutanikowo
91	297	15 Sep. 1943	1143–1245	Lagg-5	Dnepro-South
92	299	18 Sep. 1943	0711–0805	Lagg-5	Dnepro-South
93	300	18 Sep. 1943	1010–1105	Lagg-5	Dnepro-South
94	301	18 Sep. 1943	1320–1420	Lagg-5	Dnepro-South
95	301	18 Sep. 1943	1320–1420	Lagg-5	Dnepro-South
96	305	19 Sep. 1943	1416–1520	Lagg-5	Zaporozhe

(*Note:* Hartmann was shot down in Soviet territory at approximately 0615 after his ninetieth victory.)

97	305	19 Sep. 1943	1416–1520	Lagg-5	Zaporozhe
98	308	20 Sep. 1943	1305–1350	Lagg-5	Dnepro-South
99	308	20 Sep. 1943	1305–1350	Lagg-5	Dnepro-South
100	309	20 Sep. 1943	1512–1610	Airacobra	Dnepro-South
101	309	20 Sep. 1943	1512–1610	Lagg-5	Dnepro-South
102	314	25 Sep. 1943	0725–0825	Lagg-5	Novo-Zaporozhe
103	315	25 Sep. 1943	1200–1305	Lagg-5	Novo-Zaporozhe
104	316	25 Sep. 1943	1550–1650	Lagg-5	Novo-Zaporozhe
105	317	26 Sep. 1943	0635–0738	Lagg-5	Novo-Zaporozhe
106	317	26 Sep. 1943	0635–0738	Airacobra	Novo-Zaporozhe
107	318	26 Sep. 1943	0930–1035	Airacobra	Novo-Zaporozhe
108	321	27 Sep. 1943	1145–1245	Lagg-5	Novo-Zaporozhe
109	321	27 Sep. 1943	1145–1245	Lagg-5	Novo-Zaporozhe
110	324	28 Sep. 1943	1615–1710	Lagg-5	Zaporozhe
111	325	29 Sep. 1943	0635–0735	Lagg-5	Zaporozhe
112	326	29 Sep. 1943	0837–0940	Airacobra	Zaporozhe
113	330	30 Sep. 1943	0643–0715	Lagg-5	Zaporozhe
114	332	30 Sep. 1943	1353–1445	Airacobra	Zaporozhe
115	333	30 Sep. 1943	1620–1710	Airacobra	Zaporozhe
116	334	1 Sep. 1943	1200–1255	Lagg-5	Zaporozhe
117	334	1 Oct. 1943	1200–1255	Lagg-5	Novo-Zaporozhe
118	337	2 Oct. 1943	0820–0925	Lagg-5	Novo-Zaporozhe
119	337	2 Oct. 1943	0820–0925	Pe-2	Novo-Zaporozhe
120	338	2 Oct. 1943	1110–1210	Airacobra	Novo-Zaporozhe
121	339	2 Oct. 1943	1335–1425	Lagg-5	Novo-Zaporozhe
122	340	3 Oct. 1943	0030–1030	Lagg-5	Novo-Zaporozhe
123	342	3 Oct. 1943	1525–1630	Lagg-5	Novo-Zaporozhe
124	343	4 Oct. 1943	0645–0740	Airacobra	Novo-Zaporozhe
125	348	11 Oct. 1943	1240–1400	Lagg-5	Novo-Zaporozhe
126	349	12 Oct. 1943	0650–0745	Lagg-5	Novo-Zaporozhe
127	349	12 Oct. 1943	0650–0745	Lagg-5	Novo-Zaporozhe
128	349	12 Oct. 1943	0650–0745	Lagg-5	Novo-Zaporozhe
129	351	12 Oct. 1943	1415–1515	Lagg-5	Novo-Zaporozhe
130	353	13 Oct. 1943	0955–1055	Lagg-5	Zaporozhe
131	355	14 Oct. 1943	0740–0835	Lagg-5	Zaporozhe
132	355	14 Oct. 1943	0740–0835	Lagg-5	Zaporozhe
133	357	14 Oct. 1943	1505–1555	Lagg-5	Zaporozhe
134	359	15 Oct. 1943	0835–0925	Lagg-5	Zaporozhe
135	359	15 Oct. 1943	0835–0925	Lagg-5	Zaporozhe
136	360	15 Oct. 1943	1100–1200	Lagg-5	Novo-Zaporozhe
137	366	20 Oct. 1943	0630–0705	Airacobra	Kirovogard
138	366	20 Oct. 1943	0630–0705	Airacobra	Kirovogard
139	368	20 Oct. 1943	1420–1505	Airacobra	Kirovogard
140	369	21 Oct. 1943	0720–0740	Lagg-7	Beresovka
141	376	24 Oct. 1943	1355–1450	Lagg-7	Novo-Zaporozhe
142	376	24 Oct. 1943	1355–1450	Lagg-7	Novo-Zaporozhe
143	377	25 Oct. 1943	0920–1020	Pe-2	Novo-Zaporozhe
144	379	25 Oct. 1943	1500–1545	Lagg-7	Novo-Zaporozhe
145	380	26 Oct. 1943	0740–0840	Airacobra	Novo-Zaporozhe
146	380	26 Oct. 1943	0740–0840	Airacobra	Novo-Zaporozhe
147	385	29 Oct. 1943	0825–0910	Lagg-7	Kirovogard
148	386	29 Oct. 1943	1020–1120	Airacobra	Kirovogard
149	387	7 Dec. 1943	1305–1405	Lagg-7	Apostolovo
150	391	13 Dec. 1943	0923–1020	Lagg-7	Apostolovo

Here ends Erich Hartmann's first combat logbook, which is kept safely in Germany. His second logbook, containing information on the rest of his wartime career, was taken from him the last day of the war by an American or a Czechoslovakian captor, and is the subject of an urgent search by the authors.

Hartmann's victories from this point are taken from III/JG-52 records and from letters written to Fraulein Ursula Paetsch, his fiancée, whom he later married.

Victory	Date	Time	Type A/C	Location
151–153	15 Dec. 1943			
154–156	18 Dec. 1943			
157–159	20 Dec. 1943			
160	3 Jan. 1944			
161	6 Jan. 1944		Airacobra	Kirovograd
162	6 Jan. 1944		Airacobra	Kirovograd
163–165	9 Jan. 1944			
166–168	16 Jan. 1944			
169–172	17 Jan. 1944			
173–176	23 Jan. 1944		Lagg-7	Novo-Krasnoje
177	24 Jan. 1944		Lagg-7	Novo-Krasnoje
178–183	30 Jan. 1944			
184–185	31 Jan. 1944			
186–190	1 Feb. 1944			
191	3 Feb. 1944			
192	4 Feb. 1944		Airacobra	Novo-Krasnoje
	22 Feb. 1944 (Crashed on landing at Uman)			
193–202	2 Mar. 1944 (Ten victories in one day)			Kirovograd
203	23 Apr. 1944			Sevastopol
204–205	25 Apr. 1944			
206–207	26 Apr. 1944			Kolomea
208	3 May 1944			Crimea-Chersonaise
209	4 May 1944			Crimea-Chersonaise
210–215	5 May 1944			
216–221	7 May 1944			
222–223	8 May 1944		(After second victory on this date, Hartmann landed, took two mechanics into the fuselage of his Me-109 and fled the Crimea Peninsula)	
224–225	21 May 1944		Mustangs	Burcharest
226–228	29 May 1944		Lagg-7	Roman
229–231	31 May 1944		Airacobra	Roman
232–237	1 Jun. 1944		Mustangs	Ploesti
238–239	2 Jun. 1944			
240–243	3 Jun. 1944			
244–250	4 Jun. 1944		YAK-9	Bobruisk
251–256	5 Jun. 1944			
257–261	6 Jun. 1944			
262–266	24 Jun. 1944			
267–290	25 Jun. to 23 Aug. 1944			
291–301	24 Aug. 1944		Airacobra	Baranov
302–306	27 Oct. 1944			
307	8 Nov. 1944			
308–309	8 Nov. 1944			
310–311	12 Nov. 1944			
312–313	15 Nov. 1944			
314–315	16 Nov. 1944			
316	21 Nov. 1944			

Victory	Date	Time	Type A/C	Location
317–322	22 Nov. 1944			
323–327	23 Nov. 1944			
328–331	24 Nov. 1944			
332	5 Feb. 1945			
333–346	6 Feb. to 27 Feb. 1945			
347–351	4 Apr. 1945			
352*	8 May 1945	0830–0920	YAK-11	Brünn

TYPES OF AIPLANES FLOWN BY ACE
ERICH HARTMANN DURING WORLD WAR II

Bucher Bu-131
Focke-Wulf FW-44
Klemm KL-35
Arado AR-66
Focke-Wulf FW-58
Focke-Wulf FW-56
Heinkel He-46
Junkers W-34
Heinkel He-51
Heinkel He-50

Junkers F-13
Junkers W-33
Bucher Bu-133
North American NAA-64
Arado AR-96
Fiesler Fi-153
Klemm KL-25
Morane C-445
Messerschmitt Bf-108
Messerschmitt Me-109B, C, D, E, F, G
Messerschmitt Me-262 (jet)

MODELS FLOWN IN COMBAT:
Messerschmitt Me-109G-7, G-10, G-14, G-16 and Me-109R-4

* Hartmann's 352nd victory was scored on his 1405th combat mission and his 825 actual combat dogfight.

MOVEMENTS OF III/JG-52 DURING THE PERIOD
1 DEC. 1942 TO 1 JUNE 1944*

From	To	Airfield or Geographical location†
1 Dec. 1942	–4 Jan. 1943	Soldatskaja
5 Jan. 1943	–10 Jan. 1943	Mineralny Wody
11 Jan. 1943	–22 Jan. 1943	Armaviv
22 Jan. 1943	–7 Feb. 1943	Rostow
8 Feb. 1943	–14 Mar. 1943	Nikolajew
15 Mar. 1943	–31 Mar. 1943	Kertsch IV
1 Apr. 1943	–2 July 1943	Taman
3 July 1943	–13 July 1943	Ugrim
14 July 1943	–19 July 1943	Orel
20 July 1943	–2 Aug. 1943	Iwanowka
3 Aug. 1943	–5 Aug. 1943	Warwarowka
6 Aug. 1943	–12 Aug. 1943	Charkow-Rogan
13 Aug. 1943	–13 Aug. 1943	Charkow-Sud
14 Aug. 1943	–18 Aug. 1943	Peretschepino
19 Aug. 1943	–23 Aug. 1943	Kutanikowo
24 Aug. 1943	–1 Sep. 1943	Makejewka
2 Sep. 1943	–5 Sep. 1943	Stalino-Nord
6 Sep. 1943	–7 Sep. 1943	Grischino
8 Sep. 1943	–8 Sep. 1943	Boguslaw
8 Sep. 1943	–23 Sep. 1943	Dnjepropetrowsk
24 Sep. 1943	–15 Oct. 1943	Nowo Saparoshje
16 Oct. 1943	–18 Oct. 1943	Malaja Beresowka bei Alexandria
19 Oct. 1943	–31 Oct. 1943	Kirwograd
1 Nov. 1943	–6 Jan. 1944	Apostolovo
7 Jan. 1944	–9 Jan. 1944	Malaja Wiski
10 Jan. 1944	–22 Feb. 1944	Nowo Krasnoje
23 Feb. 1944	–6 Mar. 1944	Uman
7 Mar. 1944	–7 Mar. 1944	Kalinowky
8 Mar. 1944	–11 Mar. 1944	Winniza Ost
12 Mar. 1944	–23 Mar. 1944	Proskurow
24 Mar. 1944	–24 Mar. 1944	Kamenez Podolsk
25 Mar. 1944	–26 Mar. 1944	Kolomea
27 Mar. 1944	–5 Apr. 1944	Lemberg
6 Apr. 1944	–9 Apr. 1944	Roman
10 Apr. 1944	–10 May 1944	Krim Chersonaise
11 May 1944	–17 May 1944	Zarnesti
18 May 1944	–31 May 1944	Roman

* The above list indicates where the headquarters of III/JG-52
was located daily. Since III *Gruppe* was composed of three
squadrons it was necseeary that each of them generally operate
from other air bases some miles away. Those outlying bases are
not listed herein. Study of the above list indicates that III *Gruppe*
must have had an almost insurmountable problem in logistics in
trying to keep three constantly moving operational units supplied. It is almost incomprehensible to the authors that III *Gruppe*
was able to account for itself as well as it did.

All bases listed are in the Ukraine and the Caucasus regions.

† Place names are taken from III/JG-52 daily history and the
spelling is as used in that document.—Authors

PERSONAL DATA

Name: ERICH ALFRED HARTMANN
Date of Birth: 19 April 1922
Place of Birth: Weissach/Württemberg
Father's name: Alfred Erich Hartmann
Father's birth date: 1 October 1894
Father's place of birth: Ehingen/Württemberg
Mother's maiden name: Elisabeth Wilhelmine Machtholf
Mother's birth date: 16 February 1897
Mother's place of birth: Ehingen/Württemberg
Date of father's and mother's marriage: 2 September 1920
Place: Stuttgart/Württemberg
Date of Erich's marriage to Ursula Paetsch: 10 September 1944
Place of marriage: Bad Wiessee
Chronological formal education:
   April 1928–April 1932: Grade school in Weil im Schönbuch
   April 1932–April 1936: High School Gymnasium in Böblingen
   April 1932–April 1937: NPEA Gymnasium in Rottweil
   April 1937–April 1940: Gymnasium at Korntal
   Education major: Would have studied medicine but war intervened
First station and date of reporting: 10th Flying Regiment, Neukuhren, East Prussia (near Königsberg), 1 October 1940
Chronological list of stations:
   1 October 1940: 10th Flying Regiment, Neukuhren
   1 March 1941: Air War School, LKS2, Berlin-Gatow
   1November 1941: Pre-fighter School 2, Lachon-Speyerdorf
   1 March 1942: Fighter School 2, Zerbst-Anhalt
   20 August 1942: Fighter Supply Group, East Gleiwitz/Oberschleissen
   10 October 1942: 7/III/JG-52, Eastern Front
   2 September 1943: C.O. 9 Sqdn. III/JG-52, Eastern Front
   1 October 1944: C.O. 6 Sqdn. II/JG-52, Eastern Front
   1 November 1944: C.O. I *Gruppe*/JG-52, Eastern Front
   1 March 1945: transition to Me-262 Jets at Lechfeld
   25 March 1945: C.O. I *Gruppe*/JG-52
Date commissioned as an officer: 1 March 1942
Place commissioned: Fighter School 2, Zerbst
Chronological list of dates of promotion:
   First Lieutenant: 1 July 1944
   Captain: 1 September 1944
   Major: 8 May 1945
   Lieutenant Colonel: 12 December 1960
   Colonel: 26 July 1967
Date awarded Knight's Cross: 29 October 1943
Date awarded Knight's Cross and Oak Leaves: 2 March 1944
Date awarded Knight's Cross, Oak Leaves and Swords: 4 July 1944
Date awarded Knight's Cross, Oak Leaves, Swords and Diamonds: 25 July 1944

TOPS AND FIRST—LUFTWAFFE, WORLD WAR II

Top Ace of World War II—Major Erich Hartmann: 352 victories

Top Night Fighter Ace of World War II—Major Heinz Schnaufer: 121 victories

Top German Ace of Spanish Civil War (1937–1938)—Lt. Werner Moelders: 14 victories

First German Ace of World War II—Major Hannes Gentzen

First Ace to exceed Baron Manfred von Richthofen's World War I score of 80—Capt. Werner Moelders

First to score 100 victories—Major Werner Moelders 15 July 1941

First to score 150 victories—Major Gordon Gollob: 29 August 1942

First to score 200 victories—Capt. Hermann Graf: 2 October 1942

First to score 250 victories—Major Walter Nowotny: 14 October 1943

First to score 300 victories—Capt. Erich Hartmann: 24 August 1944

First to score 350 victories—Major Erich Hartmann: 4 April 1945

Most kills scored in a single day—Major Emil Lang: 18 victories

Most kills on a single mission (sortie)—Major Erich Rudorffer: 6 November 1943; 13 victories

Most kills scored on the Western (includes Mediterranean) Front—Capt.Hans Joachim Marseille: 158 victories

Most kills scored on the Russian Front—Major Erich Hartmann: 352 victories

Best kill average per sortie flown (day fighters)—Lt. Guenther Scheel: 70 missions; 71 victories (Russian Front)

Top fighter ace for number of four-engine aircraft shot down (day fighters)—Lt. Herbert Rollwage: 102 victories (44 of them four-motor bombers)

Top four-engine killer (night fighters)—Major Heinz Schnaufer: 121 victories (mostly four-engine)

Top Jet Ace of World War II (Me-262)—Major Heinz Bär: 16 victories

THE GERMAN LUFEWAFFE FIGHTER ACES— TOP AWARDS

Knight's Cross with Oak Leaves, Swords and Diamonds
Germany's Highest Military Award

Name	Victories	
Galland, Adolph	104	
Gollob, Gordon	150	
Graf, Hermann	212	
Hartmann, Erich	352	
Lent, Helmut	110	(102 at night)
Marseille, Hans Joachim	158	
Mölders, Werner	101	(plus 14 in Spain)
Nowotny, Walter	258	
Schnaufer, Heinz	121	(all at night)

Knight's Cross with Oak Leaves and Swords
The Second Highest Award

Name	Victories	
Bär, Heinz	220	(16 with Me-262 jet)
Barkhorn, Gerhard	301	
Batz, Wilhelm	237	
Bühlingen, Kurt	112	
Hackl, Anton	192	
Hermann, Hajo	9	
Ihlefeld, Herbert	130	(includes 7 in Spain)
Kittel, Otto	267	
Lützow, Günther	108	(includes 5 in Spain)
Mayer, Egon		
Müncheberg, Joachim	135	
Oesau, Walter	123	(includes 8 in Spain)
Ostermann, Max Helmut	102	
Philipp, Hans	206	
Priller, Josef	101	
Rall, Guenther	275	
Reinert, Ernst Wilhelm	174	
Rudorffer, Erich	222	
Sayn-Wittgenstein, Prinz Zu	83	(night)
Schroer, Werner	114	
Steinbatz, Leopold	99	
Steinhoff, Johannes	176	
Streib, Werner	66	(night)
Wilcke, Wolf-Dietrich	162	
Würmheller, Josef	102	

GLOSSARY

A-20: Twin-engined Douglas attack bomber, also known as a "Boston or "Havoc."

Abort: Turn back from an aerial mission before completion.

Acceptable Loss: Combat loss judged not to be high for result obtained; within the limits of affordable cost.

Aerial Combat: Combat between or among hostile forces in the air.

Aileron: Control surface on wing of an airplane.

Airacobra: Nickname for the Bell P-39 fighter airplane.

Airstrip: Generally a landing field for aircraft.

Ammo: Ammunition.

Anchor: Apply air brakes, flaps, etc., in an attempt to slow down rapidly in flight. "Throw out the anchor"—reduce speed as rapidly as possible.

Angle-off: The angular measurement between line of flight of an aerial target and line of sight of an attacking aircraft.

Anoxia: Absence of oxygen in the blood experienced by pilots while flying at high altitudes.

Attrition: The process of permanent loss of aircraft due to enemy action or other operational or defined causes, which includes accidents.

Auger-in: A slang term meaning to crash in an airplane.

B-17: Four-engined bomber by Boeing. The "Flying Fortress."

B-24: Four-engined bomber by Consolidated. The "Liberator."

B-25: Two-engined bomber by North American. The "Mitchell."

Bail or Bailout: The action of parachuting from an airplane. Sometimes written as "bale out."

Balls Out: Full speed ahead! Taken from the centrifugal governor regulating the speed of a steam engine.

Bandit: Pilot slang for an enemy aircraft.

Barrel Roll: An aerial maneuver in which an airplane is caused to make a complete roll about a line offset but parallel to the longitudinal axis, as the chamber of a revolver revolves about the barrel. Sometimes called a "slow roll," but the two are slightly different.

Belly-land: To land an airplane on its underside without the benefit of the landing gear. A skidding landing with no wheels, due to their having been shot away in combat or the lowering mechanism rendered inoperative.

Bird: An airplane is a bird to a pilot.

Blind Approach: Approach to a landing under conditions of very low visibility made the aid of instruments or radio.

Blitz, Blitzkrieg: Highly mobile form of warfare introduced by the German Army, featuring close cooperation between fast-moving armored forces and air power. Old-style army units could not cope with these new techniques, which led to rapid victories. Literally, "flash war"; generally, lighting war.

B.O.B.: Battle of Britain.

Boa Cumulus: A cloud around a mountain top.

Boston: North American Aviation Company twin-engined light bomber. The A-20.

Bogey: First sighting of an unidentified airplane in flight.

Bounce: to attack an aircraft or target on the ground from another aircraft. Especially applied to catching an enemy pilot unawares.

Brassed off: Slang for angry.

Break!: "Break right!" or "Break left!" was a signal to an airborne comrade to make an instantaneous turn in the direction indicated, a maneuver designed to avoid being shot down by an attacking enemy aircraft.

Buck fever: The tension and excitement experienced by a fighter pilot in his first few combat missions. "Buck fever" usually leads to wild firing and missed targets. A fighter pilot no longer so afflicted is said to have conquered his buck fever.

Burp Guns: Automatic machine guns usually carried by infantrymen.

Buzz: To fly low over the ground.

CAP: Combat Air Patrol.

Ceiling Zero: Atmospheric condition when cloud height or ceiling above ground is less than fifty feet to its base.

Chomp on the Binders: To apply the brakes.

Chop Up: To shoot up an aerial or ground target, the bullets tearing the target to pieces.

Clobber: To crash an airplane; to destroy or damage an area or airplane with gunfire.

Cockpit: The pilot's seat and controls in an airplane.

Cold Turkey: Without mincing words. Also, a sure kill.

Condor Legion: A volunteer air force made up from the Luftwaffe to gain experience in Spain in supporting General Franco, 1936–1939.

Contrails: Vapor trails or condensation trails visible behind an aircraft as it moves through the air.

Controlled Interception: Friendly aircraft are directed to the enemy aircraft or target by radio from a ground or air station.

Control Tower: A radio-equipped facility at an airfield manned by trained personnel to control air and ground traffic on or above the field.

Court-martial: To try or judge a person in a military court.

Damaged: As claimed in combat, an aircraft claimed as partially destroyed but subject to repair.

Deck: The ground, the cloud level, or the deck of an aircraft carrier.

Deflection: Shot: The angle of a shot in gunnery measured between the line of sight to the target and the line of sight to the aiming point.

Diaterka: A prison-of-war camp near Sverdlosk in the Ural Mountains of Russia.

Ditch: To force-land an airplane in the water with intention of abandonment.

Dogfight: An aerial battle between opposing fighter aircraft. Aerial combat. Sometimes called a rhubarb.

Ejector Seat: A seat resigned to catapult at sufficient velocity to clear the airplane completely.

Eleven O'clock Low: The clock position of a bogey or airplane sighted by a pilot.

External Store: Any fuel tank, bomb, rocket, etc., attached to the wings or fuselage of an airplane.

Fat Dog: Luftwaffe expression for large bombers loaded with bombs. Sometimes called "fat target"—a target of considerable value.

Feldwebel: Flight Sergeant.

Firewall: Fireproof wall between pilot and engine, slang, "firewall the throttle" means full throttle.

Flaking: Loss of members of a flight of aircraft as they turn back homeward before reaching the target.

Fliegerdivision: An air division.

Fliegerhorstkommandant: Airfield commandant.

Forced Landing: A landing forced upon an aircraft through mechanical failure or any other reason.

Four-motor: A four-motor bomber. In World War II these were generally the British Halifax, Stirling, Lancaster and Lincoln; American four-motors were the Boeing B-17 Fortress and Consolidated B-24 Liberator.

Führerhauptquartier: Führer Headquarters.

Fürungsstab: Operations Staff.

Full Bore: Full throttle or full speed ahead.

FW-190: The Focke-Wulf single-engined fighter plane.

Gaggle: A number of aircraft flying in loose formation.

Gandy Dancing: Skirting an issue; avoiding confrontation with a problem.

Gear: Short for landing gear, the wheels of an airplane.

General der Jagdflieger: General of the Fighter Forces.

General der Kampfflieger: General of the Bomber Forces.

Generalstab: General Staff.

Geschwader: The largest mobile, homogeneous formation in the Luftwaffe. A Wing. In the Luftwaffe a Fighter Wing (*Jagdgeschwader*) consisted of three *Gruppen.* Thus:

> A Wing consisted of three *Gruppen* (Groups)
> A *Gruppe* consisted of three *Staffeln* (Squadrons)
> A *Staffel* consisted of three *Schwarms* (Flights)
> (Each *Schwarm* consisted of four aircraft, and was divided into two *Rotten.*)

(The *Rotte* of two aircraft was the basic tactical element.)

Geschwaderkommodore: The wing commander. Usually a

colonel or lieutenant colonel; sometimes a major; very rarely, a captain.

Glycol: A thick alcohol, $C_2H_4(OH)_2$, used as a coolant in liquid-cooled aircraft engines.

Graf: German for Count.

Gray Out: Start of a blackout, the phenomenon a pilot experiences when pulling G's on an airplane, resulting in the blood leaving his head and his sight becoming lost.

Ground Loop: Loss of lateral control of an airplane on the ground resulting in the aircraft making a sudden turn, a sudden change in direction. Usually a wheel or gear strut on the outside of the turn will break and the aircraft suffers considerable damage. A nose-over or a somersault on the ground is not a ground loop, although it may result from a ground loop.

Gruppe: A Group. Usually consisted of three squadrons. Largest (thirty-six aircraft) individual operational unit of the Luftwaffe fighter force.

Gruppenkommandeur: Group commander. Usually a major, sometimes a captain.

Guards Fighter Regiment: A special group of Soviet fighter pilots selected from the best pilots.

Heck: To tolerate something; also to accomplish something, or shoot another aircraft down, especially a big bomber.

Hals und Beinbruch!: "Break your head and bones." A German saying which meant the opposite—good luck.

Havoc: Nickname for the A-20 attack bomber.

Head-on: A frontal attack.

Heavies: Bomber aircraft of the four-engined type.

Hedgehop: Sometimes called "contour chasing." Flying very low over the ground, rising up over trees, houses, hills, etc.

Hochschule: School at the college level.

Horrido!: The victory cry of the Luftwaffe fighter pilots. Also a greeting and parting word among friends and comrades of the Luftwaffe. The cry of the hunter. Similar to the British and American cry of "Tallyho!"

Hyperventilation: Excessive ventilation of the blood induced by rapid or deep breathing, often expericend by pilots while flying at high altitudes.

Hypoxia: Insufficient oxygen in the blood at high altitudes.

IL-2: The Ilyushin "Stormovik" dive bomber used by the Soviet Air Force.

Inertia Starter: Hand-operated starter used to start aircraft engines.

Inspekteur der Nachtjäger: Inspector of Night Fighters.

Inspekteur der Tagjäger: Inspector of Day Fighters.

Jabo: Abbreviation for fighter-bomber.

Jafü: Abbreviation of *Jagdführer,* "Fighter Leader." Separate fighter commands in each *Luftflotte.* Originally assigned a policy-regulating and observing role, Fighter Leaders later controlled operations and handled considerable administration.

Jagdfliegerheim: A rest and recuperation spa used by the fighter pilots, located at Bad Wiessee in Germany. fighter pilots, located at Bad Wiessee in Germany.

Jagdgeschwader: Fighter wing. Usually consisted of three or four *Gruppen* of pilots and aircraft. From 108 to 144 aircraft made up the establishment of a wing. Some were larger. See under *Gesschwader.*

Jagdstaffel: Fighter squadron.

Jägerblatt: Fighter News. A periodical published by the German Fighter Pilots' Association.

JG-26: Fighter Wing 26, known over Europe as "The Abbeville Boys."

Jink: To jerk an aircraft about in evasive action.

Jockey: To fly or pilot an airplane. Slang name for "pilot."

Joy Stick: Slang for control stick of a fighter airplane.

Jump: To attack an enemy aircraft.

JV-44: The Me-262 equipped "Squadron of Experts."

Kadetten Korps: Cadet Corps.

Karaya One: Erich Hartmann's radio call sign.

Karinhall: Goering's estate on the Shorfheide, about twenty-five miles, north of Berlin.

Kette: Basic three-ship element used in early Luftwaffe fighter tactics, the counterpart of the RAF's three-ship "Vic" formation. Replaced in the Luftwaffe before World War II by the Rotte and Schwarm formations; returned with the Me-262.

Kettenführer: Flight commander.

KIA: Killed in action.

Kill: A victory in aerial combat. Destroying an enemy aircraft in flight. Does not refer to the death of an enemy pilot.

Kite: An airplane.

Kommodore: Abbreviation of *Geschwaderkommdore.* Commanding officer of a wing.

La: Lavochkin La-5. A fighter plane employer in Russia.

Lagg-3: A single-engined Russian fighter plane designed by Lavochkin, Gorbunor, and Gudkov.

Lead (rhymes with *heed*): The action of aiming ahead of a moving target. See "deflection shot."

Leutnant: Lieutenant.

Lightning: The Lockheed P-38, a single-seat twin-boom-fuselaged fighter aircraft.

Lufbery Circle: A formation in which two or more aricraft follow each other in flight in circles in order to protect one another from enemy aircraft. Named for Major Raoul Lufbery, American ace who developed the tactic in World War I.

Luftflotten: Tactical and territorial air commands. Literally, air fleets.

Luftwaffe: Air force. The name of the German Air Force from 1935 through 1945.

Lysander: A British two-place single-engined high-wing monoplane extensively used for army cooperation.

Macchi: An Italian fighter plane manufactured by the Macchi Company.

Mach: The speed of a body as compared to the speed of sound, which is Mach 1.0.

Marauder: Popular name for the U.S.-built Martin B-26 medium bomber.

Mayday: International radiotelephone signal of distress.

Me-109: Officially known as the Bf-109, Germany's most famous single-engined. Originally designed by Bayerische Flugzeugwerke A.G. at Augsburg. Called Me-109 in this book because it is so known by most Americans and is so referred to by virtually all German aces. The term Bf-109, while historically correct, is relatively unknown in the United States.

Me-262: The Messerschmitt twin-engined jet fighter.

Methanol: A colorless, volatile alcohol injected into an aircraft engine to give it a few seconds of additional power.

MIA: Missing in action.

Mission: An air objective carryiing out a combat air mission;

a number of aircraft fly *x* number of sorties (number of aircraft committed) to carry out a mission.

Mustang: The North American Aviation Company P-51 fighter airplane.

Nachtjagdgeschwader: Night fighter wing, abbreviated as NJG, followed by the number of the wing, e.g., NJG-6.

Night Fighter: A fighter aircraft and crew that operates at night, the aircraft being provided with special equipment for detecting enemy aircraft at night.

NKVD: Russian *Narodny Kommissariat Vnutrennikh Del*, the People's Commissariat for Internal Affairs.

Nose Over: An airplane moving on the ground noses, tips over on its nose and propeller, damaging nose and prop. Sometimes it somersaults over on its back. This is not a ground loop, which is merely directional loss of control of an airplane on the ground.

No Sweat: Slang for "without difficulty."

Oberkommando der Luftwaffe: Referred to as OKL, the Luftwaffe High Command.

Oberkommando des Heeres: Referred to as OKH, the Army High Command.

Oberleutnant: First lieutenant. Not to be confused with *Obersteulnant*, lieutenant colonel.

Oberst: Colonel.

Oberstleutnant: Lieutenant colonel.

O'clock: The position of another airplane sighted in the air was called out by its clock position from the observer, twelve o'clock being straight ahead; six o'clock high, directly behind and above the observer; nine o'clock, horizontally ninty degrees left of the observer.

OKH: Army High Command.

OKL: Luftwaffe High Command.

OKW: High Command of the Armed Forces.

Open City: A city of a belligerent power declared by that power to be noncombatant, and made so in order to avoid bombing or shelling from any of the combatant forces.

OSSOAVIAKIM: Flying Association in Russia which gave thousands of youths paratroop, glider and flying training before World War II.

Overshoot: In air combat, to fly over or past the enemy plane when following through on an attack.

Pathfinder: A highly trained and experienced bomber crew that preceded the bomber formation to the target and marked it with flares or smoke bombs for easy location and attack by the main force. The RAF frequently used Mosquito fighter-bombers in the pathfinder role.

Perch: Postion of tactical advantage prior to initiating an attack on an enemy airplane.

Photo Recce: Photographic reconnaissance.

Port: The left side of an airplane facing forward. The right side is starboard.

P.O.W.: Prisoner of war.

Prang: Slang for crash or collision of airplane, also to crash-land. Also in RAF slang to down an enemy airplane or accurately hit a target, as in "wizard prang"—meaning a successful operation.

Probable: An instance in which a hostile airplane is probably destroyed. With a "probable" it is not known whether it actually crashed, but it is considered so badly damaged as to make its crash probable. USAAF claims in aerial combat listed three categories: 1. Confirmed destroyed. 2. Probably but unconfirmed destroyed. 3. Damaged.

Prop: An abbreviation for propeller.

Rack: To make a sudden, violent maneuver in a fighter plane.

RAF: Royal Air Force.

Recce: Abbreviation for reconnaissance.

Recip: Abbreviation for reciprocating engine.

Red Alert: An alert that exists when attack by the enemy is or seems to be imminent.

Red Guards Fighter Unit: A regiment made up of the best Soviet fighter aces.

Red Line: A red mark on the air-speed indicator showing the safe maximum speed of the airplane. Other flight instruments also have a red line.

Reef It In: To change direction of flight violently.

Rev: To increase the rpm of an engine; to rev it up.

Reverse: One-hundred-and-eightly-degree change of direction in flight.

Rhubarb: A dogfight or the harassment of ground targets by a flight of aircraft. A German term for aerial combat.

Robot: A mechanism, device, weapon, etc., that operates automatically. Trade name of a well-known German camera used to make sequence exposures of aerial combat and synchronized with the fighter aircraft's armament.

Roger!: Pilot language meaning "Received O.K."

Rotte: A two-plane formation. Smallest tactical element in the Luftwaffe fighter force.

Rottenflieger: Wingman.

Rottenführer: Leader of a *Rotte.* Loosely, an element leader.

R/T: Radiotelephone, or radio transmitter.

St. Horridus: The savior saint of the Luftwaffe fighter pilots and origin of the victory cry "Horrido!"

Schiessschule der Lufewaffe: Luftwaffe Gunnery School.

Schlachtgeschwader: Ground Attack Wing, or Close Support Wing. The SG-2 was commanded by famed Stuka pilot Hans-Ulrich Rudel.

Schwarm: Two-*Rotte* formation, four or five aircraft acting in a single flight.

Schwarmführer: Leader of a *Schwarm.*

Scramble: The action of getting fighter aircraft into the air quickly.

Scrub: To cancel a flight, sortie, or mission.

Shakhty Revolt: Revolt at the Shakhty prisoner-of-war camp in Russia.

Snake Maneuver: A Soviet tactic developed to get the IL-2 Stormovik fighter-bomber home when attacked by German fighters. The IL-2's would enter a Lufbery circle, then descend to a few feet above the ground and work their way home using the snake maneuver, a weaving, follow-the-leader maneuver for mutual protection.

Snaking: The tendency of an airplane to yaw in flight from side to side at a certain frequency.

Sortie: A flight or sally of a single airplane which penetrates into airspace where enemy contact may be expected. While a single plane or any number of aircraft may go on a mission, each aircraft flying is actually making a sortie. One mission may involve any number of sorties.

Split S: A high-speed maneuver in which the airplane makes a half-roll onto its back and then dives groundward, leveling off going in the oposite direction at a much lower altitude.

Stabs-Schwarm: A headquarters flight of three to six aircraft, usually of the same type that make up the *Geschwader.* The wing commander and his adjutant normally fly in the *Stabs-Schwa.m.*

Staffel: A squadron. Consisted of three *Schwarms*, made up of from twelve to fifteen aircraft. Three or sometimes four *Staffeln* made up a *Gruppe*.

Stalin Hawks: Stalinfalken, or Stalin Eagles. The top Soviet fighter aces' *nom de plume*.

Starboard: Right side of an aircraft facing forward. The left side is port.

Strafe: To dive at and machine-gun targets on the ground. Sometimes spelled "straff."

Strip: An aircraft landing field.

Stukatcha: Stool pigeon.

Tallyho!: A code expression called over the radio by a fighter pilot when he sights the enemy target. Derived from the traditional English hunting cry. The Luftwaffe fighter called "Horrido!" which in essense had the same meaning.

Throttle-jockey: Slang name for a pilot. Sometimes shortened to "Throttle-jock" or shorter yet to "Jock."

Thunderbolt: Popular name for the Republic P-47 fighter airplane. American pilots called it the "Jug."

Tiger: Eager pilot; eager to fight. Because of their general nature and quick reactions, most fighter pilots are referred to as "tigers" in aviation circles.

Tracer Bullet: A bullet containing a pyrotechnic mixture to make the flight of the projectile visible.

Turbo Fighter: The Me-262 fighter airplane.

Undershoot: To land short of the runway; to shoot under a target in aerial combat.

Unteroffizier: The lowest non-commissioned rank standing between the non-commissioned rank of sergeant and the rank of Staff Sergeant in the Luftwaffe.

Verbandsführer: Unit commander.

Vic: A V formation of three airplanes.

Waffengeneral: Technical Service General.

Wilco: Radiotelephone word of acknowledgment. Abbreviation for "Will comply" or "Will cooperate." In addition, "Roger-Wilco means "Received O.K., will comply."

Wilde Sau: Literally, "Wild Boar," name of a German night fighter unit operating without radar aids in single-engined fighters.

Window: Metal foil strips that cause a reflection on radarscopes corrupting radar information. Also called "chaff." When dropped from an airplane window it cluttered screens, giving the impression that great hordes of aircraft were in the air, completely obscuring the radar screen.

Windscreen: An airlane windshield.

Wingco: Abbreviation for wing commander.

Zerstorer: Literally, "destroyer." The name chosen for the long-range, twin-engined Me-110 fighter.

Zerstorergeschwader: Destroyer wing. Fighter wings consisting of Me-110's, Ju-87's, etc., and expressed as ZG-26, ZG-1, etc. Actually dive-bomber wings of the Luftwaffe.

INDEX

Aces, air combat: and awards, Luftwaffe, listed, 305; criteria for, 56, 119 ff.; Luftwaffe, 39–47, 49–50, 51, 52 ff., 56, 92–93, 95–104, 115, 116, 119 ff., 123–124, 133–135 (*see also* specific individuals by name); RAF, 93; Red Air Force, 90, 92, 119–32, 134 (*see also* specific individuals by name); USAF, 124

Ackerman, Colonel, 202–3

Adenauer, Konrad, 7, 266–67, 275, 277

Ahlhorn, 286, 295

Air Academy School, Luftwaffe (Berlin-Gatow), 27–28

Airacobras (P-39's), 58, 137–38, 171–172, 307

Aircraft (*see also* specific planes by designation): Russian and German compared, World War II, 119–22 ff.

Air Force Military Training Regiment, Luftwaffe, 10, 27–28

Akmet-Khan, Sultan, 132

Alelyukhin, A. V., 132

Alexander, Jean, 131

Allies (allied powers), World War II: (*see also* specific countries, individuals) bombings by, 60–61, 99, 106, 108–109, 110, 120, 144, 154, 156, 161–73; and post war Germany, 215; surrender and treatment of Germany, 181–90

Amavir, 50

Antifa movement, 198–201, 206

Arab-Israeli war (1967), 290

Ardennes offensive, 152–53

Arkhipenko, F. F., 132

Armament, 28 (*see also* Gunnery); weather and functioning of, 82

A-20 Douglas Boston attack bombers, 171–72, 307, 308

Babak, I. I., 132

Bachnik, Sergeant, 67

Bad Wiessee, 147–53

Baer, Heinz ("Pritzl"), 99, 116, 156–57; a leading ace with 220 confirmed victories, 156–57; top scoring ace in Me-262, 156–57

Baku oil fields, 35

Bänsch (West German Defense Ministry official), 277

Barkhorn, Gerhard (Gerd), 9–11, 93, 100, 104, 123–24, 133–34; and "circus" air

319

NEW FROM BALLANTINE!

FALCONER, John Cheever   27300 $2.25

The unforgettable story of a substantial, middle-class man and the passions that propel him into murder, prison, and an undreamed-of liberation. "CHEEVER'S TRIUMPH . . . A GREAT AMERICAN NOVEL."—*Newsweek*

GOODBYE, W. H. Manville   27118 $2.25

What happens when a woman turns a sexual fantasy into a fatal reality? The erotic thriller of the year! "Powerful."—*Village Voice*. "Hypnotic."—*Cosmopolitan.*

**THE CAMERA NEVER BLINKS, Dan Rather
with Mickey Herskowitz**   27423 $2.25

In this candid book, the co-editor of "60 Minutes" sketches vivid portraits of numerous personalities including JFK, LBJ and Nixon, and discusses his famous colleagues.

THE DRAGONS OF EDEN, Carl Sagan 26031 $2.25

An exciting and witty exploration of mankind's intelligence from pre-recorded time to the fantasy of a future race, by America's most appealing scientific spokesman.

VALENTINA, Fern Michaels   26011 $1.95

Sold into slavery in the Third Crusade, Valentina becomes a queen, only to find herself a slave to love.

**THE BLACK DEATH, Gwyneth Cravens
and John S. Marr**   27155 $2.50

A totally plausible novel of the panic that strikes when the bubonic plague devastates New York.

**THE FLOWER OF THE STORM,
Beatrice Coogan**   27368 $2.50

Love, pride and high drama set against the turbulent background of 19th century Ireland as a beautiful young woman fights for her inheritance and the man she loves.

**THE JUDGMENT OF DEKE HUNTER.
George V. Higgins**   25862 $1.95

Tough, dirty, shrewd, telling! "The best novel Higgins has written. Deke Hunter should have as many friends as Eddie Coyle."—*Kirkus Reviews*

LG-2